Varieties of Capitalism and Business History

T0289695

The financial crisis of 2008 brought new urgency to the question how best to organise national economies. This volume gives a business history perspective on the Varieties of Capitalism debate and considers the respective merits of the liberal and coordinated market economies. It looks at individual firms and business people as well as institutions and takes a long-term perspective by covering the whole 20th century. The authors examine both continuity and change with a particular focus on the Netherlands, a nation with an open economy, situated between two countries that oppose each other in the way they organize their economies: Germany and Great Britain. The Netherlands also provides an important case study with Dutch business maintaining strong links to the United States, widely considered to be the 'typical' liberal market economy.

Contributors address the main topics of the capitalism debate, including labour relations, corporate governance, the firm and its leaders, coordination between firms, innovation, multinationals as agents of change, and economic performance. They show that the Netherlands moved from a mostly liberal market economy before 1914 towards a coordinated market economy from the 1930s onwards, and—up to a certain extent—back again to a more liberal market economy. Under both varieties of capitalism the country experienced economic growth and stagnation, but a more equal division of wealth occurred in the coordinated market economy only. Wars and international economic crises offered moments for revaluation and changes of tack.

This book raises questions for every country around the globe: How is change being brought about? Can one see different results from a liberal or a more coordinated market economy? And most critically: which system is more effective in bringing prosperity and enabling enough people to share in the wealth?

Keetie Sluyterman is professor of business history at Utrecht University, the Netherlands, and a specialist in Dutch business history of the 19th and 20th centuries. She has written or jointly authored a large number of companies histories, and written the overview *Dutch Enterprise in the Twentieth Century* (Routledge 2005). She is past president of the EBHA and a member of the advisory editorial board of the journals *Business History* and *Business History Review*.

Routledge International Studies in Business History

Series editors: Ray Stokes and Matthias Kipping

Varieties of Capitalism and Business History

The Dutch Case

Edited by Keetie Sluyterman

Routledge
Taylor & Francis Group

NEW YORK AND LONDON

First published 2015
by Routledge
711 Third Avenue, New York, NY 10017

and by Routledge
2 Park Square, Milton Park, Abingdon, Oxon OX14 4RN

First issued in paperback 2018

Routledge is an imprint of the Taylor & Francis Group,
an informa business

Library of Congress Cataloging-in-Publication Data

Varieties of capitalism and business history : the Dutch case /
edited by Keetie Sluyterman. — First Edition.
        pages cm. — (Routledge international studies in business history ; 28)
    Includes bibliographical references and index.
    1. Capitalism—Netherlands—History—20th century.
2. Entrepreneurship—Netherlands—History—20th century.
I. Sluyterman, K. E. (Keetie E.), 1949– editor.
    HB501.V35547 2015
    338.509492'0904—dc23
    2014028658

ISBN 13: 978-1-138-34092-3 (pbk)
ISBN 13: 978-1-138-78493-2 (hbk)

Typeset in Sabon
by Apex CoVantage, LLC

Contents

Tables

Figures

Acknowledgements

This volume is the result of a decade-long research project to trace changes in capitalism in the Netherlands during the 20th century. The research project was termed 'BINT': the Dutch acronym for *Bedrijfsleven in Nederland in de Twintigste Eeuw* (Business in the Netherlands in the 20th Century). It is inspired by the intense academic debates on the various manifestations of capitalism and their respective merits. Utrecht University took the initiative for BINT and received the enthusiastic support and contribution from other institutions, including Erasmus University, the Free University of Amsterdam, the International Institute for Social History, and the Netherlands Economic History Archives. The BINT project encompasses seven subprojects, resulting in seven books published in Dutch for an academic as well as a general audience. To reach an international audience the project envisaged one concluding volume in the English language. First results of the research project on a number of themes have been published in the *Business History Review* (2010 Winter). This volume highlights the main results of the whole project and includes international comparisons as well as a chapter on the performance of Dutch capitalism during the 20th century.

During the course of the BINT project, the authors of the various Dutch books (Annette van den Berg, Bram Bouwens, Joost Dankers, Mila Davids, Jacques van Gerwen, Ferry de Goey, Abe de Jong, Harry Lintsen, Erik Nijhof, Arjan van Rooij, Jan Peet, Gerarda Westerhuis, and Ben Wubs, as well as Jan Luiten van Zanden, Hans Schenk, Lex Heerma van Vos, Maurits van Os, and Ailsa Röell) frequently met and discussed the outcomes of the various subprojects. I would like to thank them all for their contribution not only to their own parts of the project, but for their continued involvement with the project as a whole. Most of them are also included as contributors to this English-language volume. Moreover, I am particularly grateful to Joost Dankers and Jan Luiten van Zanden for their huge participation in organising this long-term project and their tireless dedication on moving it forward. My special thanks also goes to the colleagues of the European Business History Association, who over the years read and commented on many conference papers presented by the BINT researchers at the annual EBHA conferences.

In an indirect way, this volume benefited from the research money dedicated to the execution of the various Dutch volumes. In particular I would like to thank Utrecht University and the Dutch funding organisation NWO for their financial contribution. More directly this volume profited from the financial support of Jan Luiten van Zanden, who contributed some of the research money awarded to him through the NWO Spinoza Prize.

I am greatly indebted to Matthias Kipping and Ray Stokes, editors of the Routledge International Studies in Business History, for including this volume in their series and for their excellent advice. The anonymous reviewers of Routledge gave useful and much appreciated suggestions with regard to the individual contributions and the organisation of the whole volume.

Keetie Sluyterman

1 Introduction
Varieties of Capitalism and Business History: The Dutch Case

Keetie Sluyterman

INTRODUCTION

The present deep economic crisis particularly in Europe and the United States gives the study of capitalism a new relevance. Could a different organisation of the economy have prevented the present crisis? Capitalism has been a much-discussed topic in the past. For most of the 20th century, capitalism was contrasted with communism. Some academics have looked for a third way between capitalism and communism, while others discussed whether or not the two would converge into one system in due time. The fall of the Berlin Wall marked the end of communism in Eastern Europe and Russia. Capitalism came forward as, seemingly, the superior system. At the same time, the world became increasingly economically interconnected. Would all countries in the world move to one system? Would there be one best system for running the national economy? Sociologists and political scientists argued that this was not necessarily the case. Despite globalisation, national economies would remain organised in different ways. In 2001 the political scientists Peter Hall and David Soskice built a framework for comparing different national economies in their volume *Varieties of Capitalism: The Institutional Foundations for Comparative Advantage*.[1] They concentrated on developed economies. In the first decade of the 21st century, their propositions have been debated, confirmed, contradicted, and improved upon.

This volume gives a business history perspective on this debate. As group of authors, we take Hall and Soskice seriously in their wish to put the firm centre stage. We want to fill the often abstract discussion with the flesh and bone of history, with people who acted and events that took place. We look at both continuity and change: how flexible are these national capitalistic systems? How do the different elements of the national organisation of the economy interact with each other? What are the mechanisms behind change? What is the role of companies and people in forging changes?

We explore these themes in one specific country because we believe this helps to see the different aspects of the debate on Varieties of Capitalism (VoC) in their proper setting and in their relation to each other. The country we explore is the Netherlands. Why this country? First, because it is situated between two countries that are, according to the framework of Hall and Soskice, opposites of each other in the way they organise their economies: Germany and Great Britain. Second, because the Netherlands has an open economy and therefore experiences the pressures and opportunities of globalisation to the fullest extent.

We also want to look at the long term: the whole 20th century. The VoC framework typified national varieties mostly on the basis of their appearance in the 1990s. For instance, the Netherlands was typified by Hall and Soskice as a coordinated market economy. But is this true for the beginning of the 20th century? And is it still true for the start of the 21st century? The answer is 'no', as several authors have already argued.[2] And our research confirms this conclusion. But that raises new questions: how is change being brought about? How successful was the country during the 20th century? Can we see different results from the liberal or more coordinated economy? For success we have looked at economic growth and the spread of economic benefits over the whole population because economic systems matter for both of these reasons: are they effective in bringing prosperity, but also do enough people share in the proceeds?

This introduction is organised in four parts. First, it will highlight the Varieties of Capitalism framework introduced by Hall and Soskice in 2001. Next, it will follow the debates about the concept and the way the concept evolved in response to criticisms and new research. The third section will briefly introduce the Netherlands. Finally, the main findings of the different chapters will be presented.

A LANDMARK IN THE DEBATE ON VARIETIES OF CAPITALISM

The 2001 publication *Varieties of Capitalism* by Peter Hall and David Soskice set a landmark in the debates on different ways of organising the national economy.[3] In their introduction to that volume they brought together many strands of thought of the 1990s and made propositions that framed the debate for the next decade. They wanted to combine the study of comparative capitalisms by political economists with the strategies of firms from the business studies. Their emphasis on the firm as the key actor in a capitalist economy makes their approach particularly interesting for business historians.

In building up their core competencies, firms have to deal with problems of coordination. For Hall and Soskice, five areas (spheres) of coordination are central, three of which relate to the firms and their workforce. These include the coordination between employers and employees about wages and labour conditions on group level (industrial relations), the coordination on the individual level between the firm and its employees, and thirdly the coordination of the vocational training and education of the labour force. The remaining two main areas of coordination are the relation between firms and their providers of capital (corporate governance) and the interactions between firms, their suppliers, and their clients (interfirm relations). In these five spheres, coordination can take place via markets and hierarchies or via nonmarket institutions. The organisation of national economies can be compared by looking at the choices firms make in those five spheres of coordination. In their framework, not the state but the firms are central in defining the national economy.[4] This framework will be explained in some detail here because all authors of the chapters in this volume use it as their starting point with due attention to the ensuring debates.

Building further on the contrast and contest that, according to Michel Albert, existed between the Anglo-Saxon and Rhineland capitalism, Hall and Soskice introduced the more general terms of the 'liberal market economy' (LME) and 'coordinated market economy' (CME). The United States served as the prime example of a LME, and Germany stood for the CME. In both cases the firm uses the market, but in LMEs it combines arm's length, competitive relations with formal contracts, while in CMEs it prefers the use of networks and collaboration. These choices will be supported by the national institutions, organisations, and culture, which in turn will underpin the firm's choices.[5]

Two mechanisms will give durability to the national type of capitalism. First, the characteristics of the five spheres are not distributed at random but show coherence. For instance, patient capital and long-term employment go hand in hand. Institutional complementarities therefore reinforce the differences between LMEs and CMEs. Second, companies will follow strategies that make the most of the institutional context in which they operate. In doing so, they will confirm that context. Hall and Soskice take their argument one step further: because firms use the national context for creating advantages, firms in CMEs and LMEs will behave differently. For instance, firms in CMEs will invest in specific assets and those in LMEs in switchable assets. That means that differently organised economies will specialise in different products. Moreover, flexible capital and labour markets in LME countries will allow firms to focus on radical innovation, while the long-term relationships in CME countries make a focus on incremental innovation more logical.[6]

Where is the government in this framework of varieties of capitalism? Hall and Soskice discuss the role of the state by addressing economic policymaking. In their view, the principal problem facing policymakers is inducing economic actors to operate more effectively with each other. Policymakers can use the market to secure this coordination, for instance, through incentives, and that is likely to happen in LMEs. Or they can use the existing organisations, including business associations and trade unions, to encourage coordination, which is the logical choice in CMEs.[7]

Technological revolutions and liberalisation in the international economy provide challenges for national economies. Firms, however, will react differently to those challenges in accordance to their national setting. Firms in LMEs might move production units to countries with cheaper labour, while firms in CMEs might prefer to stay in their home country because of the specific skills of their workers. Hall and Soskice even argue optimistically that the pressure of the international financial markets might lead to a closer cooperation between management and works councils. External shocks might challenge the system and create change, but the most likely outcome is that the adjustment will remain relatively small and not upset the existing framework. There might be change, but there is no reason to expect convergence between LME and CME countries.[8]

Hall and Soskice do not argue that one type of capitalism is superior to the other. However, they do argue that the two types differ with regard to their capacity for innovation and their distribution of income and employment. In a later article, Peter Hall and Daniel Gingerich have calculated that countries with complementary institutions had higher economic growth. Thus, pure LME or CME countries performed better than countries with partly LME and CME characteristics. This conclusion comes with a warning to those who want to reform certain spheres of the national economy: those reforms will have impacts on other spheres and cannot be considered in isolation.[9]

On the basis of the five spheres, Hall and Soskice have clustered the OECD countries. Six were classified as LMEs: the United States, Britain, Australia, Canada, New Zealand, and Ireland, all English-speaking countries. Ten were classified as CME: Germany, Japan, Switzerland, the Netherlands, Belgium, Sweden, Norway, Denmark, Finland, and Austria. Another six countries—France, Italy, Spain, Portugal, Greece, and Turkey—were considered difficult to identify with one of the two categories. Tentatively, Hall and Soskice introduced a third type of capitalism, Mediterranean, characterised by a large agrarian sector and extensive state intervention. This showed that their framework was flexible and a 'work in progress', as they pointed out themselves.[10]

DEVELOPMENT OF THE VOC FRAMEWORK

More Variety

The VoC framework as presented by Hall and Soskice has created much debate, both positive and negative, and has unleashed many efforts to develop it further. This introduction will highlight some important discussions that led to further elaboration of the VoC framework. It will discuss the sparse choice of two options (LME and CME), the positioning of countries somewhere in this continuum, and the all-important question of change and possible mechanisms behind change.

The most obvious point for discussion was the dichotomy between LME and CME. Why two models—why not four, or five, or ten? In fact, Hall and Soskice had already hinted at a possible third model: the Mediterranean market economy. In 2003 Bruno Amable came with an alternative set of five different models: the Anglo-Saxon model, the Continental European model, the social democratic economies, the Mediterranean model, and, finally, Asian Capitalism.[11] Richard Whitley, who wrote extensively about business systems in the 1990s and onwards, developed a scheme of eight types of business systems, four types of states, and six types of innovation systems. It seemed to cover every possible angle.[12] Matthew Allen argued that VoC did not have enough variety because it paid no attention to the varieties of firms within countries. Different industry sectors within a country were often organised very differently.[13] Robert Boyer compared VoC with Regulation Theory (RT) and divided the world into four 'brands of capitalism': market-led, meso-corporatist, social democratic, and state-led.[14] Colin Crouch appreciated the theoretical parsimony of the two models but warned against determinism and functionalism. He also warned against confusing models with the reality on the ground.[15] Bob Hancké, Martin Rhodes, and Mark Thatcher concluded that the framework could easily be extended with two more models, and at the same time brought the state back in. They introduced the mixed market economies and emerging market economies, but the latter was seen as a transitory model.[16] So, over time more variations were introduced, but there appeared no consensus on one best framework. The original simple framework of two contrasting models, therefore, remains very useful for analysing how economies are organised and how this organisation develops over time.

Linked to the discussion of models was the discussion about positioning countries in the framework. The initial framework was developed with the developed countries in mind, but some authors tested the concept's usefulness for developing countries or countries that had no market economy. Labelling brought up further questions. It appeared that countries did 'fit' the bill in some periods but not in others. For instance, Hall and Soskice positioned the Netherlands as a CME. Historical studies for the Netherlands concluded that the country was indeed a coordinated market economy for much of the 20th century, but it showed many liberal characteristics at the start and at the very end of that century.[17] The chapters in this volume discuss these shifts in more detail, and the concluding chapter compares the Dutch experiences with some other countries. For instance, some authors questioned whether the United States was a LME in the middle of the 20th century. Ronald Dore, William Lazonick, and Mary O'Sullivan describe the United States in the 1950s and 1960s as a period of 'managerial capitalism', which was more characterised by collaboration than by market liberalism.[18] This exercise leads us to the all-important discussion about changes over time.

Changes over Time

Many authors criticised Hall and Soskice because they considered the VoC framework too static. As we have seen, changes were not excluded from their approach, but the emphasis was clearly on continuity as a consequence of the institutional complementarities. In any case, they argued against convergence between the liberal and coordinated market economies. In an earlier publication, Ronald Dore, William Lazonick, and Mary O'Sullivan came to a similar conclusion. They compared institutional changes in the United States, Britain, Germany, and Japan during the 20th century and found that all four countries had changed. But it was not a story of a long and steady process of gradual convergence. Instead, the four countries seemed to be heading for more convergence in the 1960s but then diverged again in the 1980s. The 1990s came with renewed convergence. The authors did not reach a firm conclusion but noticed a pattern of 'ebb and flow' that still needed to be explained.[19] As the 21st century progressed, it had become increasingly clear that national economies were changing, and most of that change meant a move from a coordinated to a liberal market economy. For instance, recent calculations by Martin Schneider and Mihai Paunescu show moves in a more liberal direction for a number of countries, including Denmark, Finland, the Netherlands, and Sweden. 'The direction and the extent of change do not appear to be consistent with the idea of stable types of capitalism', the authors conclude.[20] Other authors argue for the same movement in the same direction. By focusing on recent years, nearly all changes relate to a move from CME to LME. To get a more balanced view, it is important to also study how CMEs were created or how LMEs developed into CMEs, and for that exercise we probably need to go further back in time. This is indeed the approach chosen by the contributors to the present volume.

Can more change be included in the VoC framework? Robert Boyer contrasts the VoC approach with the Regulation Theory. While the VoC school agrees that external shocks might bring changes in the reigning type of capitalism, the Regulation Theory looks for endogenous factors to explain the two main phenomena of the late 20th century: the globalisation and the transition from manufacturing to services. For countries such as Japan and Germany, the crises of the 1990s were the result of earlier successes. Past successes were transformed into signs of weakness. Thus, change can be explained from the very successes in the past. Boyer argues for a combination of both approaches.[21]

Lack of change in the VoC framework is also a major concern for Colin Crouch in his 2005 book *Capitalist Diversity and Change*. 'Hall and Soskice were bringing to a brilliant fulfilment a project around which many of us had been skirting for the past quarter century. But now that I saw its perfectly logical culmination I was unsettled by it', he wrote.[22] He considered the main contribution of the VoC approach to be the realisation that economic actors and the market itself exist within a framework of patterns, routines, and rules that constrain the actions and choices of people. At the same time, people were threatened with becoming imprisoned in an iron cage of institutions that they cannot change. Was there an escape? Yes, some people, and Crouch named them 'institutional entrepreneurs', could bring change by combining elements of the institutions in a new way at the right moment. They have more options for recombining in new ways in economies with institutional heterogeneity. By creating new rules and following them, they bring change.[23]

In *Beyond Varieties of Capitalism* Hancké, Rhodes, and Thatcher developed the VoC framework further in order to address some of the criticisms.[24] As already mentioned above, they suggested that the original concept with two opposing models of capitalism could easily be extended by two more models. More importantly, they gave more attention to change and the mechanisms behind change. They disagreed with the view that change is not likely to happen because of the strength of the complementarities. Change is possible because the institutions that underpin coordination are subject to constant renegotiation. When sectors and industries within a national economy develop according to different paths, conflicts of interest may arise, which in turn will lead to power struggles and shifting coalitions. It implies that not all institutional arrangements that underpinned successful cross-class coalitions in the past will remain valid when economic circumstances change. Therefore, they propose to enhance the original VoC framework by paying more attention to class struggles, coalitions, and the role of state. But they hang on to their original argument that changes will play out differently in CMEs and LMEs. Nevertheless, they observe that in countries such as Germany and Switzerland, cooperation has moved from industry to firm level and that LMEs and CMEs in Europe are beginning to share an increasingly segmented labour market and rising income inequality. In their view, this does not signify the demise of the CME, or at least not yet. They end with the warning: 'Ultimately, however, an analytical framework such as the VoC is only as good as its ability to make sense of what is going on in the world around us. And that world is changing quickly'.[25]

Using the more general term comparative capitalisms (CC), Gregory Jackson and Richard Deeg moved from analysing how institutions contributed to economic performance to the question of how institutions themselves are created and change. They want to leave behind the notion of path dependence and instead focus on institutional change. By comparing the different systems of comparative capitalisms, they hope to shed more light on institutional change and to create a 'dynamic theory of institutional change'. In this context, the role of politics should receive more attention. While the VoC literature argues that the nation state would hold on to its own despite increasing globalisation, Jackson and Deeg reverse the argument and suggest that study of changing capitalism should include the international economic activity and the transnational institutions because there is such overwhelming evidence that national economies changed in response to the globalisation. The extent of these changes may not have come to light yet because the formal institutions may look the same, while the way they play out may already have become different.[26]

This last point was highlighted by Kathleen Thelen in 2004 and later in a paper with Peter Hall, in which they explain that institutions remain the same while their coordination changes, perhaps because actors either stop using the rules or else they interpret them differently. But the opposite may also occur: the formal institutions change while the old types of coordination remain the same. Whether or not institutions change depends very much on political coalitions and on their impact on the distribution of welfare.[27]

Performance

This brings us to the key question. Does it matter how an economy is organised? Is there a difference in outcome between the different types of capitalisms? Hall and Soskice expected LMEs to provide more radical innovations and CMEs more incremental innovations. In 2010 William Lazonick vigorously contested this view on the basis of US experiences. Many of the radical innovations had come from state subsidies, not from the market sector. The liberal market economy from the 1990s, or what he called the 'New-Economic Business Model', had in fact a negative impact on any innovation, be it radical or incremental. He particularly blamed the high executive remunerations and the share buy-back schemes that robbed companies from funds to invest in innovation.[28] Bruno Amable and Karim Azizi addressed the question of whether LMEs would act more countercyclical than CMEs because of their supposed greater flexibility. Their study of eighteen OECD countries over the period 1980–2002 did not confirm this hypothesis. If anything, they found a more countercyclical policy in CMEs. This result led them to call for more research into the complicated mix of economic institutions, macro-economic policies, and political systems.[29] Hall and Gingerich concluded that countries that belonged firmly to the liberal or coordinated market economies would be economically more successful than hybrid countries that were something in between. Jeroen Touwen, however, concluded that a CME country could introduce market-based solutions, as happened in the Netherlands during the 1980s and 1990s, without damaging its economic performance. Touwen saw the introduction of changes as part of a learning process among many groups in society through which the country moved from an 'immobile corporatism' in the 1970s towards a 'responsive corporatism' after 1982.[30]

What comes across as a new research agenda to which business historians might contribute? The consensus that market economies are in flux right now highlights the importance of analysing shifts in the past and studying people who were instrumental in creating those shifts. Working from the supposition that there is some coherence between the various institutions of a national economy makes it logical to study the various institutions in their national context. But it is equally important to keep in mind the international context and the impact of globalisation. Politics, power struggles, and class have also been put back on the agenda. The final question that needs to be solved is: how does it all affect us and our welfare? This volume is not going to answer all of those questions, but it intends to increase insight on a number of them from the perspective of one particular country.

THE NETHERLANDS IN THE LONG 20TH CENTURY

The country we have chosen as case study is the Netherlands. Located in Northwestern Europe, the country forms part of one of the most prosperous regions of the world in the 20th century. It is a small country with an open economy. Though the country is small in square miles, it is densely populated. Its population grew from around 5 million in 1900 to 16.6 million in 2010.[31] The country belongs to the mid-sized economies. In 2012 the Netherlands ranked twenty-sixth in the World Bank rankings of the world's largest economies. The country was a world leader in the 17th century, when it reached its summit in economic power, political influence, and rich cultural life after a revolt against the Spanish empire. Its ships sailed the world, combining dominance over bulk trades with a strong position in the more specialised colonial trade. The Dutch East India Company (VoC), established in 1602, was among the first multinational companies, though with some justice it could also be called the first 'national champion' because it thrived on a state-supported monopoly position. It exercised a military presence around the centres of foreign trade, which in due time would lead to the establishment of a colonial empire. The Dutch Republic took over the leading role from older trade centres such as Venice, Genoa, Augsburg, and Antwerp and was in turn superseded and surpassed by Britain in the 18th century.[32] In 1795 the French troops of Napoleon occupied the country, shutting the country off from the sea and introducing French laws and the metric system.

The Netherlands did not begin to industrialise in the late 18th century as did Britain. Historians have agonised over why the country was so slow to follow Britain's example and when at last its 'industrial revolution' took off.[33] The most recent contribution, based on reconstruction of the national accounts, underlines the importance of institutional factors in retarding growth during the first part of the 19th century, until the political and economic liberalisations between 1840 and 1870 paved the way for a rise in productivity and economic growth after 1860. In this economic upswing, agriculture, trade, and transport, helped by the colonies overseas, played a leading role and manufacturing followed.[34] The turn of the 20th century marked the beginning of the four large multinational companies that dominated the Dutch economy for much of that century. Three of the four— Royal Dutch Shell, Unilever, and AKU (the later AKZO Nobel)—were early examples of cross-border mergers, and the first two retained their double Dutch-British nationality. The fourth, Philips Electronics, was Dutch but actively involved in international cartel arrangements, further proof of the international character of Dutch business. The four multinationals were basically active in different industry sectors and therefore could easily work together on general issues and help each other in specific circumstances without harming their own positions. The success of those four multinationals also meant that the Dutch economy was characterised by four really large companies on the one hand and many much smaller firms on the other. With the rise of multinationals in the service sector in the 1980s and 1990s, including banks and insurance companies, and the slimming down of the manufacturing multinationals, the economic structure became more varied.

Around the start of the 20th century, employment in the Netherlands was equally divided between the economic sectors, as Table 1.1 shows. Dutch developments are compared with those of two of its most important trading partners and neighbouring countries: Britain and Germany. Being a latecomer in industrialisation, the Netherlands was behind Britain in employment in manufacturing throughout the whole period, but in particular until 1913. It was, however, ahead of Germany in 1870, but no longer in 1913. The share of manufacturing in employment in the Netherlands rose from 29 per cent in 1870 to 40 per cent in 1950 but remained somewhat behind Britain and Germany. Though not visible in Table 1.1, employment in manufacturing reached a level of 41 per cent in 1960 and diminished thereafter.[35] The Netherlands was very similar to Britain in its importance of the service sector, including the nonmarket services, as a source of employment. Its share was already 34 per cent in 1870 and gradually increased to 72 per cent in 1992. In contrast, employment in agriculture steadily declined, though it remained higher than in Britain and somewhat lower than in Germany. By 1992 agriculture was less than 4 per cent of employment in all three countries. However, the agricultural sector remained important in the Netherlands. The country is still one of the

Table 1.1 Breakdown of employment by major economic sectors, the Netherlands compared to Britain and Germany, 1870–1992, in percentage of total employment

	1870	1913	1950	1992
1. *Agriculture, forestry, fisheries*				
Britain	23	12	5	2
The Netherlands	37	26	14	4
Germany	49	35	22	3
2. *Manufacturing, mining, construction and utilities*				
Britain	42	44	45	26
The Netherlands	29	34	40	24
Germany	29	41	43	38
3. *Market and nonmarket services*				
Britain	35	44	50	72
The Netherlands	34	40	46	72
Germany	22	24	35	59

Source: A. Maddison, *Monitoring the world economy, 1920–1992* (OECD, 1995), p. 39.

largest exporters of agricultural products such as cheese, meat, tomatoes, flowers, and, of course, the famous bulbs.[36]

One important characteristic of the Netherlands, shared with many other small and medium-sized countries, was the 'small country dilemma': the country is strongly dependent on international developments, while at the same time being unable to influence these developments. While large countries like the United States could export the cost of economic change to other countries through ad hoc protectionist policies, small European states had to be flexible and adjust their industrial policies to adapt to changes in the world economy.[37] International trade was hugely important for the Netherlands because of its attractive geographical position along major rivers and the sea, surrounded by prosperous nations. Figure 1.1 highlights the imports and exports of the Netherlands during the past two centuries as percentage of GDP.

After 1860 international trade rose to a substantially higher level, roughly amounting to between 50 and 80 per cent of GDP until 1914. This illustrates how much Dutch business relied on international trade. It was often involved in just a small part of the supply chain, buying raw materials or intermediate products abroad, upgrading them to the next level, and exporting them again as intermediate or final products. To put this figure in perspective: the US level of import and export varied roughly between 4 and 8 per cent of GDP between 1870 and 1914. US exports peaked at slightly over 20 per cent in 1920,[38] while Dutch exports were seldom below that level. Dutch figures for the two world war periods are lacking, but both wars seriously interrupted the flow of goods. International trade did not

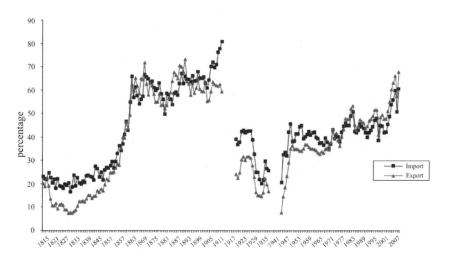

Figure 1.1 Dutch import and export as percentage of GDP, 1815–2010

Source: CBS, *Tweehonderd jaar statistiek in tijdreeksen, 1800–1999*, Voorburg CBS, 2001; CBS StatLine, Import, Export and GDP, 1999–2010.

return to the very high level it had before the First World War until the start of the 21st century.

The two world wars of the 20th century impacted the country in different ways. During the First World War, the country remained neutral, but it was hindered in its overseas trading as well as it contacts with its colonies. That created problems but also opportunities for the home industry. It was a time in which government, businesspeople, and trade unions were thrown together to find solutions for the sudden disruption. During the Second World War, the Netherlands was occupied by the Germans and became a cog in the German war machines. The occupation led to the exploitation of the Dutch economy and the impoverishment of the whole population. Part of the Dutch working population was forced to work in German factories, and some groups of the population were fervently prosecuted, including all Jewish people, many of whom were deported to Germany and murdered in concentration camps.[39] The Second World War also meant the beginning of the end of the Dutch colonial ties with Indonesia. From its existence as a modest colonial power, the Netherlands suddenly became a 'small country'.

During the 20th century, the country went through a number of economic crises. First there was the short but fierce crisis of 1921, caused by the huge fall in commodity prices that followed the boom period directly after the end of the First World War. In particular trading companies and banks came into heavy water because of the price fall. The crisis led banks to withdraw from investment banking, in which they had become engaged since the early years of the 20th century. Of longer duration was the crisis of the 1930s following the stock market crash in the United States in 1929. The crisis did not reach the Netherlands until 1931, but it continued longer than elsewhere because of the deflationary policy of the government. To overcome the negative effects of the crisis, the government encouraged businesses to form cartels and reach collective agreements with their employees.[40]

The two oil crises of 1973 and 1979 affected the manufacturing industry that struggled to keep its export position because of high labour costs and a strong currency. After 1979 the country moved into an economic slump that reached its nadir in 1982. Though economic growth resumed, unemployment remained relatively high during the 1980s.[41] With a large financial sector, it was unlikely that the Netherlands would escape the international housing and banking crisis of 2008, which quickly developed into an economic crisis, and it did not. As happened elsewhere, the Dutch government stepped in to rescue the banks and safeguard the savings of the population. The economic crisis fuelled fresh debates on the role of government, the efficiency of markets, and the division of incomes and wealth that are still ongoing.

In Table 1.2 the Dutch performance in economic growth and labour productivity in the period 1913–1994 is compared with an average of eleven Northwest European countries and the United States.

Table 1.2 The Netherlands within Northwest Europe and the United States, 1913–1994 (unweighted averages of annual compound growth rates)

	The Netherlands	Northwest Europe*	United States
Population	1.14	0.59	1.22
GDP	2.99	2.80	3.05
GDP per capita	1.83	2.00	1.80
GDP per hour worked	2.55	2.67	2.19

* Includes Austria, Belgium, Denmark, Finland, France, Germany, the Netherlands, Norway, Sweden, Switzerland, and the United Kingdom
Source: B. van Ark and H. J. de Jong, *Accounting for Economic Growth in the Netherlands since 1913*. Research Memorandum GD-26, Groningen Growth and Development Centre, Groningen: Universiteit Groningen, 1996, p. 20.

The average annual growth in Gross Domestic Product (GDP) was higher than in Northwest Europe, but the Dutch rise in population was much higher as well, and as a consequence the GDP per capita was lower than in the Northwest Europe, though slightly higher than in the United States. The rise in labour productivity, measured as GDP per hour worked, was somewhat lower than in Northwest Europe, but significantly higher than in the United States. These general figures conceal different periods of alternating fast growth and stagnation, which will be further discussed in chapter 8. Overall, they show that the Netherlands succeeded in providing a growing population with rising incomes and that its labour productivity has been relatively high.

THE NETHERLANDS AND THE VOC DEBATES

The chapters in this volume delve deeper into the question of whether the Netherlands was a coordinated or liberal market economy during the 20th century and what that meant for its economy and its people. Industrial relations, vocational training, and employee representation are central elements in defining the difference between the liberal and coordinated market economy. In chapter 2 in this volume, Erik Nijhof and Annette van den Berg deal with these issues at the macro, meso, and micro level. They show how the First World War brought government and organisations of employers and employees together. The three parties gradually created the coordinated economy that blossomed in the 1950s and 1960s, and became contested in the 1970s. The evolution of the Dutch business system after 1980 can be considered as the transition from a state-directed type of neo-corporatism to a kind of 'soft coordination', with a prominent role for the representatives of the employers and the employees. Nijhof and Van den Bergh conclude that these two groups have now become crucial actors in the field of labour relations. In education and vocational training, the Netherlands followed neither the German nor the British system. Before 1980 the state and the denominational organisations (charities) were the dominant parties in education and vocational training, but in recent years local employers have taken on a dominant role. Again, a different coordination, but still involvement of business. In worker's representation, the relevant laws and regulations have assigned increasing power to the employees, continuing into the present. In this respect the Netherlands resembles Germany more than Britain. In labour relations, Nijhof and Van den Bergh do not see an outright shift from LME to CME and back again to LME, but they see changes in the way the economy is coordinated with a less prominent role of the government and more negotiations directly between employers and employees. These results lead them to end with the crucial question: who is coordinating and within what legal and mental framework?

The fact that the legal power of the work's councils was increased rather than diminished during the 1980s and 1990s, leaves us with the important question what happened to the position of the other stakeholders in the company, and in particular the shareholders. In chapter 3 in this volume, Abe de Jong, Ailsa Röell, and Gerarda Westerhuis discuss changes in Dutch corporate governance from the perspective of shareholders in listed companies. They examine the power of shareholders to exert influence over key corporate decisions, and they do that by analysing the discussions in annual meetings of shareholders. In a LME shareholders are supposed to have a dominant position, and the company is managed to further their interests, while in a CME managers are supposed to balance the interests of the various stakeholders. Their research confirmed that the position of Dutch shareholders in the early 20th century was more characteristic of a LME, while after World War II the other stakeholders became more important. Finally, after the 1980s, the shareholders became once again more powerful. However, they immediately nuance this general picture because they found different shareholders for different periods, from family owners at the start of the century, to large institutional investors at the end. Also, less powerful shareholders did not go hand in hand with more power to the other stakeholders because the real power came in the hands of the managers. Even though in recent years shareholders have become more vocal, and debates at the annual meetings of shareholders are decidedly livelier, shareholders still have limited influence on corporate decisions.

Though the authors don't highlight this conclusion, they show that the corporate laws from 1928 and 1971 solidified past practices and views on how the corporate governance should work at the very moment in time that these views began to shift slowly into a different direction. Whether that also will be the case with the Tabaksblat Code of 2003 has yet to be seen.

The listed companies, central in chapter 3 in this volume, have been very important in the Netherlands during the 20th century, in particular the big four multinationals, but they are not the only sources of business. Chapter 4 in this volume, written by Jacques van Gerwen and Ferry de Goey, analyses the role of entrepreneurial individuals and their companies. Their approach includes small and medium-sized companies. They formulated four hypotheses about how entrepreneurs would behave in respectively liberal and coordinated market economies. They expected entrepreneurs in LMEs to enjoy a higher social status and be less constrained by their social background than those in CMEs. In LMEs entrepreneurs would receive educational programmes and schooling more often than in CMEs, and they expected the share of entrepreneurs in the working population to be higher in LMEs than CMEs. Supposing that the Netherlands and Germany were CMEs and Britain and the United States were LMEs, they tested their four hypotheses and found that none were confirmed. They found no homogeneity in types of entrepreneurs and enterprises, something that would have occurred if the institutional complementarities had been strong. They concluded that in fact all four countries were hybrids, and that, moreover, institutions were not static. One of their findings is that in the Netherlands the number of self-employed people as percentage of civilian employment was higher than that in the United States, though lower than in the United Kingdom. So it seems that the country doesn't lack enterprising people, despite some misgivings in this respect.

Companies don't work in isolation. They are linked to other enterprises such as suppliers and clients but can also work together to reduce the competition or gain more market power. Interfirm relations are one of the five spheres Hall and Soskice distinguish, and in chapter 5 in this volume, Bram Bouwens and Joost Dankers look at collaboration and competition between companies in the Netherlands to analyse their strategies with regard to business interest associations (BIAs), cartels, and mergers and acquisition. They consider those three instruments together because BIAs can easily lead to cartels, while mergers can be used as alternative for cartels. BIAs and cartels are typically seen as instruments for a coordinated market economy, while mergers and acquisitions are more associated with a liberal market economy. Can we therefore identify a liberal or coordinated market economy by analysing these instruments? To a certain extent that is indeed the case, but the story is also more complex. As Bouwens and Dankers show, BIAs provided different services to their members over time, and mergers and acquisitions could be the result of friendly collaboration or of hostile struggles on the stock markets. The development of these instruments confirms the general conclusion that the Dutch economy became more coordinated in the interwar period and moved slowly (and reluctantly) to a more liberal market approach in the 1990s, in part also under pressure of the European legislation.

One of the functions of BIAs is offering a network and platform for discussion. As such they played an important role in the diffusion of knowledge, as Mila Davids and Harry Lintsen explain in chapter 6 in this volume, on the Dutch knowledge infrastructure and institutional change. They use the Dutch case to test the argument of Hall and Soskice that companies in coordinated market economies work more closely together to exchange knowledge and technology and are more inclined to set up joined R&D projects than those in liberal market economies. Moreover, governments in coordinated market economies are more involved in the development of the knowledge infrastructure. In liberal market economies, however, knowledge transfer more often takes place via licensing, and the government is mostly absent in innovation policy. Davids and Lintsen did not find one pattern for all Dutch firms but rather elements of both liberal and coordinated market economies. They looked at both the public and private knowledge infrastructure. The innovation strategy of large multinationals fitted in a liberal market economy, but the small and medium-sized companies relied more on their BIAs. In some cases the government supported initiatives of these associations. After the Second World War, the Dutch government became more closely involved with the knowledge infrastructure, as society had high expectations of the benefits of fundamental research. After 1970, however, both companies and government reduced their expenditures on research, while the government at the same time became more directive in steering innovation. The increased importance of commissioned research, also at public institutes, led to the creation of a market for knowledge, only accessible when paid for. Comparing the Dutch developments with those in the United States, the authors found more similarities than they had expected, nuancing further the contrast between the liberal and coordinated market economy.

The changing views on the importance of R&D and on the expenditures on fundamental research demonstrate similarities between the United States and the Netherlands. That may not surprise us because multinationals, in particular Royal Dutch Shell and Philips, held a prominent place in the Dutch knowledge infrastructure because of their large research centres. That raises the question to what extent multinationals act as intermediaries between different business systems and agents of change, the subject of chapter 7 in this volume, by Keetie Sluyterman and Ben Wubs. In analysing the impact of multinationals working in the Netherlands on the business system, they found both change and constancy. Constant was the willingness of Dutch companies to engage in international business, to invest abroad, and to work abroad. Constant also was the acceptance of foreign investment in the Netherlands and the willingness of the Dutch to work for foreign companies.

Important changes took place in the internal organisation of the multinationals and in their impact on the organisation of the economy. The First World War and the subsequent protectionism formed the first important turning point in the relationship between multinational companies and national governments. The subsidiaries of Dutch multinationals engaged with the local interests in the various countries in which they operated and adjusted to local ways of doing business. Foreign multinationals in the Netherlands followed comparable strategies. In line with their wish to be locally embedded, they underpinned the coordinated market economy. The second turning point during the 1980s is more diffuse. The combination of economic recession and technological change led to a reexamination of the role of government and the rise of a global economy. Multinationals shaped the construction of international markets and were at the same time influenced by them. The global markets and global public scrutiny pressured them into creating more homogeneity in their own companies. As a consequence of international pressure they—also in the Netherlands—became advocates of shareholder value, performance-related pay structures, and flexibility in the labour market.

The analyses made in chapters 2 to 7 in this volume confirm that the Netherlands moved from a mostly liberal market economy before 1914 towards a coordinated market economy from the 1930s onwards, and—up to a certain extent—back again to a more liberal market economy. The financial crisis of 2008 may well turn out to be a new turning point. The organisation of the economy is thus not cast in iron, and not only did the intensity of the coordination change over time but also the parties involved in the coordination process. The turning points in time differed somewhat between the different spheres, but wars and economic crises were in all cases moments for revaluation and change of tack. As the various chapters make clear, individual choices of companies and people played an important role in those changes. In some cases—as during the First World War—the need to take practical measures to protect the population led to new patterns of behaviour that successively led to new views on organising the economy. In other cases, as in the late 1970s and early 1980s, the economic stagnation led to a rethinking of the costs and benefits of the welfare state and the respective roles of government, business, and employees, which in turn led to a different behaviour.

In most cases, changes took place to further economic growth and general welfare. How well did they succeed? In chapter 8 in this volume, Jan Luiten van Zanden discusses the performance of the Dutch business system during the 20th century. Did the Netherlands perform better as coordinated market economy than as liberal market economy, and if so, in what ways? As always, the answers are not clear cut. Measured in terms of economic growth, the Netherlands did very well, also in comparison with its European neighbours, in the 1920s and the 1960s and 1970s, but also in the 1990s, so both in periods of a coordinated and liberal market economy. In contrast, in the 1930s and the early 1980s, the Netherlands lagged behind its neighbours. As an open economy, the Netherlands was apparently vulnerable to international economic crisis, and perhaps more so than its neighbours. The same vulnerability to adverse economic periods was visible in the unemployment figures. For investment in R&D, the high point was in the 1950s and 1960s, while in the 1970s, the decline in R&D investment set in, coinciding with the move from a coordinated to a liberal market economy. The frequency of strikes as indication of social unrest was high before the Second World War and low afterwards, and remained low during the 1990s. Income inequality was reduced between 1910 and 1985, but increased somewhat since, though not as much as, for instance, in the United Kingdom.

This volume's concluding chapter 9 by Keetie Sluyterman places the Dutch results in an international perspective. From the comparisons with the experiences of the other countries, in the various chapters as well as in the final chapter, it becomes clear that the generalisations of Hall and Soskice captured a moment in time and described the developments in the 1990s. Their analytic framework remains useful because it is parsimonious and flexible. It works well as a common starting point to compare different periods as well as different countries, and it highlights the many varieties in market economies. But even Germany and the United States never fitted completely into the model.

Is it possible to reconcile the idea of institutional complementarities with the overwhelming evidence that change is taking place all the time? Is there a logic in the system? The historical evidence presented in the chapters of this volume suggests that there is indeed some logic in the way the coordinated economy took shape gradually. The organisation of labour found a response in the organisation of employers, and once employers reached agreements on higher wages, they were bound to seek agreements on other costs and sources of income. We see how coordination in one area was followed by coordination in other areas: collective labour agreements were followed by cartel agreements, and in the 1930s both were supported by the government. The opposite movement took place from the 1980s onwards with less government, more flexible and individual labour arrangements, and tougher measures against collusive behaviour of companies. In short, the coherence between the various spheres was certainly not absent, but it was less constraining than the varieties of capitalism framework supposes. Businesses and people have choices. Analysing the past helps in highlighting those choices.

Wars and economic crises were moments for reflection and changing paradigms, in the Netherlands and in other countries, as chapter 9 in this volume shows. Views on the best organisation of the economy were shared between countries, companies, and people. The Dutch case in particular demonstrates the continuous influx of ideas from other countries. But sharing ideas does not mean that all countries drew the same conclusions or took the same measures. Globalisation does not necessarily come with a convergence of all national business systems, but it has an impact on the (in)dependence of countries and their room for manoeuvre, which in turn cannot fail to have an impact on how they organise their economies. What therefore needs further analysis is the question to what extent the international position of countries in terms of political power, economic size, and international trade determines their national organisation of the economy.

NOTES

1. Hall and Soskice, *Varieties of Capitalism*.
2. Sluyterman, *Dutch Enterprise*, 254–257; Touwen, 'Varieties of capitalism'; Touwen, 'How does a coordinated market economy evolve?'.
3. Hall and Soskice, *Varieties of Capitalism*.
4. Hall and Soskice, 'Introduction', 1–7.
5. Hall and Soskice, 'Introduction', 8–17.
6. Hall and Soskice, 'Introduction', 17–27.
7. Hall and Soskice, 'Introduction', 45–50.
8. Hall and Soskice, 'Introduction', 54–66.
9. Hall and Gingerich, Varieties of capitalism and institutional complementarities, 29, 37–38.
10. Hall and Soskice, 'Introduction', 2, 19–21.
11. Amable, *Diversity of Modern Capitalism*.
12. Whitley, *Business Systems and Organizational Capabilities*, 86–113.
13. Allen, 'Not enough variety?', 87–108.
14. Boyer, 'How and why capitalisms differ'.
15. Crouch, *Capitalist Diversity*, 4.
16. Hancké, Rhodes, and Thatcher, 'Introduction: Beyond varieties', 24–28.
17. Sluyterman, *Dutch Enterprise*, 243–257; Touwen, 'Varieties of capitalism', 100–104.
18. Dore, Lazonick, and O'Sullivan, 'Varieties of capitalism'.
19. Dore, Lazonick, and O'Sullivan, 'Varieties of capitalism', 102–120.
20. Schneider and Paunescu, 'Changing varieties of capitalism'.
21. Boyer, 'How and why capitalisms differ'.
22. Crouch, *Capitalist Diversity*, 1–2.
23. Crouch, *Capitalist Diversity*, 3–4, 22–24.
24. Hancké, Rhodes, and Thatcher, *Beyond Varieties of Capitalism*.
25. Hancké, Rhodes, and Thatcher, 'Introduction: Beyond varieties', 38.
26. Jackson and Deeg, 'How many varieties of capitalism?', 5–7, 37–39.
27. Thelen, *How Institutions Evolve;* Hall and Thelen, 'Institutional change', 7–34.
28. Lazonick, 'Innovative business models', 675–702.
29. Amable and Azisi, 'Are some economies more procyclical than others?'.
30. Touwen, 'How does a coordinated market economy evolve?'
31. CBS, StatLine, Population 1900–2010. http://statline.cbs.nl/statweb/.
32. Davids and Lucassen, *Miracle Mirrored*.
33. Griffiths, 'Backward', 1–22.
34. Van Zanden and Van Riel, *Nederland 1780–1914*.
35. Van Ark and De Jong, *Accounting for Economic Growth*, Table 10, 32.
36. Besamusca and Verheul, *Discovering the Dutch*, 33–34.
37. Katzenstein, *Small States in World Markets*, 17–37.
38. Bordo, Eichengreen, and Irwin, 'Is globalization today really different?', 59.
39. Klemann, *Nederland 1938–1948*.
40. Sluyterman, *Dutch Enterprise*, 88–91, 111–113.
41. Sluyterman, *Dutch Enterprise*, 191–196.

20   *Keetie Sluyterman*

REFERENCES

Allen, M., 'The varieties of capitalism paradigm: Not enough variety?', *Socio-Economic Review*, 2 (2004): 87–108.
Amable, Bruno, *The Diversity of Modern Capitalism* (Oxford: Oxford University Press, 2003).
Amable, Bruno and Azizi, Karim, 'Varieties of Capitalism and Varieties of Macro-economic Policy: Are Some Economies More Procyclical Than Others?', *MPIfG Discussion paper*, 11/6 (2011).
Ark, Bart van and Herman J. de Jong, *Accounting for Economic Growth in the Netherlands since 1913*. Groningen Growth and Development Centre (Groningen: University of Groningen, 1996).
Besamusca, Emmeline and Jaap Verheul, eds., *Discovering the Dutch: On Culture and Society of the Netherlands* (Amsterdam: Amsterdam University Press, 2010).
Bordo, M. D., Eichengreen, B., and Irwin, D. A., 'Is globalization today really different than globalization a hundred years ago?', *NBER working paper series*, 7195 (1999): 1–73.
Boyer, Robert, 'How and Why Capitalisms Differ', *MPIfG Discussion paper* 05/04 (2005).
Crouch, Colin, *Capitalist Diversity and Change. Recombinant Governance and Institutional Entrepreneurs* (Oxford: Oxford University Press, 2005).
Davids, Karel and Jan Lucassen, eds., *A Miracle Mirrored. The Dutch Republic in European Perspective* (Cambridge: Cambridge University Press, 1995).
Dore, R., Lazonick, W., and O'Sullivan, M., 'Varieties of capitalism in the twentieth century', *Oxford Review of Economic Policy*, 15, 4 (1999): 102–120.
Griffiths, Richard, 'Backward, late or different?', in: Jan Luiten van Zanden, ed., *The Economic Development of the Netherlands since 1870* (Cheltenham: Elgar, 1996) 1–22.
Hall, Peter A. and Daniel W. Gingerich, 'Varieties of Capitalism and Institutional Complementarities in the Macroeonomy', *MPIfG discussion paper* 04/05 (2005).
Hall, Peter A. and David Soskice, 'An introduction to varieties of capitalism', in: Peter A. Hall and David Soskice eds., *Varieties of Capitalism. The Institutional Foundations of Comparative Advantage* (Oxford: Oxford University Press, 2001) 1–68.
Hall, Peter A. and David Soskice, eds., *Varieties of Capitalism. The Institutional Foundations of Comparative Advantage* (Oxford: Oxford University Press, 2001).
Hall, P. A. and Thelen, K., 'Institutional change in varieties of capitalism', *Socio-economic Review*, 7 (2009): 7–34.
Hancké, Bob, Martin Rhodes, and Mark Thatcher, eds., *Beyond Varieties of Capitalism. Conflict, Contradictions, and Complementarities in the European Economy* (Oxford: Oxford University Press, 2007).
Hancké, Bob, Martin Rhodes, and Mark Thatcher, 'Introduction: Beyond Varieties of Capitalism', in: Bob Hancké, Martin Rhodes, and Mark Thatcher, eds., *Beyond Varieties of Capitalism. Conflict, Contradictions, and Complementarities in the European Economy* (Oxford: Oxford University Press, 2007) 3–38.
Jackson, Gregory and Richard Deeg, 'How Many Varieties? Comparing the Comparative Institutional Analyses of Capitalist Diversity', *MPIfG Discussion paper*, 06/02 (2006).
Katzenstein, Peter, *Small States in World Markets: Industrial Policy in Europe* (Ithaca: Cornell University Press, 1985).
Klemann, Hein A. M., *Nederland 1938–1948. Economie en samenleving in jaren van oorlog en bezetting* (Amsterdam: Boom, 2002).

Lazonick, W., 'Innovative business models and Varieties of Capitalism: Financialization of the US corporation', *Business History Review*, 84, Winter (2010): 675–702.

Schneider, M. R. and Paunescu, M., 'Changing varieties of capitalism and revealed comparative advantages from 1990 to 2005: A test of the Hall and Soskice claims', *Socio-Economic Review*, 9 (2011): 1–23.

Sluyterman, Keetie E., *Dutch Enterprise in the Twentieth Century. Business Strategies in a Small Open Economy* (London and New York: Routledge, 2005).

Thelen, Kathleen, *How Institutions Evolve* (Oxford: Cambridge University Press, 2004).

Touwen, J., 'How does a coordinated market economy evolve? Effects of policy learning in the Netherlands in the 1980s', *Labor History*, 49, 4 (2008): 439–464.

Touwen, J., 'Varieties of capitalism en de Nederlandse economie in de periode 1950–2000', *Tijdschrift voor Sociale en Economische Geschiedenis*, 3, 1 (2006): 73–104.

Whitley, Richard, *Business Systems and Organizational Capabilities: The Institutional Structuring of Competitive Competences* (Oxford: Oxford University Press, 2007).

Zanden, Jan Luiten van and Arthur van Riel, *Nederland 1780–1914. Staat, instituties en economische ontwikkeling* (Amsterdam: Uitgeverij Balans, 2000).

2 Variations of Coordination
Labour Relations in the Netherlands

Erik Nijhof and Annette van den Berg

INTRODUCTION

In their now classic volume on Varieties of Capitalism, Hall and Soskice unreservedly classify the Dutch business system as a coordinated market economy.[1] Other authors, who investigated the Dutch economy in detail, saw a turn towards a more liberal market economy after 1980, but not an outright transition.[2] Especially with regard to labour relations, there was a strong resilience of the consultative institutions that were seen as the cornerstone of this business system.[3]

In this chapter, we will concentrate on labour relations. In order to determine the crucial stages in the evolution of the labour relations in the Netherlands, we have chosen to investigate the developments of three key aspects of the labour relations, on the three relevant levels of the business system: *the macro, meso, and micro levels*. On the *macro (national) level* we concentrate on organisations of employers and employees and on the development of the central institutions of the Dutch consultative economy, the Labour Foundation (Stichting van de Arbeid), and the Social and Economic Council (Sociaal-Economische Raad, SER); on the *meso level (industrial sectors)* we study the changes in the field of vocational training and education; on the *micro level (plant or company)* we focus on the works councils and their growing competencies, including in the field of health and safety.

These three aspects of labour relations largely overlap with three of the five 'spheres' that were distinguished by Hall and Soskice (2001), as set out in the introductory chapter of their book. These three areas are related to the interaction between businesses and their workforce and concern, in succession, the sphere of the industrial relations on the national level, the sphere of vocational training and education of the labour force, and the sphere of coordination between employers and employees at company level. According to Hall and Soskice, liberal and coordinated market economies (LMEs and CMEs) each have their own specific constellation of institutions in every single one of these spheres. The way these scholars classify the Netherlands as a CME needs further elaboration because they fail to adequately take historical changes into account. In our contribution, we will try to correct this and show that it is fruitful to distinguish between different forms of coordination.

A DANCE FOR THREE: THE CONSULTATIVE INSTITUTIONS

Before 1914, most employers bluntly refused even to talk with trade unions. However, during the First World War they had to cooperate with the state and these unions in order to preserve the neutrality and the social stability of the country. The shock of the Russian and German revolutions and an abortive attempt of the Dutch socialists to seize state power resulted in a wave of social legislation. A milestone was the introduction of the universal suffrage in 1917 for men, and in 1919 for women, as well as that of the eight-hour working day. In this changed climate, many employers came to see the advantages of bargaining with the trade unions, which were in majority moderate and pragmatic organisations.[4] This became apparent by the growing number of trade-based collective labour agreements (CLAs) in the 1920s. Already in 1907, labour contracts between individual employers and one or more trade unions became legally possible, only binding the contracting parties. In 1927, the scope of the law was extended to the whole workforce of the contracting company. Ten years later a new law enabled the government to declare a CLA legally binding for the whole trade, to avoid free-rider behaviour among the employers. From then on, the CLA became a crucial vehicle for the growing coordination within the Dutch business system, by constantly incorporating new regulations, such as the pension schemes and the sickness insurance.[5]

A new development was the introduction of a pension fund in a branch of industry, jointly founded and administered by employers and trade unions. The first arrangement of this kind came into being for civil servants in 1922: the ABP (Universal Pension Funds for Civil Servants), which was to become highly successful and has even become one of the biggest pension funds in the world. The branch-based character implied information sharing among all participants: on the numbers and age composition of the personnel, the sum total of the premiums paid, and, hence, the wage structure; but most important was the long-term commitment of all partners in the funds, to guarantee the promised benefits over some decades—all of them characteristic features of a CME.[6]

Another sign of the consciousness of common interests was the joint initiative in 1921 of two national leaders of employers and employees, Folkert Posthuma and Evert Kupers, to design a bill to compensate for loss of income due to sickness leave. The premiums would be paid by the employers, and the implementation of this insurance was left to 'trade associations', co-administered by representatives of the trade unions and the employers. This Sickness Law, carried in 1931, was a crucial element of social security, but its painful implementation reflected the big controversies in Dutch society around this issue; on the costs of medical treatment no consensus could be reached; this desideratum was fulfilled only ten years later, by a decree of the German occupiers.[7]

In the 1930s, the government stepped in with ad hoc regulation and then with coordination. Successive right-wing cabinets, most of them headed by Hendrik Colijn, made two important strategic choices: first, to hold on to the gold standard and, hence, to support the national currency; and second, to protect essential sectors of the economy (agriculture and shipbuilding) and to introduce a quota system in other sectors, all without resorting to high tariffs, that would be inappropriate for a small, open economy highly dependent on foreign trade. These measures implied monitoring and control of the economic activities in the protected sectors, which was only possible with adequate coordination, and this, in turn, required more staff members in the government departments.[8]

Another measure was to stimulate cooperation in business. So in 1935, the government proposed a bill that regulated production cartels: when companies in a certain branch of industry agreed on a cartel, they had to request government approval; when it was granted, it applied to the whole trade, in order to avoid free-rider behaviour. Until 1940, seven cartel agreements were approved. But the logic of regulation did not stop at this point: in order to create a level playing field, there also needed to be a similar regulation with respect to the labour agreements. As a consequence, a bill was adopted in 1937, which enabled the government to declare a collective labour agreement binding for the whole branch of industry, as became the rule.[9] In the same vein, the government favoured the extension of the scope of the CLA—for instance, by incorporating pension schemes.

Behind this pragmatic cooperation between the three main actors, there was also deeper, ideological rapprochement that had gone on from the late 19th century: under the influence of Social-Christian ideas, the denominational organisations of employers and employees were strongly pressed to reconsider their mutual relations in favour of class cooperation instead of class struggle; joint institutions were seen as the best solution to social problems. So, on the national level, two advisory bodies had been founded in the interwar years. First, the High Council of Labour (1920) for social questions; after long discussions, it laid the foundation of unemployment insurance (agreement in 1939, realisation in 1952). Second, 1932 saw the birth of its pendant, the Economic Council, which advised on the 1937 law regarding the CLAs. Both bodies had as its members government-appointed experts and representatives from the leading organisations of employers and employees. These tripartite bodies could only give advice when asked for by government; their effectiveness was further reduced by internal disagreements. But both councils continued to function, notably in many subcommittees, where informal contacts were maintained. Perhaps the latter aspect was most important in preparing the ground for the success of the postwar consultative economy.[10]

Of equal importance was the ideological turn of the Social Democrats: after their failed 'revolution' in 1918, they gave up all perspectives of radical socio-political revolution and opted for a more regulated capitalism. This changing attitude became visible in the participation in the institutions mentioned above: perhaps at first as a pragmatic move but then gradually as a positive choice for a coordinated capitalism within a parliamentary democracy.[11]

All of these developments, however, did not yet result in a fully coordinated market economy in the field of labour relations. The first measures were taken ad hoc, in the fight against the Depression, but after 1935, these took a more permanent character. The end of the Christian-liberal coalition, in power since 1918, and headed by the orthodox-Protestant Colijn since 1933, was a turning point. The latter was a staunch defender of *laissez faire* capitalism, free trade, and a solid currency, but he was confronted with a growing opposition from Catholics, who in 1939 changed sides and started a coalition with the Social Democrats. The economic depression of the 1930s had severely undermined the trust of the public in *laissez faire* capitalism and had made clear that new socio-political coalitions were necessary.[12]

The German Occupation: Imposed Coordination[13]

The outbreak of the Second World War and the German occupation of the Netherlands put an abrupt end to this process of gradual rapprochement between these parties and organisations striving for more coordination. First, all of these parties were forbidden and forced to terminate their (visible) activities; second, the German occupiers introduced their own variety of a coordinated economy: the state apparatus, dominated by dedicated Nazis and supported by a handful of collaborators, claimed absolute authority to impose whatever measures that they deemed necessary to help Germany win the war and to attain its ideological goals. They outlawed all established political parties and forced the trade unions to merge into one organisation under national-socialist control: the National Labour Front. But their success was limited: the leaders of these unions exhorted their members to resign, an appeal which was widely followed, and these unions lost most of their members within a few weeks (with the exception of the agricultural labourers). The Germans also set out to reorganise the whole structure of the economy in line with their corporatist principles, but the leading figures of Dutch business were not so keen to cooperate; in the end the Germans ran the economy themselves.[14] Other measures in the field of labour relations turned out to be so useful that they were maintained after May 1945: obligatory insurance of medical treatment,[15] new pension funds,[16] and strict wage control.[17]

Postwar Society: New Forms of Coordination

During the German occupation, the contacts between the outlawed parties and organisations were continued secretly and became more intensive as the defeat of the Nazis seemed a matter of time. And at the end of the Second World War, leaders of the employers' organisations and the trade union federations held clandestine meetings on the postwar system of business relations. They agreed on the necessity of creating a platform for mutual consultation, which they baptised the Labour Foundation (Stichting van de Arbeid) and for which draft statutes were made; it officially came into being in 1945. Both parties solemnly declared that they would stimulate joint consultations on the macro and meso levels in order to avoid conflicts on labour relations. On micro level, however, the authority of the employers in their companies would not be questioned.[18]

In the meantime, the government in exile had launched its own plans for a new postwar society in 1944, which also came to incorporate the Labour Foundation. In order to rebuild the damaged country as quickly as possible, and to restore the export industry that was considered crucial to the Dutch economy, a policy of fixed and low wages was launched. The State Board of Arbitration was given the authority to compare all draft CLAs with the government guidelines. The Labour Foundation was only given the right to advice on these drafts, but the government had to approve every single labour agreement. Strikes to obtain better terms were difficult: the decision of the State Arbiters was binding for all contracting parties. Thus, the official trade unions relied only upon negotiating; wildcat strikes and strikes launched by nonofficial unions were still possible but could not result in a better contract, as a CLA could only be signed by the official unions in the Labour Foundation.[19] The official labour organisations had agreed with the loss of autonomy and the low wages because they expected that employment would benefit from the recovery of the export industries if labourers were cheap and did not strike. Moreover, the employers and the new government had solemnly and publicly promised that a comprehensive programme of social security would guarantee a decent and secure living to all citizens; the unions went along with this promise and accepted the unavoidable time-lag before the first measures in this field could be realised.[20]

The immediate situation after liberation showed a society in a state of turmoil: impoverished and radicalised workers often called wildcat strikes, notably in the harbours; a new trade union federation presented itself as the alternative to the prewar unions that hesitated to reestablish themselves; a new political formation was announced, which should unite all progressive people regardless their religious beliefs. But the strikes failed, the new unitary trade union federation became only a newcomer amidst the old federations that returned, and the Labour Party (Partij van de Arbeid) was not so different from the prewar Social Democratic party, though it had attracted some Christians. But one thing had changed fundamentally: the coordinated system of labour relations and the prospect of a welfare state that would guarantee a decent living for all citizens. This explains best the return of social peace, as it responded to the widely expressed desire for more righteous and better-coordinated social and economic relations.

ones (with the Industrial Union organising workers in all manufacturing industries as its apex), and in 1979, the Social Democratic and the Catholic federations constituted the FNV (Federation of Dutch Trade Unions) as the outcome of a long and complicated evolution that turned bitter enemies into close allies; on the meso level, all of their trade unions had to merge into greater unions.[31] The employers' organisations VNO and CNW (Christian employers, after a merger of the Catholic and Protestant organisations in 1967) intensified their cooperation and finally merged into one organisation in 1995. Paradoxically, this formation of power in both camps enhanced the perspectives of a consultative economy, as there were now at both sides solid organisations with leaders who had great authority and representativeness towards their own followers.

In 1979, there were a number of strikes, partly spontaneous, that were lost by the trade unions. In combination with the bad economic situation, the balance of power began to shift in favour of the employers; the years around 1980 may be considered the end of an era of working-class radicalism. The leaders of the union federations were the first to recognise the new realities. Plant closings went on, as did inflation, and the successive governments used their right to intervene in labour agreements twelve times between 1970 and 1982.[32]

It was against the background of these dire prospects that a growing number of trade union leaders came to the conclusion that they could ask something back from the employers rather than being left empty handed by the government.[33] As for the employers, they were opposed to central wage setting long since because of the diverging interests within their ranks (such as between those operating on the domestic versus foreign markets; big versus small enterprises; labour intensive versus capital intensive industries). The system of central wage setting had always put a heavy strain on their internal cohesion; to be sure, this was also the case for the trade union federations. But the government itself became more and more reluctant to intervene in the negotiations on the terms of employment, and on many occasions, the possible implementation of such a measure was announced rather as an incentive for both parties to reach an agreement that was acceptable within the actual set of government priorities. Without this all too obvious threat by the Lubbers government, the Wassenaar Agreement would not have been reached so easily.[34]

The Wassenaar Agreement and Its Aftermath

Under these conditions, Chris van Veen, the first full-time president of the VNO, and Wim Kok, president of the FNV, met secretly in the former's residence in Wassenaar, near The Hague, accompanied, if needed, by specialists. They did this on their own account, without mandate of their organisations. During these talks, they agreed that the employers would promote shorter working hours and part-time work, in order to maximise employment, while the workers would accept moderate wage increases that would not always keep up with rising prices, as well as a nominal wage decrease if they worked less hours. The government readily responded to this agreement with promulgating an act that enabled the breaking up of existing labour agreements to suspend the automatic price compensation. Without any doubt, the concessions made by the workers' organisations were the most substantial, in conformity with the changed balance of power: the workers accepted lower real wages; the employers promised to promote employment by spreading the existing jobs over more workers, at the latter's cost. At both sides there was at first much distrust, which could only be overcome by the personal prestige of their respective leaders. In short, the era before 1982 had been a learning process during which both parties came to realise that they could only win by a long-term mutual understanding and, hence, by a certain level of trust.[35]

In the eight years after the Wassenaar Agreement, real labour costs decreased with 1.2 per cent per annum, and the percentage of unemployed sunk from 12.0 to 7.5 per cent of the working population.[36] There has been much discussion as to what extent this Agreement contributed to the economic recovery since 1985. Compared with the other OECD countries, between 1985 and 1994, Dutch GDP grew faster (2.53 per cent yearly against 2.20 per cent), just like the exports (4.62 per cent against 4.11 per cent), whereas the growth of the imports showed the opposite direction (4.27 per cent versus 4.87 per cent).[37] Most authors agree on the conclusion that the changed socio-political climate was very helpful in mobilising forces for this recovery: even when, in the 1990s, the economy was booming, there were no big wage demands and strikes were nearly absent.

The Labour Foundation took the lead in the consultative system. The rather vague recommendations of the Wassenaar Agreement were followed by more precise and concrete agreements: on youth unemployment (1984), interruption of pension accrual due to job change (1985), retraining of long-term unemployed (1986), ethnic- and gender-based unemployment (1990), reduction of sickness absenteeism (1991), and more flexible labour contracts (1994).[38] All of these recommendations were specific elaborations of the agenda set by the Wassenaar Agreement.

But to be sure, this never implicated absence of struggle. When in 1990 the government again tried to enforce a general wage freeze, the employers reacted by boycotting the tripartite consultation in the SER in 1991 and 1992, with the result that the government gave way and recognised the principle of free wage bargaining on the meso and plant level.[39] Another bone of contention was the reform of the social security system, necessary because it had grown beyond all original prognoses and had become too big a burden to the public treasury. The reform of this system was a painful operation, which aroused fierce protests, such as the limited liability to disability allowances in 1987. But in the end disputes were settled by cutting off the sharp edges, or by compensations within the CLAs.[40]

The 'Polder Model' as Decentralised Coordination

Probably the greatest significance of the Wassenaar Agreement was that it generated this joint energy and opened new perspectives for a consultative economy. As long as the leaders of employers and trade unions could reach agreements in the Labour Foundation, they were able to keep the government out; but when they disagreed, the SER could play a prominent role, with the government-appointed independent members in a key position. And in the meantime, the SER advised on more general issues, when asked by the government.[41] The Wassenaar Agreement had thus paved the way for a new type of consultative economy in the field of labour relations, in which the 'social partners' (organisations of employers and employees) tried to reach agreements in the Labour Foundation and also in the SER, together with the government-appointed experts. In 1996, this system gained international recognition under the name 'Polder Model', which had succeeded in combining good economic performance with a decent level of social security, accomplished with a minimal level of social struggle owing to joint consultation.[42] The coordination comes from a delicate interplay between the relevant actors on all levels, with the government in a monitoring role, only intervening where it is legally possible and necessary when things are going wrong. We may typify this as a form of decentralised coordination. Crucial is not so much its structure as its belief in the necessity of broad support for changes.[43]

VOCATIONAL TRAINING AND EDUCATION: NEW INSTITUTIONS[44]

Skill Formation and the Business System: The United Kingdom and Germany

The way workers acquire the necessary skills to adequately perform their jobs varies widely from country to country.[45] In a LME like the United Kingdom, older workers, mostly on an ad hoc basis, train the young on the spot; as a consequence, the new skills are plant specific and not easily transferable to other jobs. More generally, acquiring skills is seen as a personal investment into one's career; employers are always afraid that a competitor would hire workers they have invested in, thereby reaping the benefits of their own efforts to raise the skill of their labour force. This distrust, together with a deep-rooted desire for autonomy that also prevails in the trade unions,[46] has prevented the rise of common institutions of training and educating workers on the level of a branch of industry.

The historical roots of this arrangement go back well into the 19th century. The traditions and mentalities of the guilds survived also among the workers in the new industries. This manifested itself in a strong sense of professional exclusivism of small, craft-based unions that clung to traditional, once-acquired prerogatives. Often they struggled with rivalling unions over demarcation lines and the right to represent certain catego-ries of workers. But one of their most effective rights was the control of the influx of newcomers by selectively admitting apprentices, who were trained on the job by experienced workers. Thus, in these trades, the level of skills and the entrance to the labour market were under control of the elder union members. This made sense in manual crafts with relatively sta-ble, labour-intensive skills: here the technology was located in the heads and hands of experienced workers. But where employers introduced new, capital-intensive technologies, as a rule in large factories, they wished to control the skills needed for the expensive machinery they had invested in. So it is not surprising that especially in the metallurgical sector, the employ-ers began to challenge this monopoly of the workers in the late 1890s; and after repeated and protracted struggles, they succeeded to break it, although without creating alternative arrangements of skill formation in their branch. In labour-intensive sectors such as mining, dock work, and printing, the workers preserved this monopoly, at least until the 1970s and 1980s.[47]

At the other end of this spectre, in CME Germany, skill formation is firmly embedded in a legal framework that entrusts the task of skill forma-tion to small and medium-sized enterprises that teach workers the general skills of the trade; in exchange, they are allowed to pay lower wages, and as a rule, after the training period, these apprentices are employed by big-ger enterprises that are also involved in establishing vocational qualification standards on branch level. This system was created in 1897 (*Handwerker Schutzgesetz*) as a device to strengthen the crafts that were considered as bulwarks against socialism. Small and medium-sized industries had to par-ticipate in vocational training schemes with branch-specific certification. But in Wuerttemberg, Baden, Bavaria, and Thuringia, modern and export-oriented firms, mostly family owned and medium-sized, adapted this system to their own needs and thus laid the foundation of what would become the cornerstone of the German business system.[48] Despite two world wars and abrupt regime changes, the system survived, prospered again after 1950, and in 1969, it acquired a nationwide basis.[49] The German apprentice system is now generally considered essential to the successful export of high-quality products.[50]

When we compare both systems of vocational education, we see that in LMEs there is only general education on different levels on the one hand, and plant-specific training on the job on the other, whereas CMEs tried to bridge this gap by creating intermediate bodies for branch-specific voca-tional training and education, thus sharing the risks and costs for individual employers.[51] The role of government was crucial: in the United Kingdom, it remained aloof and let employers and unions fight their battle; in Germany, the government actively interfered to battle the rising socialist movement by strengthening the guild-inspired crafts, but modern, market-oriented firms transformed the original, backwards-looking measure into a modern strategy to strengthen their competitiveness.

Technical Schools in the Netherlands: Dominance of Ideology

The early decades in the Netherlands showed a totally different picture than either the United Kingdom or Germany. Some local charity organisations had set up evening schools for young male workers to provide some additional education, and there were also employers who organised vocational training courses with a wider curriculum than was needed in their factory. More important were the 1901 Education Act that made school attendance up to the age of twelve compulsory, and the successive raising of that age up to fifteen years, which necessitated additional educational arrangements. For the young who would become workers, there were now three options. The simplest one was to follow three additional years of lower education. The second option was the Lower Technical School (LTS), established by a law in 1919 and subsidised by the state. The 1919 law also made possible dual learning trajectories, but few pupils followed these. The LTS gained ground in the following decades: between 1920 and 1940, their numbers of pupils rose from almost 12,000 to 38,000, but there was no even coverage over the country or between the branches of industry, as it was local groups that initiated the founding of a LTS.[52] Successive governments reduced their support of this kind of vocational education by cutting their subsidies and lowering the school age from fifteen to fourteen years; supervision on the content of the curricula was hardly exerted.[53]

After 1945, the landscape of vocational training and education drastically changed. The postwar reconstruction era saw a drastic reappraisal of the value of labour, due to its relative scarcity and also as a reaction to the Great Depression with its massive layoffs. The position of the young (male) workers was considered crucial: to integrate them fully into society, and to prevent them from falling into nihilism or even communism, secure employment was needed in combination with a form of vocational education that imbued them with values such as cooperativeness, loyalty, and obedience, and taught them some basic manual skills and general knowledge. These became the main elements of the curricula of the Lower Technical Schools that now spread rapidly all over the country: between 1946 and 1955, the number of these schools rose from 132 to 202, and their pupils from 36,772 to 68,969.[54] Driving forces behind this rapid expansion were the different denominational currents: the Catholics, the Protestants, and the Social Democrats developed, despite their differences, parallel policies of educating and elevating the young working people.

The employers could exert little influence on the content of the LTS curricula: although paid by public means, the Catholic and the Protestant schools were independent entities with their own boards, and they founded their own schools in every town with the intention to create their own sphere of influence among the young workers. The Social Democrats were staunch defenders of public technical schools, which resorted under the local municipalities. In all cases, employers could exert no influence whatsoever. Their voice could only be heard in some temporary advisory committees, but here they were not able to speak with one voice: the big enterprises tended to stress general education and functional attitudes, relying on their internal training schemes, whereas the representatives of small businesses were keen on more specific skills that required minimal additional training on the spot. In the discussions on reform of the whole educational system, which eventually resulted in the 1963 'Mammoth Law' (a nickname hinting at its all-embracing scope), the perspectives of the employers hardly played a role.

The 1981 report, 'Towards a new industrial spirit', was a turning point. It launched many recommendations to revitalise Dutch industry, and some important items had to do with creating a better match between technical education and the job requirements at plant level. But the fine-tuning of these still-vague recommendations was in need of many more efforts. The Wassenaar Agreement assured trade union support for reforms of the system of vocational training, and the next years witnessed rounds of 'open consultation' between representatives of employers, trade unions, educational institutions, and the government. In 1984, an agreement was reached: the employers were to have a crucial role in determining the kind of required skills, and in exchange they would create a sufficient number of apprenticeships, acknowledging that all young workers should have an opportunity to acquire a basic vocational qualification, be it in regular curricula or during apprenticeships in a dual trajectory (combining regular education with one or two days of vocational training on the spot). The government, for its part, launched a program to subsidise all efforts to enhance employment (such as apprenticeships for the young, retraining for older workers in endangered trades of industry and reintegration for the unemployed).

It took considerable time to translate these propositions into practice. In the 1980s, the Labour Foundation and the SER played their role by making useful recommendations about reducing youth unemployment and creating a better match between job requirements and education. In the meantime, a new committee had been installed, named after its president, Ferdinand Rauwenhoff (from Philips Company), which translated all proposals to concrete measures down to the local level, and it succeeded in gaining support of all relevant parties for an agreement to reach the following goals. First was the founding of independent *combined schools for education and vocational training* on a regional or urban scale (Regional Education Centres, RECs), which brought together activities that were formerly separated. They provided for the educational component within the dual learning trajectory (paid for by the Ministry of Education) and for retraining unemployed workers (paid for by the Ministry of Social Affairs and Employment); in addition, they should also develop curricula with relevant knowledge on branch or trade level. Second, under the slogan of *co-makership*, these independent centres were encouraged to conclude contracts with employers on the desired vocational training at branch level, as well as to offer updating courses for older workers; in doing so, they would behave like commercial suppliers on a market. Third, *dual learning trajectories*, combining general education with training on the spot at plant level, should be extended and be practiced on all levels of education, universities included. Finally, the courses of vocational training and education should guarantee every pupil the possibility of acquiring a *basic qualification to perform a job*, for each person on his or her own level.

The Result: Decentralised Education, More Coordination

The most visible manifestation of this new approach was the appearance of RECs all over the country: these centres tended to become ever bigger via mergers of vocational schools, in order to attain economies of scale. In the boards of these RECs, local employers now gained prominent positions, together with the trade unions and professionals from the educational (and other) fields. This drastically reduced the influence of the once-so-powerful denominational organisations, entrenched in the boards of institutions they had founded: a side effect that was certainly welcomed by the employers.

This new approach also induced the creation of a whole range of new institutions, not only on the local and regional levels but also as joint committees on the meso level and umbrella organisations on the national level. Important topics of discussion were the needs of the local labour market, apprenticeships, the desired vocational profiles, the distinction between plant-specific skills and those on branch or sector levels, and, most important of all, the sharing of the costs in order to solve the free-rider problem. The latter problem was solved by the principle: whoever benefits will pay. On the plant level the employers had to pay for specific training, for which the RECs bargained a contractual price. On the branch level joint funds were created, as a rule on an obligatory basis, to which the employers contributed via a levy on the paid wages for education according to the needs of the specific branch of industry. This was a typical CME solution to the free-rider problem; it required mutual bargaining between rivals, exchange of plant-based information (such as the number of trainees, the desired skills, the terms of examination, etc.), and, hence, a degree of trust to invest in these forms of institutional cooperation. Public money was brought in for general education or reintegrating the chronically unemployed.

All of these developments implied a remarkable growth of mutual and decentralised coordination in this field. While before 1980 the main actors were the state and the denominational organisations, in the new setting, there were many players on all levels of the system, who were in permanent discussion with each other, with the employers as the dominant party. So we may conclude that the latter, when they were in a position to set the agenda, only to a limited degree opted for a liberal market solution (free contracting between the RECs and local employers on specific curricula). On the whole, their solution went into the direction typical of a coordinated market economy: joint and decentralised vocational training based on cost sharing and mutual consultation. In a report of the EU organisation for vocational training (CEDEFOP), this new educational system was quite straightforwardly labelled as 'neo-corporatist'.[55] This seems a bit exaggerated: on the plant level, vocational education was a market commodity, as in most LMEs; the state still played a role in reschooling as a part of reintegrating the unemployed into the labour market; only on the branch and sector levels were there joint institutions of all stakeholders. This rather pragmatic mix is characteristic of the Dutch variant as CME in the field of vocational education. But on the whole, the transition after 1980 from a centralised technical education to a more decentralised system in which the employers were able to give rein to the job requirements, seems in line with the development we discerned in the preceding section on the macro level. We now turn to the plant and company level, with regard to the development of worker involvement.

WORKER INVOLVEMENT IN THE FIRM[56]

Stereotypic Notions

In the VoC literature, in a typical LME, all discretionary powers lay with the employers.[57] At best, they negotiate with trade unions about the terms of employment of their personnel. On the whole, employees are viewed as production factors that can be exchanged for others; therefore, there is not so much investment in human capital. Only if employers see fit will they consult their employees on an ad hoc basis, but more often than not they make decisions unilaterally. By contrast, in a typical CME, employers are much more focused on creating worker commitment so they will invest in their personnel, aiming to increase their loyalty to the firm. One way to reach that goal is to give workers a say in company policies and in labour conditions.

This stereotype dichotomy mainly reflects the contemporary period and not necessarily the past. Therefore, in the following we will investigate how labour relations evolved at the plant level over time, both in the Netherlands and in its neighbouring countries. When interpreting our findings, we will address the question of to what degree developments on the micro level correspond with the developments that we discerned on the macro and meso levels.

Early Initiatives towards Worker Participation

By and large, the Dutch prewar era was characterised by voluntary initiatives as far as worker participation in the company was concerned.[58] In several firms, 'factory councils' had been erected as early as the last quarter of the 19th century, but their numbers remained modest. The motives of the entrepreneurs, who installed such councils, were mixed. Some employers were quite progressive and rational, reasoning that giving their core workers a modest say would be to the benefit of both the employees and themselves. Other employers installed a council in order to uplift the workers, as a result of their religious conviction. Still other entrepreneurs, however, thought it a good idea only because it could discourage workers to join a union, which in turn could subdue the influence of trade unions. This was exactly the reason why the early labour movement did not support the creation of factory councils. This attitude changed during the First World War, when unions gradually started to conclude more CLAs and they realised that workers inside the firm could monitor the employers' compliance with the agreement. From then on, unions tried to stimulate the installation of councils through the CLA, stipulating that this body would be granted some advisory rights while the unions would keep the prerogative of bargaining over the terms of employment. This was fine by the employers, as they did not want a powerful workers' body inside their firm.

Dutch politicians, in the meantime, debated during the interwar era about the question of whether worker involvement should be made legally mandatory, either on the firm level (socialists were in favour of this, and pointed at the situation in Germany where this was already effectuated), or on the sector level (Christian parties, of which the Roman-Catholic party was influenced by papal encyclical letters, carefully embraced the idea of businesses as organic entities, in which workers and management should cooperate in harmony).[59] Neither liberal nor Christian employers, however, supported these ideas enough, as they insisted on their autonomy in decision making; this contributed to the delay of legal enactments. Yet, over the course of the 1930s, the Great Depression gradually changed the mind-set of people and parties involved. In 1933, the *Bedrijfsradenwet* (a law on industry advisory boards) was introduced, aiming at the installation of joint committees on the sector level that could give advice on social security matters and in case of conflicts. However, only a few boards were set up, and they did not really function well. Still, the persistence of the economic crisis made leaders of all ideological denominations, representatives of workers, and employers alike, start to gather in order to intensify cooperation.[60] This development was not completely disrupted by the start of the Second World War, since the aforementioned representatives kept on seeing each other in clandestine meetings during the war, as was explained earlier in this chapter. Moreover, despite the German occupation and the subsequent abolition of the established trade unions, at the plant level, numerous employers kept on consulting their factory councils.[61]

Comparing early Dutch developments in the field of worker involvement with those in the neighbouring countries gives the following picture. In Belgium and the United Kingdom, just like in the Netherlands, neither unions nor employers were very much in favour (if at all) of giving workers a say in company matters. While in both countries entrepreneurs held onto their prerogative of being one's own master (leaving aside the few progressive industrialists who did give their workers a modest say), Belgian unions opted foremost for influence at the sector level, while British unions were plainly against cooperation with the employer inside firms, as this would undermine their independence. Attempts by the British government during the first four decades of the 20th century to stimulate cooperation at the sector and national levels through so-called Whitley committees lost out to the force of the enduring class struggle between capital and labour. In Belgium, at the end of the First World War, the strong socialist union demanded large reforms (inspired by the Russian revolution), so politics had to make a concession by introducing joint advisory industry boards, while the unions received the exclusive right to bargain over the terms of employment on behalf of the workers. During the 1930s, just like in the Netherlands, Belgian politicians had long discussions on the extent to which business life should be regulated according to corporatist ideas, in which workers and employers would cooperate extensively, both on the sector level and on the national level, but here as well the commencement of the Second World War prevented the materialisation thereof.[62]

By contrast, the situation in the other neighbouring country, Germany, was different. Here, early turmoil among mining workers made the government introduce a first law on factory councils inside the mines in 1900, which was extended to all firms with more than fifty workers during the First World War. It implied that workers were allowed to inspect safety at the workplace, and in addition they gained some advisory rights and were supposed to help in solving conflicts. Shortly after the war, the revolutionary threat drove the employers into the arms of the moderate-minded unions, who were demanding legal worker participation rights in all firms with more than twenty workers. This 'coalition' enabled the introduction of the first official Works Council Act in 1920, with co-decision rights in quite a number of social and financial issues. The influence of workers (and in the background, the unions) was, however, much larger on paper than in practice, due to a combination of powerful employers and often untaught works council members. During the Nazi regime, the works council was replaced by a worker body presided by the employer, with fewer powers.[63]

From this first comparison, we may conclude that the United Kingdom already acted as a typical LME from an early stage despite some government efforts to induce coordination, while Germany figured as a typical CME from an early stage, despite the peculiar interlude during the Nazi regime. For Belgium and the Netherlands, the seeds for the development of a CME were sown in the course of the interwar period, while the German occupation also spurred rapprochement between employers and employees.

The Introduction of Works Councils: Coordination Enforced by Dutch Law

During and right after the war years, the leaders of the employers' and workers' associations in the Labour Foundation mutually agreed on intensive cooperation at the national and sector levels. In order to acquire this influence at the macro and meso levels, the union movement renounced its claim to have a say at the micro level.[64] Nevertheless, Dutch politics decided after several years of intense debates that employees should have representation inside the firm, which led to the first Works Council Act of 1950. This law was clearly a big compromise since the employers had been against law enforcement from the start. So, the law granted hardly any serious rights to workers (just a few information and advisory rights in social matters), the employer would chair the works council, and it was supposed to act completely in the service of the company (hence, should not purely defend the workers' interests). On top of this, in case of failure to install a works council (obligatory for firms employing at least twenty-five workers), no penalty was imposed, and over the course of the 1950s and 1960s, it became clear that, overall, more than 50 per cent of the eligible employers, especially in the smallest firms, had not set up such a body.[65]

In those decades, the viewpoint on the role of employees started to shift. All parties, even employers' associations, acknowledged that the Act focused too much on the interests of the employer and undervalued the possible contribution by workers to the operation of the firm. Gradually, parties came to agree that a well-functioning works council would promote goodwill and enhance productivity. So, in 1971, the second Works Council Act was adopted, in which the threshold was lifted to firms with at least one hundred employees, as a gesture to the employers in the small firms, who preferred to consult their personnel in an informal way. Worker representatives were now specifically expected to serve the interests of the firm at large, including the interests of their rank and file; and they gained more influence because next to information and advisory rights, they also received co-decision rights with respect to social issues such as pensions, holidays, and working conditions. Within just a few years, 85 per cent of all eligible (100-plus employees) firms had installed a council.[66]

The 1970s witnessed a radicalisation of labour relations, both in the Netherlands and abroad. There was a call for more industrial democracy, and the progressive Den Uyl government responded to that by preparing yet another amendment of the Act, which Parliament adopted in 1979, again after a lot of discussions between advocates and opponents. In the new version of the law, much to their discontent, employers were removed from the chair of the works council, turning it into a pure worker representation body. But apart from these meetings of the works council, at least six consultative meetings a year had to be held between the employer (or his mandated representative) and the council; both parties had to agree on the agenda and the chairmanship of each consultative meeting; the council would not publish its views on the issues at stake before this meeting was held, and the employer had to take the advice and views of his employees into account.[67] The council also saw its rights extended, with respect to information, initiative, advice, and co-determination, as well as better possibilities to appeal in case of disagreement with the employer.[68]

Several more adjustments to the law were made during the 1980s and 1990s, mostly enlarging the council's room for manoeuvre some more. Each time, the Social and Economic Council was asked for advice, and usually this ended up in a report with mixed recommendations, as the employers' and workers' representatives in the SER typically had different opinions on the matter. A notable exception to that 'rule' concerned the allotted role for works councils in the field of health and safety, about which employers and unions were fully in agreement. As a consequence of EU regulations, all member states had to introduce worker bodies that would have important monitoring and consultation functions with respect to working conditions. In the Netherlands, these functions were assigned to the works councils, endowing them with quite extensive consultation and co-decision rights in this area.[69]

By the turn of the century, the Works Council Act could be considered as a very good example of far-reaching coordination imposed by the government. Before each amendment of the law, the parties involved were almost always sceptical, but afterwards dissenting voices were usually silenced. The latest amendments have ensured that an ever larger group of workers is covered: since 1995, all government organisations are included, and since 1999, temporary workers in all firms are also included. After several different thresholds throughout the years, the cut-off point has now, already for some time, been set at fifty employees, irrespective of whether they work full or part time. Below that number, organisations may opt for the voluntary regime and install a personnel representation body, which then endows the members thereof with several of the rights a works council has, albeit less far reaching.[70]

How Typical Is Dutch Worker Involvement?

Comparing once again the neighbouring countries, we aim to determine to what degree they have come to be compatible with the ideal types of the CME and the LME over the (postwar) years. Shortly after the German defeat, the occupying forces of the Western allies encouraged industrial democracy in the various *Länder* by dismantling the large industrial conglomerates and reinstalling the works councils that had existed prior to the Nazi regime. In addition, in the British zone, worker representatives were placed in the supervisory boards of large companies, a feature that was confirmed and extended later on by German governments and that has become so exemplary for Germany as the country with far-reaching rights for employees. This construction induced Hübner to say, 'One of the ironies of the time may be . . . [that T]hese British initiatives however found no response in the system of the United Kingdom, but remained a permanent feature in Germany',[71] which underlines the persistent liberal character of the British and the coordinating character of the German business system. Much earlier than in the Netherlands, German works councils were granted comprehensive rights, and on top of that, they formed a pure worker body right from the start. However, the Works Council Act of 1979 and later versions have made the Dutch works councils comparably strong, so that we can safely state that in the sphere of coordination between employers and employees at the company level, the two countries are well matched. Both have mostly managed to defy the pressures from neo-liberalism to make labour relations more flexible, as employers keep on coordinating company policies with their employees. The fact that in both countries the unions do not (or hardly) interfere with company policies certainly helps in maintaining trust relations on the company floor.

The situation in the United Kingdom and in Belgium is different, to a larger or smaller degree, respectively. In these two countries, there was on the whole stronger resistance against more worker involvement at the company level, especially in the United Kingdom. British unions have never been much in favour of delegating participation rights to workers inside the firm, as they wanted to stay in control themselves. British employers have always insisted on their autonomy in decision making, but since the 1980s, they have voluntarily erected some 'joint consultative committees' (JCCs), and these appear to be working rather well. But management chairs these JCCs, and the worker members do not enjoy much power. The only meaningful influence actually exerted by workers in the firm is the result of the 1974 Health and Safety at Work Act, endowing trade unionists with advisory powers in this particular field. The introduction of the EU Directive on Information and Consultation after 2005 hardly had any effect because the way in which these guidelines were translated into British law ensured that information and consultation bodies hardly came about, as this required the active request of workers in the firm, which does not often happen. In Belgium, the employers tried in vain to prevent the introduction of this particular EU Directive because it implied that workers would gain influence in firms with more than fifty workers, whereas this used to be the case in the firms with more than one hundred workers only. In 1948, after long discussions, mandatory works councils were implemented here as well, but even today they are still chaired by the employer and have clearly been endowed with less prerogatives than in Germany and the Netherlands. This most probably has to do with the fact that the union movement is strong in Belgium and quite politicised. The law grants them much influence in collective bargaining, and works council candidates must be union members. So, although the Belgian law enforces coordination, employers have never embraced it wholeheartedly.[72]

From this postwar comparison in the field of worker involvement on the micro level, we may conclude that the United Kingdom was and remained a typical representative of a LME, and Germany was and remained a typical CME. Whereas Belgium seems to occupy a position somewhat in between, the Netherlands can clearly be categorised in the CME group: in the first decades after the war, cautious steps were taken to introduce modest legal participation rights, but the position of workers became steadily stronger, especially after the amendment of the Works Council Act in 1979. So, ever since the 1980s, Dutch workers have consolidated their position and play a serious role in coordinating business at the plant or company level.

IN CONCLUSION: MANY KINDS OF COORDINATION

After 1945, all continental countries outside the Soviet zone developed their own variety of coordinated capitalism, with Social Democratic parties often in key positions. By nationalising industries, especially in the sectors of energy, (means of) transport, banking, and insurance, the governments of Italy, France, and the United Kingdom acquired a firm grip on their economies; employers and employees kept their antagonistic positions, without intermediating institutions. In smaller countries like Sweden, Norway, Denmark, Belgium, and Austria, government favoured the creation of central consultative institutions between employers and employees, where agreements were made to exchange moderate wage rises for social security arrangements, to be completed in the future.[73] The Netherlands quite obviously belonged to the latter category, but its power to determine the wages was unparalleled in democratic countries west of the Iron Curtain. Together with the long duration of this rigid policy, the ultimate result was that in 1963 wage costs in The Netherlands were lowest in comparison to the other countries of the Common Market and the United Kingdom.[74] In the years that followed, wages exploded, and the postwar promise of creating a social security system was fulfilled. In the field of vocational training, the Netherlands had a very centralised school system, with a strong position of denominational organisations, which was a unique phenomenon. On the plant or company level, Dutch workers' legal participation rights did surpass those of Belgian and British workers, but they lagged far behind those in Germany.

The 1970s and 1980s were an epoch full of turbulence in most countries, but the differences are striking. In the Netherlands, coalmining was terminated because it was unprofitable; the government provided the financial support to close the mines. In the early 1980s, the newspapers made the transition to electronic typesetting, thus making the typographers redundant; the trade unions then bargained successfully on a trajectory of retraining the younger typographers and early retirement of the elder ones. The same issues were at stake in the United Kingdom, but they caused protracted and vehement strikes in the mines and in London, which were lost by the unions. In the Netherlands, there were also radicalised trade unions, but in the end they always bargained with the employers; the Labour Foundation and the SER did not break up. On the meso level, the employers succeeded in putting through their agenda of reforming the vocational training system, and on the plant and company level we see the legal rights of worker involvement being extended to a degree that turned the backwards position of the Netherlands into its opposite.

From 1980 onwards, many other continental CMEs were engaged in a painstaking process of reforming their welfare state and labour market arrangements, but nowhere did the free consultations between employers' and employees' organisations play a comparable role; the driving force was always a government consisting of political parties that had won the elections with a program of reform. In these other CME countries, vested interests often entrenched themselves, using all veto points and other means at their disposal to retard or even frustrate the reforms, which made the outcome uncertain. The international reputation of the 'Polder Model' as successful management of reform of a neo-corporatist system rose when it became clear that the constant bargaining to reach compromises, often criticised because of its sluggishness, in the end produced better results, with less social frictions.[75]

We may conclude that the development of the Netherlands shows at least three types of coordination: the German regime with its claims of a total control of the economy, corporatist and strictly top down (1940–1945); the state-led but parliament-controlled wage policy with its complementary programme of social security (1945–1963); and the decentralised coordination between employers, employees, and government on different levels and in different institutions (from 1982 onwards). In addition, there have been periods of transition (before 1940 and between 1963 and 1982), during which intense debates took place on the desirability and the specific nature of coordination.

As a matter of fact, the specific form of coordination has varied widely over time, as has been the case in many continental European countries that have developed along their particular lines, and has shown much more dynamism and change than is often assumed. Crucial should be the questions: who is coordinating, and within what legal and mental framework? It is obvious that the government is playing a crucial role in any CME, but then a great number of questions arise. What are the legal competencies to intervene? Is this authority top down (be it still under parliamentary control), or are there intermediating institutions that give room for consultation with the social and economic parties involved, such as the Labour Foundation and the SER? What mechanisms of coordination prevail in a specific country (cf. the pivotal position of the CLA in the Netherlands or the institutions of vocational training in Germany, or the stringent labour market policy in Sweden)? And perhaps least tangible, and thus often overlooked, but nevertheless crucial: what are the prevailing sentiments and mentalities in a country? Do they foster interventions in a market economy, and to what extent, and at what price? For this kind of comparative research in varieties of coordination, much work is still to be done.

NOTES

1. Hall and Soskice, 'An Introduction to Varieties of Capitalism', 19–21.
2. Sluyterman, *Dutch Enterprise in the Twentieth Century*, 256; J. Touwen, 'Varieties of capitalism en de Nederlandse economie', 101–104.
3. Nijhof, 'Het menselijk kapitaal', 303–305.
4. This applied also to the Social Democratic trade unions, which were not in favour of the revolutionary attempt of November 1918; see Harmsen and Reinalda, *Voor de bevrijding*, 130.
5. Nijhof, 'Het Nederlandse stelsel', 54–56.
6. Nijhof, 'Pensions and providence', 265–303.
7. Bruggeman and Camijn, *Ondernemers verbonden*, 106–110.
8. De Hen, *Actieve en reactieve industriepolitiek*, 118–124.
9. Windmuller, *Labor Relations*, 73–78; Sluyterman, *Dutch Enterprise*, 111–113.
10. Camphuis, *Tussen analyse en opportuniteit*, 44–55.
11. Knegtmans, *Socialisme en Democratie*, 247–255.
12. Blom, 'The Netherlands since 1830', 439–444; Wielenga, *Die Niederlande*, 140–148.
13. For this section, see Windmuller, *Labor Relations*, 87–103.
14. Klemann, *Nederland 1938–1948*, 519–524.
15. Klemann, *Nederland 1938–1948*, 409–410.
16. In 1942 the German authorities introduced a corporate tax on profits; companies were allowed to deposit part of these reserves into pension funds without taxation, which resulted in the creating of many new pension funds; see: Nijhof, 'Pensions and providence', 293.
17. Windmuller, *Labour Relations*, 289–292.
18. Windmuller, *Labour Relations*, 106–107.
19. Fase, *Vijfendertig jaar loonbeleid in Nederland*, 204–214.
20. Windmuller, *Labour Relations*, 116–117.
21. Camphuis, *Tussen analyse en opportuniteit*, 32–75; Jaspers, Van Bavel, and Peet, *SER 1950–2010*.
22. Nijhof, 'De hoogtijdagen van het overleg', 348–354.
23. Camphuis, *Tussen analyse en opportuniteit*, 32–75; Jaspers, Van Bavel, and Peet, *SER 1950–2010*.
24. Windmuller, *Labour Relations*, 390–398.
25. Van der Velden, *Stakingen in Nederland*, 323.
26. Hueting, De Jong Edz. and Neij, *Naar groter eenheid*, 353–356.
27. To be sure, employers did not oppose all wage raises: where labour was short, they wanted to pay more, but on an incidental scale, so that it could be undone whenever they wanted; but the automatic indexation also had to be applied in trades that were not so booming, and the indexation automatically increased the employers' contributions to the social insurances.
28. Bootsma and Breedveld, *De verbeelding aan de macht*, 129–132; for the political side of the story, see also Cox, *The Development of the Dutch Welfare State*, especially chapters 6 and 7.
29. This inquiry was commissioned to the Scientific Council for Government Policy (WRR).

30. Bruggeman and Camijn, *Ondernemers verbonden*, 258–259; Nobele, *Onder-nemers georganiseerd*, 223–230.
31. Hueting et al., *Naar groter eenheid*, 372–392.
32. Bruggeman and Camijn, *Ondernemers verbonden*, 265.
33. Van Bottenburg, *Aan den arbeid*, 193.
34. Van Bottenburg, *Aan den arbeid*, 192–196.
35. Van Bottenburg, *Aan den arbeid*, 194–197; see also Visser and Hemerijck, 'A Dutch Miracle'.
36. Van Bottenburg, *Aan den arbeid*, 198.
37. Van Zanden, *The Economic History of the Netherlands*, 175.
38. Van Bottenburg, *Aan den arbeid*, 198–199.
39. Bruggeman and Camijn, *Ondernemers verbonden*, 287–289.
40. Visser and Hemerijck, 'A Dutch Miracle', 134–151.
41. Camphuis, *Tussen analyse en opportuniteit*, 490–493.
42. Visser and Hemerijck, 'A Dutch Miracle', 81–83.
43. Cf. Woldendorp, *The Polder Model*, 265–273.
44. This section is based on Nijhof, 'Scholing en opleiding', 259–285. Where references from books in English are available, these are given when useful. Important EU Reports are: C. van Dijk, T. Akkermans, and B. Hövels, *Sociale partners en beroepsonderwijs in Nederland* (CEDEFOP, Berlin 1987) and T. Moerkamp and J. Onstenk, *Beroepsonderwijs en scholing in Nederland* (CEDEFOP, Thessaloniki 1999); CEDEFOP stands for the 'Centre Européen pour le Développement de la Formation Professionnelle', a European organisation with the status of an 'agency' founded in 1975. Both reports contain a summary in English.
45. For skill formation in different countries, see: Streeck, *Social Institutions and Economic Performance*; Thelen, *How Institutions Evolve*.
46. This latter point is stressed by Oude Nijhuis, *Labor Divided*, 26–40.
47. More, *Skill and the English Working Class*, 41–52; Lovell, *Stevedores and Dockers*, 30–58; Thelen, *How Institutions Evolve*, 144–147.
48. Thelen, *How Institutions Evolve*, 39–49.
49. Thelen, *How Institutions Evolve*, 267–268.
50. Streeck, *Social Institutions and Economic Performance*, 115–125.
51. The leading theorists on skill formation, Becker, *Human Capital*, and Mincer, *Schooling, Experience, and Earnings*, argued mainly from the viewpoint of a dichotomy between the private effects of schooling activities for employers and those for employees.
52. Thanks to the 1917 Law on Private Education, which stipulated that the state would finance these private schools when there was enough local support for them, and the 1919 Law on Vocational Education, which allowed for some state supervision on the content of the curricula.
53. Meijers, *Van ambachtsschool tot L.T.S*, 68–86; Wolthuis, *Lower Technical Education in the Netherlands 1798–1993*, 169–171.
54. Meijers, *Van ambachtsschool tot L.T.S*, 68–86.
55. Van Dijk et al., *Sociale partners en beroepsonderwijs*, 103.
56. This section is based on van den Berg, 'Op weg naar medezeggenschap', 179–225.
57. Hall and Soskice, 'An introduction', 24–25, 29–30.
58. Most information about the early period stems from Van den Bergh, *De medezeggenschap der arbeiders in de partikuliere onderneming* and in second instance from Van Putten, *Het kernwezen in de particuliere onderneming* and Knaapen, *De ondernemingsraden en de ontwikkeling van de medezeggenschap in de particuliere onderneming in Nederland en België*.
59. Windmuller, De Galan and Van Zweeden, *Arbeidsverhoudingen*; Van der Ven, *Economische en sociale opvattingen*.

60. Windmuller et al., *Arbeidsverhoudingen*; Roebroek and Hertogh, '*De beschavende invloed des tijds*', 206–214.
61. Van Putten, *Het kernwezen*, 23; Windmuller et al. *Arbeidsverhoudingen*, 93; Knaapen, *De ondernemingsraden*, 32–33.
62. Sources on the early history of the United Kingdom and Belgium are the following: Knudsen, *Employee Participation in Europe*; Mills and Montgomery, *Organized Labour*; Hübner, *Worker Participation*; Dambre, *Geschiedenis van de ondernemingsraden in België*; Luyten, 'Bedrijfsorganisatiewet', 27–47.
63. Sources on early Germany are the following: Knudsen, *Employee Participation in Europe*; Hübner, *Worker Participation*; Addison, *The Economics of Codetermination*, 5–7; Müller-Jentsch, '1918–1952. Mitbestimmung', 47–51.
64. Windmuller et al., *Arbeidsverhoudingen*, 95–97.
65. Windmuller et al., *Arbeidsverhoudingen*, 361–365; Engelen, *De betekenis van de ondernemingsraad*, 1–2, 144; Plasman, *Medezeggenschap in het geding*, 57–58.
66. Looise, *Werknemersvertegenwoordiging op de tweesprong*, 226–230; Van der Linden, 'De ondernemingsraad', 17–18.
67. Visser, 'The Netherlands: From paternalism to representation', 79–82.
68. Windmuller et al., *Arbeidsverhoudingen*, 221 ff; Harmsen and Reinalda, *Voor de bevrijding van de arbeid*, 385–389; Van der Linden, 'De ondernemingsraad', 25; Nijs, 'Medezeggenschap', 116–121.
69. SER, *Advies inzake vernieuwing van de wetgeving*; Popma, *Het arbo-effect van medezeggenschap*, 74, 79–80.
70. Bakels, Asscher-Vonk, and Fase, *Schets van het Nederlands arbeidsrecht*, 251–280; Vink and Van het Kaar, *Inzicht in de ondernemingsraad*.
71. Müller-Jentsch, '1918–1952. Mitbestimmung'; quote in Hübner, *Worker Participation*, 52. And for a short English summary of the whole German postwar era, see Addison, *Economics of Codetermination*, 7–14.
72. Sources on postwar United Kingdom are the following: Knudsen, *Employee Participation*, 53–54; Kersley et al., *Inside the Workplace*, 123–134; Hall, 'Assessing the information and consultation of employees regulations', 103–126. Sources on Belgium include Van Putten, *Het kernwezen*, 96–97; Dambre, *Geschiedenis*; Mus, *Plus est en vous*, 122–124.
73. Van der Wee, *De gebroken welvaartscirkel*, 202–230; Eichengreen, *The European Economy since 1945*, 31–39.
74. Windmuller, *Labour Relations*, 391.
75. Visser and Hemerijck, '*A Dutch Miracle*', 179–185.

REFERENCES

Addison, J.T., *The Economics of Codetermination* (New York: Palgrave Macmillan, 2009).
Bakels, H.L., I.P. Asscher-Vonk, and W.J.P.M. Fase, *Schets van het Nederlands arbeidsrecht* (Deventer: Kluwer, 2000).
Becker, G., *Human Capital. A Theoretical Analysis with Special Reference to Education* (Chicago: University of Chicago Press, 1964).
Berg, A. van den, 'Op weg naar medezeggenschap. Van kernen naar ondernemingsraden', in: E. Nijhof and A. van den Berg, *Het menselijk kapitaal. Sociaal ondernemersbeleid in Nederland* (Amsterdam: Boom, 2012) 179–225.
Bergh, G. van den, *De medezeggenschap der arbeiders in de partikuliere onderneming* (Amsterdam: Proefschrift Universiteit van Amsterdam, 1924).

Blom, J.C.H., 'The Netherlands since 1830', in: J.C.H. Blom and E. Lamberts eds., *History of the Low Countries* (New York: Berghahn Books, 2006) 393–470.

Bootsma, P. and W. Breedveld, *De verbeelding aan de macht. Het Kabinet-Den Uyl 1973–1977* (The Hague: SDU Uitgevers, 1999).

Bottenburg, M. van, *Aan den arbeid. In de wandelgangen van de Stichting van de Arbeid* (Amsterdam: Bakker, 1995).

Bruggeman, J., and A. Camijn, *Ondernemers verbonden. 100 jaar centrale ondernemersorganisaties in Nederland* (Wormer: Inmerc, 1999).

Camphuis, W., *Tussen analyse en opportuniteit. De SER als adviseur voor de loon- en prijspolitiek* (Amsterdam: Aksant, 2009).

Cox, R., *The Development of the Dutch Welfare State: From Workers' Insurance to Universal Entitlement* (Pittsburgh: University of Pittsburgh Press, 1993).

Dambre, W., *Geschiedenis van de ondernemingsraden in België* (Antwerpen: Kluwer, 1985).

Dijk, C. van, T. Akkermans, and B. Hövels, *Sociale partners en beroepsonderwijs in Nederland* (Berlin: CEDEFOP, 1987).

Eichengreen, B., *The European Economy since 1945: Coordinated Capitalism and Beyond* (Princeton: Princeton University Press, 2007).

Engelen, J.A.M., *De betekenis van de ondernemingsraad* (Nijmegen: Proefschrift Katholieke Universiteit Nijmegen, 1961).

Fase, W.J.P.M., *Vijfendertig jaar loonbeleid in Nederland* (Alphen aan den Rijn: Samson, 1980).

Hall, M., 'Assessing the information and consultation of employees regulations', *Industrial Law Journal*, 34, 2 (2005): 103–126.

Hall, P, and D. Soskice, 'An introduction to Varieties of Capitalism', in: P. Hall and D. Soskice eds., *Varieties of Capitalism. The Institutional Foundations of Comparative Advantage* (Oxford: Oxford University Press, 2001) 1–68.

Harmsen, G. and B. Reinalda, *Voor de bevrijding van de arbeid. Beknopte geschiedenis van de Nederlandse vakbeweging* (Nijmegen: SUN, 1975).

Hen, P. de, *Actieve en reactieve industriepolitiek in Nederland* (Amsterdam: Arbeiderspers, 1980).

Hübner, J.W., *Worker Participation. A Comparative Study between the Systems of the Netherlands, the Federal Republic of Germany and the United Kingdom* (Leiden: Proefschrift Universiteit Leiden, 1981).

Hueting, E., F. de Jong Edz, and R. Neij, *Naar groter eenheid. De geschiedenis van het Nederlands Verbond van Vakverenigingen, 1906–1981* (Amsterdam: Van Gennep, 1983).

Jaspers, T., B. Van Bavel, and J. Peet, eds., *SER 1950–2010. Zestig jaar Denkwerk voor draagvlak, advies voor economie en samenleving* (Amsterdam: Boom, 2010).

Kersley, B. et al., *Inside the Workplace: Findings from the 2004 Workplace Employment Relations Survey* (London and New York: Routledge, 2006).

Klemann, H., *Nederland 1938–1948* (Amsterdam: Boom, 2002).

Knaapen, A.L.M., *De ondernemingsraden en de ontwikkeling van de medezeggenschap in de particuliere onderneming in Nederland en België* (Assen: Van Gorcum, 1952).

Knegtmans, P.J., *Socialisme en Democratie. De SDAP tussen klasse en natie (1929–1939)* (Amsterdam: Stichting Beheer IISG, 1989).

Knudsen, H., *Employee Participation in Europe* (London and New Delhi: Sage, 1995).

Linden, J.M. van der, 'De ondernemingsraad: taak, samenstelling en bevoegdheden. Een inleiding', in: W.J.C. Schouten, ed., *Ondernemingsraad ter sprake* (Scheveningen: Stichting Maatschappij en Onderneming, 1977) 6–42.

Looise, J.C., *Werknemersvertegenwoordiging op de tweesprong. Vakbeweging en vertegenwoordigend overleg in veranderende arbeidsverhoudingen* (Alphen aan den Rijn: Samson, 1989).

48   Erik Nijhof and Annette van den Berg

Lovell, J., *Stevedores and Dockers, a Study of Trade Unionism in the Port of London, 1870–1914* (London: Macmillan, 1969).
Luyten, D., 'De bedrijfsorganisatiewet: werknemersparticipatie of instrument van syndicale economische democratie?', in: M. Stroobant, M. De Samblanx and P. Van Geyt, eds., *Bedrijfsorganisatie aan de vooravond van de 21e eeuw. Ontstaan en evolutie van een experiment van werknemersparticipatie* (Antwerpen-Groningen: Intersentia, 2000) 27–47.
Meijers, F., *Van ambachtsschool tot L.T.S. Onderwijsbeleid en kapitalisme* (Nijmegen: SUN, 1983).
Mills, H.A. and R.E. Montgomery, *Organized Labor* (New York and London: McGraw-Hill, 1945).
Mincer, J., *Schooling, Experience, and Earnings* (New York: National Bureau of Economic Research, 1974).
Moerkamp, T. and J. Onstenk, *Beroepsonderwijs en scholing in Nederland* (Thessaloniki: CEDEFOP, 1999).
More, C., *Skill and the English Working Class 1870–1914* (London: Croom Helm, 1980).
Müller-Jentsch, W., '1918–1952. Mitbestimmung für eine neue Wirtschaftsordnung nutzen', *Magazin Mitbestimmung* (January 2008): 47–51.
Mus, E., *Plus est en vous. Coördinatie en diversificatie binnen het sociaal overleg in België* (Gent: Proefschrift Universiteit Gent, 2010).
Nijhof, E., 'De hoogtijdagen van het overleg (1940–1965)', in: A. Knotter, ed., *Mijnwerkers in Limburg. Een sociale geschiedenis* (Nijmegen: Van Tilt, 2012) 330–385.
Nijhof, E., 'Het menselijk kapitaal en het Nederlandse *business system*: een slotbeschouwing', in: E. Nijhof and A. van den Berg, eds., *Het menselijk kapitaal. Sociaal ondernemersbeleid in Nederland* (Amsterdam: Boom, 2012) 293–305.
Nijhof, E., 'Het Nederlandse stelsel: instituties en overleg', in: E. Nijhof and A. van den Berg, eds., *Het menselijk kapitaal. Sociaal ondernemersbeleid in Nederland* (Amsterdam: Boom, 2012) 41–79.
Nijhof, E., 'Pensions and providence: Dutch employers and the creation of funded pension schemes', *Enterprise and Society*, 10, 2 (2009): 265–303.
Nijhof, E., 'Scholing en opleiding', in: E. Nijhof and A. van den Berg, eds., *Het menselijk kapitaal* (Amsterdam: Boom, 2012) 259–291.
Nijs, W.F., 'Medezeggenschap', in: W.H.J. Reynaerts, ed., *Arbeidsverhoudingen, theorie en praktijk* (Leiden-Antwerpen: Stenfert Kroese, 1987) 81–150.
Nobele, P.W.M., *Ondernemers georganiseerd. Een studie over het Verbond van Nederlandse Ondernemingen in de periode 1973–1984* (The Hague/Moordrecht: VNO, 1987).
Oude Nijhuis, D., *Labor Divided. Union Structure and the Development of the Postwar Welfare State in the Netherlands and the United Kingdom* (Leiden: Proefschrift Universiteit Leiden, 2009).
Plasman, J., *Medezeggenschap in het geding. Een bedrijfspastorale, toegepaste sociaal-ethische studie over medezeggenschap* (The Hague: Boekencentrum, 1988).
Popma, J., *Het arbo-effect van medezeggenschap. Over de bijdrage van ondernemingsraden aan het arbeidsomstandighedenbeleid* (Alphen aan den Rijn: Samson, 2003).
Putten, W.M. van, *Het kernwezen in de particuliere onderneming* (The Hague: Fundatie Werkelijk Dienen, 1952).
Roebroek, J. and M. Hertogh, *'De beschavende invloed des tijds'. Twee eeuwen sociale politiek, verzorgingsstaat en sociale zekerheid in Nederland* (The Hague: VUGA, 1998).
SER, *Advies inzake vernieuwing van de wetgeving betreffende de gezondheid en de veiligheid bij de arbeid* (The Hague: Staatsdrukkerij, 1976).

Sluyterman, K, *Dutch Enterprise in the Twentieth Century. Business Strategy in a Small Open Economy* (Abingdon and New York: Routledge, 2005).

Streeck, W., *Social Institutions and Economic Performance. Studies of Industrial Relations in Advanced Capitalist Economies* (London: Sage, 1992).

Thelen, K., *How Institutions Evolve. The Political Economy of Skills in Germany, Britain, the United States and Japan* (Cambridge: Cambridge University Press, 2004).

Touwen, J., 'Varieties of Capitalism en de Nederlandse economie in de periode 1950–2000', *Tijdschrift voor Economische en Sociale Geschiedenis*, 3, 1 (2006): 73–104.

Velden, S. van der, *Stakingen in Nederland. Arbeidersstrijd 1830–1995* (Amsterdam: Stichting Beheer IISG, 2000).

Ven, F.J.H.M. van der, *Economische en sociale opvattingen in Nederland. De Nederlandsche volkshuishouding tussen twee wereldoorlogen* (Utrecht and Brussel: Spectrum, 1948).

Vink, F.W.H. and R.H. van het Kaar, *Inzicht in de ondernemingsraad. Een toelichting bij de Wet op de Ondernemingsraden* (The Hague: SDU Uitgevers, 2005).

Visser, J., 'The Netherlands: From paternalism to representation', in: J. Rogers and W. Streeck eds., *Works Councils: Consultation, Representation, and Cooperation in Industrial Relations* (Chicago and London: University of Chicago Press, 1995) 79–114.

Visser, J. and A. Hemerijck, *'A Dutch Miracle'. Job Growth, Welfare Reform and Corporatism in the Netherlands* (Amsterdam: Amsterdam University of Chicago Press, 1997).

Wee, H. van der, *De gebroken welvaartscirkel. De wereldeconomie, 1945–1980* (Leiden: Nijhoff, 1983).

Wielenga, F., *Die Niederlande. Politik und politische Kultur im 20. Jahrhundert* (Münster: Waxmann, 2008).

Windmuller, J.P., *Labor Relations in the Netherlands* (Ithaca, New York: Cornell University Press, 1969).

Windmuller, J.P., C. de Galan, and A.F. van Zweeden, *Arbeidsverhoudingen in Nederland* (Utrecht/Antwerpen: Het Spectrum, 1983).

Woldendorp, J.J., *The Polder Model: From Disease to Miracle? Dutch Neo-Corporatism 1965–2000* (Amsterdam: Thela Thesis, 2005).

Wolthuis, J., *Lower Technical Education in the Netherlands 1798–1993. The Rise and Fall of a Subsystem* (Leuven-Apeldoorn: Garant, 1999).

Zanden, J.L. van, *The Economic History of the Netherlands. A Small Open Economy in the 'Long' Twentieth Century* (London and New York: Routledge, 1998).

3 The Evolving Role of Shareholders in Dutch Corporate Governance, 1900–2010

Abe de Jong, Ailsa Röell, and Gerarda Westerhuis

INTRODUCTION

The goal of this chapter is to describe the development of corporate governance in the Netherlands over the 20th century. We approach this topic from the perspective of shareholders and in particular firm ownership structure, the annual shareholder meeting, and shareholder rights. The main theme of this chapter is thus the role and power of shareholders over time, relative to management, labour, and banks, and their relationship to broad ownership trends for listed companies.

The role of shareholders lies at the heart of the debate on Varieties of Capitalism (VoC), which distinguishes between liberal market economies (LME) and coordinated market economies (CME) as two hypothetical models.[1] In an LME, firms organise their activities mainly via markets and hierarchies, and in a CME, they are more dependent on nonmarket relations. In LMEs, firms look to financial markets for investment capital, and therefore transparency is important and share prices are a primary yardstick of firms' performance. When shareholders are dissatisfied with share price performance, they will sell their shares in the market, and the market for corporate control is a dominant mechanism for disciplining management. Thus shareholder value is paramount. In contrast, in a CME bank lending, retained earnings and family capital are more important as sources of funding relative to publicly held security issues, and the different stakeholders in the firm coordinate decisions and activities. Since the firm balances the interests of various stakeholders, continuity of the firm is the most important goal. The shareholders in this model are only some of the many stakeholders, i.e. managers, shareholders, banks, labour, and the state.

Our focus is on Dutch exchange-listed corporations. The motivation for this is that, in these firms, the shareholders are potentially most far removed from the firm's management. Thus, in these companies, the LME and CME ideal types can really accord very different roles to the shareholders involved. When a firm's shares are exchange listed, the shares can be freely bought and sold amongst outside shareholders and hostile takeovers are in principle possible. In contrast, Dutch corporations can also decide not to list their shares and/or bonds on the exchange, and they can adopt a closed form, requiring authorisation from the corporation for the transfer of shareholdings.

In this chapter, we argue that the role of shareholders in the corporate governance and VoC debates requires a nuanced discussion. We demonstrate this by considering three main topics.

The first topic is the ownership of companies: who are the shareholders? Are they small or large, or family, or dispersed small shareholders, or institutions? Until recently it was not easy to determine how dispersed share ownership in Dutch listed companies was, since the shares were generally not registered, but bearer shares, and even if the owners of the shares were registered, there was no legislation compelling companies to make the information public. Identifying the shareholders of Dutch listed companies, therefore, is rarely possible for much of the 20th century.

Our second topic is the annual shareholder meeting. Strätling identifies three important functions of general meetings in corporate governance today: (i) to inform shareholders about the performance of the company over the past year; (ii) to obtain approval for the report over the past year, as well as for decisions that are beyond the authority of the board of directors; and (iii) to provide a forum for discussion between directors and shareholders.[2] We will discuss the development of shareholder meetings over the 20th century and explain whether the functions mentioned by Strätling were relevant.

Our third topic is shareholder rights and the various measures used to concentrate power in the hands of corporate insiders. In an LME setting, control rights of shareholders are a fundamental determinant of companies' goals, strategies, performance, and overall direction. When shareholders in a publicly traded company have the undisputed power to hire and fire boards and management at will, companies are forcibly driven towards maximising current shareholder returns; if not, the shares can profitably be purchased on the market by activist investors who will either replace the current management team in a hostile takeover or else force the incumbent team to realign its strategy. In order to trace shareholder rights as a typical LME characteristic versus alternative modes in a CME, we will touch upon takeover defences, disclosure, and dividend policy. But we will not cover networks of influence via positions on boards of directors; for these the reader is referred to Westerhuis.[3]

Four main sources of data and information are used. First, we consider selected cases for which archival records are available. Second, in order to describe the development of shareholder meetings over the 20th century, we analyse the minutes of 143 shareholder meetings over the period 1903–1973 from publicly accessible archives. This sample is created as follows. Using the annual *Van Oss Effectenboek* (issued from 1903 until 1976), all exchange-listed nonfinancial firms were selected. Next, a keyword search on the company name and Dutch words for shareholder meeting for these firms in www.archieven.nl, a digital search portal to the archives of more than eighty institutions including the National Archive and many municipal archives, was performed in the summer of 2012. In total we visited fourteen archives. Although we found minutes of shareholders' meetings for forty-seven firms, we selected twenty-one firms based on coverage over the 1903–1973 period and industries. For these firms we analysed the minutes from 1903 onwards at five-year intervals. Third, in order to measure the occurrence of complaints and stronger dissents, we compiled an inventory of all shareholder meetings of public companies in the year 1966 using *Financieel Archief van Systemen Keesing*. This source is a regularly appearing booklet (101 bi-weekly issues during 1966) whose goal is to inform shareholders about relevant developments, including summaries of shareholder meetings. We have found 329 ordinary shareholder meetings and 45 extraordinary meetings. Finally, we use statistical overviews from published sources.

We will divide our period of enquiry, which starts at the turn of the 20th century, into four periods and trace the above-mentioned topics over time, both in broad outline and in anecdotal detail culled from a reading of archival records of meetings of shareholders, directors, and management.

INSIDER DOMINANCE (UNTIL 1920)

Industrial development came somewhat later to the Netherlands than to neighbouring countries such as the United Kingdom and Belgium, but it accelerated during the last decades of the 19th century.[4] At the turn of the century, most industrial companies in the Netherlands were closely held family enterprises, and shareholders were typically the founders, their families, and other individuals closely involved in the business of the firm, such as wholesale customers. Thus ownership and control were typically concentrated in a very limited circle of closely connected individuals. Most firms grew organically using internal financing, and only when retained earnings were insufficient to satisfy the need for capital—as was the case, for example, for railroad infrastructure and Indonesian plantations and extractive ventures—did they seek substantial amounts of outside finance from a broader set of investors.[5]

Such outside investment was hampered by the fact that there was very little in the way of formal shareholder protection. Accounts were not always transparent or informative, and outside shareholders could not easily verify whether they were receiving their rightful share of profits. At the time it was common practice for the corporate charter to explicitly prescribe the *winstverdeling* or division of profits. Indeed, the then reigning 1838 Commercial Code (Article 42d) stated that profits would fall to the benefit of shareholders, unless the articles of incorporation would determine otherwise, a stipulation that was at the time interpreted as requiring a 100 per cent payout of reported profits in the form of a dividend. But in practice

such prescriptions had limited bite, since the accounting was subject to substantial managerial discretion (in particular, the creation of secret reserves,
as well as latitude in determining depreciation and write-offs), and the law
did not offer shareholders any protection in the form of public disclosure of
standardised accounts.[6] Thus even though the company's annual accounts
were subject to approval by the shareholder meeting, and typically on display to shareholders in the run-up to the annual meeting, shareholders'
power to intervene was generally limited by a lack of insight into the underlying state of affairs.

In the early decades of the 20th century, preferred stock was a widely
used financing instrument, not just in the Netherlands but also in, for example, the United Kingdom.[7] When outside investors cannot reliably verify
the level of profits to be shared out, the appropriate way to induce them
to contribute money is by issuing fixed-income instruments whose payout
is senior to corporate insiders' claims. As Townsend and Gale and Hellwig
have demonstrated, a fixed-payout claim such as debt is an optimal contract
in terms of economising on investors' verification costs because such costs
arise only in situations where the company cannot meet its obligations.[8]
Preferred shares promise a fixed stream of payments and thus do not normally require any insight into company accounts by investors, as long as
the promised payments are made. Given that before World War II there was
no corporate income tax,[9] the tax deductibility of interest, which nowa-
days renders preferred shares overwhelmingly less attractive than bonds as
sources of financing, was not a relevant consideration. Moreover, the fact
that a missed preferred dividend would not trigger an immediate descent
into a costly bankruptcy process conferred an advantage on preferred shares
over debt financing.

Even when shares were not formally preferred, the company statutes
often called for a fixed percentage of par (rather than profit) to be paid out
to shareholders first, if enough profit was made; the remaining *overwinst*
(excess profit), if any, was then divided among the shareholders, the management and directors, and the reserves in a specified way.[10] The corporate
charter of the Amsterdam brewery 't Haantje provides an example of the
detailed profit division in a typical corporate charter drawn up in 1910:

> Article 28. *Of the profit, in the first place five percent of the paid in
> capital shall be distributed to shareholders.* Out of any excess, fifteen
> percent goes to the management, to be divided amongst its members,
> as specified at each appointment or reappointment; fifteen percent to
> the directors jointly, fifty five percent to the shareholders, ten percent to
> the reserve fund mentioned below, five percent to the founders shares
> jointly. If the reserve fund has increased to the maximum described in
> article 30 [. . . half the paid in capital . . .], then of the amount that
> comes free as a result, one third goes to the management, to be divided
> amongst its members in the same proportions as the prescribed fifteen

percent, one third to the supervisory board directors jointly and one third to the shareholders.[11]

Shareholders' cash flow rights were specified in such a way as to safeguard their claims in an environment of low transparency and minimal shareholder influence. But now let us turn to the explicit influence and powers of the shareholders in determining corporate policies.

In this respect it is useful to distinguish inside shareholders—the founders and their family, the executives in charge of running the company, and the board members providing oversight and guidance—from outside investors. A common practice for companies that went public was to create two (sometimes more) classes of shares. The insiders generally held a limited class of registered (*op naam*) shares with enhanced control rights—*priority shares or founders' shares*—which were usually small in number (the norm was around ten or twenty) and not freely transferable, changing hands only when board and management were reshuffled, or in the wake of retirement or death of the holder. The publicly held shares, which sometimes included a separate class of preference shares, were generally freely transferable (*aan toonder*) to enhance their liquidity, or allowed the holder to switch from registered to unregistered status at will. The most common enhanced control right of the priority shares was the *bindende voordracht*, which gave the priority shareholders' meeting the power to nominate candidates for election to the board of directors. This meant that the ordinary shareholders could only choose between candidates nominated by the priority shareholders, effectively hollowing out their right to determine the composition of the board. A motivating factor for restricting outside shareholders' influence in this way was the fear of foreign influence, which helped firms to legitimise the build-up of devices to restrict shareholder influence.[12]

Apart from control of the slate of nominations, a number of other measures were commonly used to limit the decision rights of outside shareholders. One common device was *certification*, the issuance of nonvoting certificates to shareholders by a so-called *Administratiekantoor (AK)*. In particular companies themselves would set up AKs whose management was closely allied with the company leadership. Often the certificates were *niet-royeerbaar*, that is, they could not be traded in for the underlying voting shares upon request by the holder—a clear example where voting rights were permanently abrogated.

Another factor influencing shareholder power, the *voting cap*, limited the influence of large investors in particular. In most cases, a cap of six votes per shareholder was, before the legal reform of 1928, enshrined in the law, a feature inherited from the French commercial code.

In our analysis of shareholder meetings, we have chosen in the first period to include firms active in industries with large investments needs, such as shipping, railway, and shipbuilding. In Table 3.1, for example, the Almelo-Salzbergen railway company is present from 1903 until 1923. In the five meetings, the percentage of shares present in the meeting is 2 per cent on average, ranging from 1 per cent to 5 per cent over the years. On average eight shareholders are present, ranging from five to sixteen. Clearly, in the earliest years of the 20th century, for many firms, the shareholders' meetings were not well attended and typically were a formality. We have found few in-depth discussions of company strategies but rather rubber stamping of proposed new board members and consensus approval of the accounts.

In Table 3.1 the ratio of votes to shares represented is on average 0.81, which implies that about four out of five shares could be voted. For this firm, the voting cap of six votes did not seem to affect the meeting, though it is possible that some large shareholders who attended the meeting simply did not register all their shares, given that they would only be allowed to vote six shares anyway. In Table 3.2 the period 1903–1918 is characterised by average shareholder turnout percentages of between 11 per cent and 15 per cent, with eight to ten shareholders present. Most striking is that the percentage of votes present relative to the maximum number of votes possible is 2 per cent to 3 per cent. The maximum would only be reached if all shareholders were present and all had at most six shares.

Under the circumstances it is not surprising that the typical ordinary shareholders' meeting was a rather anodyne affair. A typical meeting moved uncontentiously from the approval of the minutes of the previous meeting, to the management's report on the year's business, the approval of the accounts, (re-)appointments to the board and senior management, and a general opportunity for shareholder queries. Most issues were approved close to unanimously. Indeed it is often only the 'rondvraag' at the end of the meeting that gave any signs of concern on the part of ordinary shareholders.

Such concerns most often revolved around two points: first, a wish to see higher dividends declared; and second, general frustration at the lack of informativeness of the accounts. Tekenbroek points out that shareholders were generally passive in good times when the economy was booming and firms' profits increasing. Only when dividends were disappointing were shareholders moved to try to exercise their control rights, by arguing in favour of greater payouts or withholding their votes for (re-)appointment of board members and executives.[13] However, the dissenting shareholders were invariably very much in the minority, so that their protests were symbolic at best.

In short, Dutch exchange-listed firms in the early 20th century displayed relatively little separation of ownership and control. The insiders—often founders of founding families—were dominant both in management and as financiers. Therefore, the role of shareholder meetings was typically limited to a formality. However, we also note that the power of outside shareholders in these years was increasingly curtailed by legal barriers raised by the insiders, as well as by their lack of information about companies' performance due to low transparency standards and practices. Arguably this era

Table 3.1 Shareholder meetings 1903–1973 per firm

Name	Branch	From	Till	Percentage shares			Number of shareholders			Shares/votes
				Average	Min	Max	Average	Min	Max	Average
Spoorweg-Maatschappij Almelo-Salzbergen NV	Transport	1903	1923	2%	1%	5%	8	5	16	0.81
N.V. Nederlandsche centraal Spoorwegmaatschappij	Transport	1903	1928	12%	10%	14%	5	1	7	0.06
N.V. Rotterdamsche Lloyd	Transport	1903	1938	27%	0%	52%	11	8	14	0.15
Werkspoor N.V.	Transport industry	1903	1942	6%	0%	28%	6	2	9	0.67
N.V. Koninklijke Maatschappij 'De Schelde'	Transport industry	1903	1958	70%	35%	99%	11	4	17	0.58
Rotterdamsche Droogdok Maatschappij N.V.	Transport industry	1908	1973	17%	2%	100%	10	1	26	0.36
N.V. Nederlandsche Maatschappij voor Kunstmatige Oesterteelt	Agriculture/fishing	1913	1933	13%	7%	23%	7	3	16	0.20
N.V. Billiton-Maatschappij	Mining	1913	1963	4%	1%	11%	31	15	47	0.43
Ogem NV	Utility	1913	1973	24%	2%	52%	11	4	17	0.74
N.V. Kaashandel Maatschappij Gouda	Food	1918	1942	6%	5%	10%	14	12	15	0.59
N.V. Lyempf	Food	1928	1933	39%	27%	51%	15	15	15	0.09
Maatschappij tot Exploitatie der Vereenigde Majang-Landen NV	Agriculture/fishing	1928	1958	14%	7%	24%	9	6	15	0.09
De Korenschoof NV	Food	1928	1968	3%	1%	5%	8	2	14	0.69

N.V. Handelsvennootschap vh Maintz & Co	Trade	1933	1938	2%	1%	3%	8	7	8	0.91
N.V. W.A. Scholten's Aardappelmeelfabrieken	Food	1933	1953	6%	1%	21%	9	5	12	0.69
Koninklijke Vereenigde Tapijtfabrieken NV	Textiles	1933	1968	5%	1%	16%	12	10	17	n.a.
N.V. Carton- en Papierfabriek	Paper	1942	1958	3%	3%	4%	5	4	5	1.00
Stoomvaart Maatschappij Zeeland NV	Transport	1942	1968	67%	58%	77%	n.a.	n.a.	n.a.	n.a.
Heineken NV	Food	1948	1963	49%	44%	51%	11	7	19	1.00
Van Nelle NV	Food	1953	1973	43%	1%	72%	15	9	21	n.a.
NV Betonfabriek De Meteoor	Cement	1958	1973	19%	12%	26%	6	5	9	1.00

Table 3.2   Shareholder meetings 1903–1973 per year

Year	Obs	Percentage shares			Number of shareholders			Percentage votes	Shares/votes
		Average	Min	Max	Average	Min	Max	Average	Average
1903	5	11%	1%	35%	8	5	11	3%	0.40
1908	6	11%	1%	35%	9	5	16	3%	0.41
1913	9	15%	1%	52%	9	4	15	2%	0.34
1918	10	11%	1%	37%	10	5	20	2%	0.34
1923	10	16%	0%	61%	13	3	41	2%	0.31
1928	12	19%	0%	81%	10	1	23	2%	0.30
1933	14	18%	0%	85%	11	2	26	11%	0.56
1938	12	15%	0%	88%	11	3	24	11%	0.53
1942	11	21%	1%	76%	8	5	11	16%	0.69
1948	11	23%	1%	97%	11	5	38	20%	0.71
1953	12	28%	2%	98%	12	5	36	21%	0.60
1958	12	30%	3%	99%	13	4	42	23%	0.60
1963	8	32%	3%	77%	20	6	47	20%	0.55
1968	7	46%	3%	100%	11	1	21	45%	0.79
1973	4	42%	5%	100%	5	1	9	54%	1.00
Total	143	22%	0%	100%	11	1	47	12%	0.53

was an LME period if the power of the insider owner-manager is considered in isolation, without taking into consideration the interests of other shareholders. Other stakeholders—in particular 'unorganised' employees and the liberal state—had little or no influence on decision making in the firm.

NEW LEGISLATION AND CRISIS (1920–1945)

In the period between 1920 and the Second World War, Dutch business initially benefited from the international growth after World War I and from the Netherlands's neutrality during that war. Despite a brief banking crisis in 1920–1921, the economy grew until the crisis years in the 1930s. In these years family firms were still important in the industrial landscape, while at the same time, many private firms with activities in the Indonesian colonies were established and listed on the Amsterdam exchange.[14]

The debate on the disclosure of accounts had been simmering since the second half of the 19th century, when the delayed advent of the Industrial Revolution in the Netherlands created a need for large-scale outside capital, in particular for railway companies. It was clear that reform was required if ownership was to be separated from management, but it was not until 1928 that the law was to be overhauled. The new law, as modified in 1929, required the reporting of eleven specified items on asset side of the balance sheet. In addition, the voting cap was abolished as a universal legal requirement, although it was still possible to include such a cap in the corporate charter.

Meanwhile, the disclosure provisions of the new law were far from universally welcome. While it was generally agreed that companies that sold shares or bonds to the general public had a duty to give investors insight into their affairs, many companies felt that public scrutiny of their accounts was undesirable. It could attract the unwelcome attention of actual and potential competitors—encouraging them to enter a market that looked profitable and/or to stage a knockout competitive attack against any financially struggling companies—as well as labour and the tax authorities. A modification clause introduced in 1929 responded by somewhat weakening the publication requirement for companies that did not have outside shareholders or bondholders.[15]

In the interwar years, the fear of foreign influence was often the justification for introducing oligarchic measures. For example, in 1927, Glasfabriek Leerdam NV moved to alter the corporate statutes to institute a separate class of priority shares with the right to make binding nominations. The company's chief executive explained to the shareholder meeting of 26 March 1927 that it was desirable to take measures to prevent any foreign group from taking control of the company:

[w]hat we want to prevent is that on the Exchange a number of shares are bought up by an arbitrary group, so that they, once they felt strong enough, could assume the leadership of the shareholders meeting. It cannot be denounced strongly enough, that in such a case the interests of the factory could be caught between the existing management and another which works from abroad and could undo the decisions of the current management whenever it wished to, indeed it could even move to bring to a halt the company in part or in full.[16]

In the discussion of the proposals, two shareholders objected strenuously to the attendant loss of shareholder rights, arguing that current management had not always worked in the interests of the shareholders (losses were mounting over the years, and the preferred dividend had been passed repeatedly with no immediate prospect of restoration), and voted against the binding nomination proposal. However, their 8 votes were but a tiny minority of the 423 votes represented at the meeting.[17]

An alternative defensive construction that developed in the interwar period and that was initially motivated by concerns about foreign influence was the *Gemeenschappelijk Bezit*, a pyramid-type ownership device that typically limited ownership of the operating assets to Dutch residents. Over time it too was converted for broader goals.

Tables 3.1 and 3. 2 present the shareholder meeting characteristics for the ordinary shares in our sample. Turnout at the shareholder meetings increased over 1922 to 1942 and ranges between 16 per cent and 21 per cent.[18] The number of shareholders present also increased slightly but is still around ten shareholders. In this period, our sample includes food companies as well as a cultivation company with activities in the Dutch Indies.

The percentage of votes relative to the maximum number of votes possible in Table 3.1 shows that the percentage of votes represented is 2 per cent on average until 1928 and then jumps to 11 per cent. This effect demonstrates the impact of the abolition of voting caps. It is, for example, visible for De Schelde, a firm with 1,615 shares represented by 11 shareholders in 1928, and 1,703 shares with 10 shareholders in 1933. The voting cap of six shares gives a theoretical maximum of 66 votes in 1928 (if all shareholders present owned at least six shares); in actual fact 43 votes could be cast, so that the ratio of votes to shares represented was 0.03. In 1933 all 1,703 shares yielded one vote, for a ratio of votes to shares of 1.

In summary, the interwar period saw an increased participation of investors in the securities markets. A recurring theme in governance debates is the poor transparency of listed firms, which improved somewhat following new legislation in 1928–1929 but could not satisfy external investors. The Dutch economy at the time exhibited many of the defining characteristics of an LME. Although ideas concerning the involvement of labour in company-level decision making were taking shape, it was not until after World War II that centralised coordinating institutions that involved representatives from labour, employers, and government came into prominence.

TOWARDS A STAKEHOLDER MODEL (1945–1980)

The reconstruction of the economy in the wake of World War II required a concerted national effort and a big inflow of new investment capital. This need for funding meant that many companies that had until then been family enterprises decided to list their shares and seek financing from a broader public shareholder base.[19] In addition, the postwar reconstruction effort involved an unprecedented level of coordination between firms, labour unions, and the government. In particular, centralised agreements to restrain wage increases contributed importantly to the competitiveness of Dutch industry in the two decades following the end of the war. In return, labour was given an increasingly active role in decision making at the company level.[20] Thus the Dutch economic system moved more towards a CME.

The separation of ownership and control became much more pronounced as the number of shareholders increased and management became a task for professionals rather than for the large shareholders who had traditionally led the family firm. This meant that both the nature and the influence of shareholders changed dramatically. Originally, shareholders were few in number and personally connected to the company, holding substantial stakes and intimately involved in company decision making—they were in effect company insiders (often members of the founding families), with enough voting power to exercise control. As companies broadened their investor base, the share capital was dispersed, and the power and influence of the new outside shareholders was markedly less than that of the original company insiders. Thus the VEB,[21] an association for the protection of shareholders, which started publishing the shareholder advocacy magazine *Beleggers Belangen* (Investors' Interests) in 1957, pointed out in its first year of publication, that the greater dispersion of share ownership 'has led to a gain in influence of the day-to-day leadership (the management) at the expense of the actual owner (the shareholder)'.[22] In its opening issue, the magazine set out the specific projects that the VEB felt it should undertake in its efforts to protect shareholder interests.[23] The goals pursued by the VEB, however, remained out of reach, and in particular shareholder control rights continued to be under attack. In theory, the most important decision-making powers within the company (the appointment and removal of management, the right to modify the corporate charter, the approval of the annual financial statements, and the decision to issue new shares) devolved upon the shareholders' meeting.[24] In the first half of the century, defensive mechanisms had already become an ever more popular means of curtailing these powers and shifting them to the management and the board of directors. This trend continued.

Over time, an increasing number of defensive measures were installed. Both the use of share certificates and the concentration of nominating power in the priority shareholders' meeting rose steadily and considerably in the postwar era. *Beleggers Belangen* roundly criticised Wilton Fijenoord for its circular to shareholders asking them to exchange their shares for *niet-royeerbare* (nonconvertible) nonvoting certificates. Certificates had originally been issued as a means of ensuring that the company would not fall under foreign control, but the article noted that '[t]he Überfremdung is no longer an issue, and the proposed exchange will only mean that you will assist the administration office in making management all-powerful', adding the suggestion that shareholders would find the certificates more liquid and widely traded seemed specious given that roughly equal amounts of shares and certificates were in circulation.[25]

Thus small shareholders became steadily more powerless while large or controlling shareholders imposed their will. As an illustration, *Beleggers Belangen* pointed out disapprovingly that at a shareholder meeting of Scholten-Honig, the name of the new candidate for the management board was first unveiled at the meeting and then directly subjected to a vote.[26] But this does not mean that shareholder meetings lacked excitement. At a dramatic meeting of the shareholders of Stokvis in 1969, large losses in

Venezuela and Belgium were revealed, and one of the shareholders clamouring for the resignation of the board of directors suffered a fatal heart attack in the process.[27]

In addition, a number of new mechanisms to curtail shareholder rights were developed. A major innovation was the use of defensive preference shares—not to be confused with the prewar use of financial preference shares. This device was first used in January 1969 by Rijn-Schelde NV and was quickly adopted by many other listed companies.[28] The idea was to counter any hostile takeover threat by putting overwhelming voting power temporarily in friendly hands, by issuing preference shares. The motive for their preferred status was that a stable preferred dividend would cover the interest incurred on a loan taken out to pay for the purchase cost of the shares. Thus they were not intended as a source of capital but as a cheap and self-financing means of safeguarding control, triggered by a takeover threat.

We turn now to the motives given by companies for inserting statutory takeover defences into their charter.[29] Before World War II, the primary motive given was the need to safeguard the national character of the company or, more generally, to safeguard it against the threat of a hostile takeover, either by foreign or domestic raiders. This motive remained important, but other justifications were increasingly mentioned.

One motive given for constructing takeover defences was the change in shareholders' mentality. Before the emergence of very large companies, the NVs had a strong personal and family character, and the shareholders were intimately involved in the affairs of the company. As the companies grew larger and the shareholder base became more dispersed, shareholders took on the role of investors rather than co-owners and became less concerned with the broader interests of the company; their goal shifted more towards obtaining immediate financial rewards in the form of dividends and share price increases. Such shareholders tended not to attend shareholder meetings very much, especially if they were satisfied with the level of dividend payments. This absenteeism created a real danger that a chance majority based on a relatively small proportion of the shares could make important decisions that were not necessarily in the interest of the company. Thus one motive for installing defensive devices was to insure against the consequences of an accidental majority in the shareholder meeting, and thus counter the potential instability in decision making resulting from absenteeism. This motive was already put forward before the First World War, but it became ever more prominently mentioned as time went on and absenteeism increased.

A study of the attendance of shareholders at the annual meeting to approve the 1954 annual report for forty-three listed companies found that in 75 per cent of meetings, six or fewer shareholders were present; and in 65 per cent of meetings, those shareholders who attended represented less than 10 per cent of the issued capital. An SMO follow-up survey in 1969 found that of the seventy-four companies responding, only seven had a turnout representing more than 50 per cent of the shareholders; and in forty-one cases, those present represented 10 per cent or less of the out-standing share capital.[30] For a small set of companies, Tables 3.1 and 3.2 also display shareholder turnout for our sample, which gradually increased from 23 per cent in 1948 to 42 per cent in 1973. In some meetings, larger numbers of shareholders were present, and the range is between five and twenty shareholders. The instances of high turnout in our sample are driven by the presence of a large shareholder, and indeed there are some cases with 100 per cent turnout as a result of the presence of a successful bidder in the last meeting before the firm was taken over.

The SMO survey also inquired into the motives for the use of defen-sive measures. The 1,138 companies that responded to the survey (671 declined) listed one or more of the following motives: retain national char-acter (15 per cent of the companies); protect against hostile attack (35 per cent); prevent unstable policymaking (42 per cent); safeguard the quality of board and management (42 per cent); protection of interests (48 per cent); and other motives (7 per cent).[31] Thus the desire to safeguard the quality of management and directors was important: the leadership of the company did not wish to leave the right to nominate candidates to a random and often very variable subset of the shareholders who showed up at meetings. In addition many companies wished to protect the interests of certain stake-holders in the company, but unfortunately not much is known about the nature of these interests.

In line with this trend towards less shareholder influence, in the decades after World War II, the Dutch economy increasingly moved in the direction of a CME. Centralised collective bargaining over wages and working condi-tions ensured a long era of wage restraint that helped Dutch companies to recover from the war and expand and compete internationally. Coordinated decision making included an enhanced role for labour and government in influencing key company policies such as working conditions, restructur-ing, mergers, and layoffs. Much relevant policymaking took place at a cen-tralised level where industry and labour representatives negotiated wages and working conditions, social policies and the division of influence, and decision-making rights in the company—an economic system of seeking consensus between broad social groups that was to become known as the *Polder Model*.

These developments strengthened the role of a broader set of stakehold-ers in the firm and were accompanied by a further weakening of the role of the shareholder meeting as the preeminent power in company decision mak-ing. In 1949, in its decision in the case of the Doetinchemse IJzergieterij, the Dutch Supreme Court broached the idea that the shareholders' meeting need no longer be the highest decision-making organ of the NV: the supervisory board was permitted to go ahead with a share issue that it deemed in the interests of the company as a whole, even though the majority shareholder had voted against this dilution of his stake. The Supreme Court explicitly suggested that the board should consider the interests of the company as a whole, not just its shareholders.[32] This view was later enforced in the Forumbank case in 1955, when it was held that a share repurchase decision was the province of the management and that the shareholders' meeting had exceeded its powers in trying to impose its will.[33]

These developments supporting a stakeholder view of company objectives were mirrored by growing conviction that labour should play an active role in company-level decision making. A major development in redefining the powers of the shareholders' meeting was the introduction of the *structuurregime* (structured regime) in 1971 with the new *Wetboek van Koophandel*. While the stated objective of the new law was to increase the control rights of labour by giving them a seat at the decision-making table, in practice it considerably weakened shareholder rights without giving labour much more than the power to comment on decisions. The new law obliged large Dutch companies to nominate new supervisory board members by co-optation, that is, by the existing board. This clearly reduced shareholder power, and empirical evidence suggests shareholders may have suffered a discount in the share price as a result.[34]

Also, the supervisory board of companies that fell under the structured regime received the important decision-making powers within the company that rested with the shareholders before: to appoint and remove management, to approve the annual financial statements, and to decide on fundamental management decisions. This broadening of its function was already visible with the judgment of the Supreme Court in the above-mentioned cases, and was in 1971 thus formalised in the structured regime.[35]

Two other aspects of the new company law of 1971 are of note. First, in 1971, the Enterprise Chamber of the Amsterdam Court of Appeals was set up, and the right of inquiry (*recht van enquête*) gave shareholders representing a sufficient proportion of the share capital an organised power of appeal. That is, a judicial inquiry can be set in motion to look into shareholders' concerns, if the chamber deems that those requesting it are qualified (i.e., large enough shareholders; but recently, the Works Council and unions have also sometimes been allowed to request an inquiry) and that there is sufficient cause to justify launching an investigation. Over time the practice has become more liberal so that not all that much grounds for suspicion is needed in order to launch an inquiry. This can be costly for a company, as the obligation to reveal the information requested during an investigation is not a trivial burden. Moreover, the inquiry is paid for by the company that is the target of investigation. The judges call on an informal roster of qualified experts they have on file, but sometimes this can be quite difficult, as those best able to understand the issues are most likely to be compromised by conflicts of interest: the business elite is not that large and very interlinked. Moreover, the investigative committees do not seem to be able to stay within their mandate, which is fact finding; they have a strong tendency to see their role as bringing a judgment rather than uncovering the facts.[36]

The new company law of 1971 did give companies the opportunity to escape the more onerous disclosure provisions by converting to a new legal form, the Besloten Vennootschap (BV). It was taken up by the vast majority of NVs that did not have shares or bonds issued to the general public in bearer form.

On the issue of disclosure of financial information to shareholders of NVs, a new law in 1970 finally addressed a situation that still left much to be desired. In general, in the 1950s and 1960s, the financial press took a very critical view of company financial reporting. As a striking example, at the annual shareholder meeting of bicycle producer Fongers in 1957, following a 50 per cent cut in the dividends, a shareholder tried to gain further insight into the accounts, but was rebuffed on the grounds of the threat from competitors:

> [the Chairman] responded that the management had made some improvements to the financial report but that nevertheless one should keep in mind the competition. That obliges one to keep certain issues private. A breakdown of the profits by division was in his opinion altogether inappropriate ...
>
> Another shareholder very much wanted to know if the company had made a profit or a loss in the preceding year. The Chairman was not prepared to give a clear answer to this question.[37]

To give some more insight into what happens at a typical shareholder meeting, we consider the year 1966. A characteristic of shareholders' meetings is that even though many meetings are mere formalities, they do give disgruntled shareholders the opportunity to voice their complaints and—as an ultimate sanction—to vote against the discharge of the management board. In order to measure the occurrence of complaints and stronger dissents, we have made an inventory of all shareholder meetings of public companies in the year 1966 using *Financieel Archief van Systemen Keesing*. This source is a regular booklet (101 bi-weekly editions during 1966) whose goal is to inform shareholders about relevant developments. This implies that in addition to annual reports, press releases, and new appointments, shareholder meetings are summarised. We have found 329 ordinary shareholder meetings and 45 extraordinary meetings.

In terms of the discussions between shareholders and the board, the most prevalent topics are dividends (thirty-seven explicit discussions in the summary) and transparency and accounting (nineteen discussions). Most likely these numbers are a fraction of the total number of discussions in the meetings because *Keesing* reports only on the most salient ones. Clearly, large shareholders and defensive measures dominate the proceedings: in many companies there is a lot of criticism but no voting. The reports of the meetings mention votes cast against the board's proposals in only eight meetings. Again, this may be an underestimate. We have one case of a management proposal that was withdrawn and one counterproposal by shareholders that was accepted.

The most extreme outcome—refusal to grant discharge—is rare, with only one instance in 1966: in September, the accounts of the cultivation company Ngombezi NV were not approved because a large shareholder had objections to the management's strategy.[38]

Interestingly, the *Vereniging voor Effectenbescherming* and in particular Mr. W. C. Posthumus Meyjes frequently plays a vocal role in the shareholder meetings in 1966. Posthumus Meyjes gives his perspective on the customs during shareholder meetings in the 1960s and adds some best practices.[39] In his view the best practice is to welcome shareholders as guests of the firm: 'the management needs to be fully aware that it is on the one hand a host, and on the other it needs to justify itself to the owners of the company'[40] and 'also provide for sufficient cigars and cigarettes (not just on the management table!)'.[41] Clearly, this was not the actual mores because 'it is often noteworthy to experience the deplorable way in which normal politeness is left behind and it is evident that the shareholder meeting is merely considered a necessary evil'.[42] Posthumus Meyjes also envisages a responsibility for dissenting shareholders as 'a shareholder must be aware of the responsibility he takes on if he opts for opposition'.[43]

After World War II, an ongoing shift to the stakeholder model can be discerned. It seems that if companies are to have the autonomy needed to take a broader, stakeholder viewpoint of their goals, they need to have in place some defensive measures to protect them from the threat of hostile takeovers. That is, shareholder rights need to be curtailed. This shift was in particular reflected in the changing function of the supervisory board, which now had to consider the interests of all stakeholders, among them the shareholders. Minority outside shareholders became larger in number, but had very little influence on corporate decisions.

TAKING STEPS TOWARDS A LIBERAL MARKET (FROM 1980 ONWARDS)

Although the 1980s initially saw an economic decline, towards the end of the century, economic conditions improved rapidly. In the Netherlands, a number of large multinational corporations, both nonfinancial and financial, were leading players in the world markets. At the same time, new companies were established and in specific industries, such as information technology and telecommunication, these companies grew rapidly. As a result of the developments in the 1960s and 1970s, the top managers of large firms were powerful in the corporate world because the stakeholder perspective and the strong impact of coordination with labour representatives and bankers on firm policies provided the managers with a pivotal position.[44] However, a series of corporate failures during the crisis years of the early 1980s led shareholders to question the competence of these managers. As a result, there was a shift in the direction of a more liberal system, while the influence of employees remained strong.

In this period, several key developments drove significant changes.[45] First, similar to developments in countries such as the United Kingdom and the United States, the Dutch shareholder base changed due to the increased presence of more vocal institutional investors relative to traditionally less engaged small shareholders. Second, capital markets internationalised, primarily as a consequence of the formation of the European Community and, in particular, the Monetary Union in 1999. Moreover, Dutch firms' reliance on external financing increased, enhancing the importance of public capital markets.[46] As a result, the role of passive and distant shareholders was being reconsidered. In its annual report of 1985, the Amsterdam Stock Exchange initiated a discussion of enhanced shareholder rights.[47] The Netherlands was in a situation—unlike that of the United States and the United Kingdom—where financial markets could not exert discipline on management because of the presence of highly effective takeover defences. At the same time EU member states discussed the pros and cons of moving in the direction of the more shareholder-friendly Anglo-Saxon model but could not agree on a clear direction.[48]

A first step was taken by a government committee led by legal scholar W. C. L. van der Grinten, which recommended in 1988 that the power of some of takeover defences should be reduced, and suggested that companies should reduce the number of defence mechanisms they deployed.[49] Because these recommendations would weaken the entrenched position of corporate boards, there was opposition from business leaders, and not until 1992 was a compromise reached that capped the number of takeover defences but still permitted the use of very powerful ones. However, an irreversible trend had set in.

The 1990s saw an increased dispersion of share ownership. Data on ownership concentration became publicly available with the implementation of the EU disclosure directive (*Wet Melding Zeggenschap*) in 1992. Table 3.3 presents ownership information for a selection of years. Data on this subject before that time are hard to obtain because until then, as a rule, Dutch companies only publicly listed their bearer shares and did not reveal registered shares. Between 1992 and 2007, the average total stake held by blockholders (shareholders with a stake of 5 per cent or more) was relatively stable between 45 per cent and 50 per cent, while there was a decline in the stakes of the largest shareholders.[50]

The 1990s also saw the emergence of the internationalisation of share ownership. In 1995, 37 per cent of the shares of twenty-five of the largest publicly listed companies were held by foreigners, increasing to 75 per cent in 2005.[51] Moreover, the stake of Dutch and continental European shareholders diminished, while the number of Anglo-American shareholders increased sharply. At the same time, Dutch institutional investors were

Table 3.3 Ownership structure and takeover defences

Panel A: Mean and median blockholdings per year

	C1	C3	Block	> 50	30–50	10–30	< 10
1992	28.88	41.64	46.55	19%	21%	35%	24%
	22.85	39.18	48.61				
1995	27.23	40.65	47.42	19%	20%	34%	28%
	19.40	36.11	48.80				
1998	24.90	38.89	45.51	16%	16%	36%	32%
	15.00	32.46	44.33				
2001	25.10	38.85	48.38	16%	15%	35%	34%
	14.70	32.48	50.26				
2004	23.18	38.23	50.03	15%	12%	42%	31%
	14.96	34.44	51.38				
2007	23.92	39.45	51.60	15%	11%	47%	28%
	14.29	32.78	53.21				

Note: C1 is largest owner, C3 are three largest, and Block is all stakes over 5 per cent.
Source: C. van der Elst, A. de Jong, and T. Raaijmakers, 'Een overzicht van juridische en economische dimensies van de kwetsbaarheid van Nederlandse beursvennootschappen,' in: Sociaal-Economische Raad, *Evenwichtig ondernemingsbestuur: Externe consultatie en (onderzoeks) rapportages* (Den Haag: SER, 2008).

Panel B: Takeover defences

	Priority shares	Preference shares (protective)	Certificates	Voting caps	X per cent rule	Structuurregime (obliged)	Structuurregime (voluntarily)	Structuurregime (mitigated)	Pyramide	Cross-holding
1992	42%	64%	39%	7%	9%	40%	12%	1%	13%	1%
1995	39%	62%	40%	6%	8%	48%	12%	3%	13%	2%
1998	33%	58%	33%	4%	5%	42%	14%	4%	8%	2%
2001	34%	65%	23%	3%	5%	39%	12%	3%	8%	2%
2004	31%	59%	18%	3%	1%	n.b.	n.b.	n.b.	9%	2%

Source: C. van der Elst, A. de Jong, and T. Raaijmakers, 'Een overzicht van juridische en economische dimensies van de kwetsbaarheid van Nederlandse beursvennootschappen,' in: Sociaal-Economische Raad, *Evenwichtig ondernemingsbestuur: Externe consultatie en (onderzoeks) rapportages* (Den Haag: SER, 2008).

reducing their investments in Dutch publicly listed companies.[52] Dutch-listed companies were under pressure to interest foreign investors in buying their shares. Whereas in the 1970s and 1980s, managers' primary interest was increasing sales and expanding their labour force, in the 1990s, the focus shifted to creating shareholder value by targeting the short-run stock price. The rising attention to shareholder value was associated with an increase in the fraction of firms paying dividends, especially in the late 1980s.[53]

In 1996, a committee on corporate governance chaired by J. F. M. Peters, former CEO of the insurance company AEGON, was formed.[54] The key conclusion of the committee's report was that companies should aim to rebalance power between managements and investors. The commission made forty nonbinding recommendations, and few of their suggestions were acted on during the following years. The report's main function was to create awareness about international developments and to pinpoint the idiosyncrasies of the Dutch case.

Until around 2000, most Dutch institutional investors were relatively passive, despite their increasing large holdings. A first initiative of the institutions in 1998 was to join forces in a foundation for pension funds interested in governance issues regarding the firms in their portfolio, SCGOP (*Stichting Corporate Governance Onderzoek Pensioenfondsen*).[55] The strategy changed when the ABP explicitly indicated a desire to engage in a dialogue with firm management, outside the shareholder meetings. Although interest groups for retail investors reacted negatively because these closed-door meetings could lead to an information differential between large and small investors and undermine the role of shareholder meetings, the institutions insisted that the meetings would serve to express their preferences and ideas.[56]

In 2002, the changes in governance in the five years following on the Peters committee report were evaluated, and the Minister of Finance concluded that little progress had been made, despite the need to keep up with international developments.[57] His call for a new committee gained momentum with the collapse of Royal Ahold in February 2003. Although preparations for a new committee were under way, there was an enormous sense of urgency, and public pressure for transparency and more binding rules was strong. Former Unilever CEO M. Tabaksblat took the lead and established a committee, which included representatives from listed firms, labour, and investors. The committee prepared a governance code with both general principles and explicit provisions for implementing these principles.[58] Companies either had to comply with these provisions or explain in their annual report the reasons for noncompliance.

Proxy advisory firms, or agencies supporting minority shareholders, had already become active in the Dutch market in the mid-1990s. Initially Déminor, a Belgian-based company, had a small Dutch branch providing advice to shareholders on governance issues and published comparative research on minority rights.[59] Later, other international players entered the Dutch scene, including Davis Global Advisors, Glass Lewis, and ISS (currently Risk Metrics). In 2005, ISS bought Déminor, making this firm a monopolist in the Netherlands. These agencies perform three roles. First, they advise minority shareholders—mainly the large institutional investors—on governance issues in specific companies. Second, they facilitate the actual voting for institutional investors. The international differences and specific rules on share registration make actual voting highly complicated for institutions with thousands of companies in their portfolio. Often, these companies register their holdings with a voting agency and automatically follow their advice for foreign shareholdings. They receive reports on their voting, allowing them to pretend to be active monitors. Third, they conduct and publish research on governance, in relation to best practices and firm performance.

Interestingly, the passivity of many international institutional investors in following the advice of the voting agencies makes the opinion of these agencies very important. In 2008, a collective of Dutch institutional investors managed to block proposed new compensation policies at Philips Electronics that would disconnect option grants from share price developments, by convincing Risk Metrics to advise negatively—57.8 per cent of the votes were cast against the proposal.[60]

The changes in the role of shareholders have had a clear effect on the use of takeover defences. Panel B of Table 3.3 presents the prevalence of takeover defences over 1992–2004 in detail.[61] Priority shares have become less important, declining from 42 per cent to 31 per cent. Preferred shares have remained stable at 64–59 per cent, but these instruments are only activated during a hostile takeover attempt. The strongest decline is found for certificates: from 39 per cent to 18 per cent. In the discussions about shareholder influence, these certificates were often the centre of criticism. As we have described, in the 1990s and early 2000s, both the concentration of ownership and the use of takeover defences decreased. It is important to note that these characteristics jointly reduced the degree of entrenchment for corporate management.[62]

One of the outcomes of the governance debates is that the Minister of Finance and the respective governance committees have commissioned a number of studies on annual meetings of shareholders with detailed information about the turnout rates and the discussions during the meeting.[63] In Table 3.4 we reproduce results from the first study covering 1998–2002 and 245 annual general meetings held by 54 Dutch listed firms.[64]

The turnout percentages are very high for the firms with certificates, which simply reflects the presence of the *Administratiekantoor* that has a dominant stake in the firm. In the shareholder meetings of these firms, we observe that all proposals are accepted, mostly without any voting taking place. In the firms without certificates, the turnout varies between 31.0 per cent and 36.5 per cent, which implies that on average one-third of the share capital is represented. The foundation for retail investors, *Vereniging van Effectenbezitters*, is present in almost all meetings, while Dutch pension

Table 3.4   Shareholder turnout

	1998	1999	2000	2001	2002
Percentage of share capital, certificates					
Average	89.83	88.15	94.06	92.82	94.03
Median	97.76	97.34	98.62	97.26	98.41
Number of companies	13	14	11	10	9
Percentage of share capital, without certificates					
Average	31.86	36.51	33.52	31.00	33.17
Median	26.63	33.25	37.50	30.42	33.96
Number of companies	25	28	24	25	26

Source: De Jong, A., G.M.H. Mertens, and P.G.J. Roosenboom, 'Shareholders' voting at general meetings: Evidence from the Netherlands', *Journal of Management and Governance*, 10 (2006): 353–380.

funds and mutual funds attend regularly. In these five years, a total of 1,583 proposals are brought to the table. Only nine proposals are not approved because they are withdrawn prior to the meeting or rejected. Six of these nine proposals concerned the authorisation to issue new capital, giving management a free hand to raise equity in the coming year.

In conjunction with the development of the Dutch corporate governance code, a number of regulatory changes have also been implemented. The new legislation for the structured regime adopted in 2004 gives the shareholder meeting the right to approve the annual accounts, while in firms subjected to the structured regime, the supervisory board had been entrusted with this task. And for structured-regime firms, the works council now has a right to recommend persons for at least one-third of the supervisory board. In addition, the shareholder meeting is empowered to remove the entire supervisory board for reasons of a lack of confidence. Following fierce societal debates on remuneration, firms now have to define a remuneration policy, which is subject to shareholder approval. Interestingly, the new rights for the works council to recommend board members under the structured regime has led to the exit from the structured regime by some firms that had voluntarily subjected themselves to the regime despite the exemption for firms with the majority of the employees outside the Netherlands. Apparently, allowing labour to be represented in the supervisory board is too high a price to pay for staying within this regime.[65]

To conclude, from the 1980s onwards, the role of shareholders has changed in Dutch firms, but the composition of the shareholder base has also changed, with increased dispersion and internationalisation. Although shareholder influence has improved due to the reduction of takeover defences, the shareholder meetings are still not a platform for real dialogue between firm management and shareholders but rather an inevitable ritual dance. In the movement towards a more liberal regime, the role of labour has also been strengthened via new legislation.

CONCLUSION

The development of corporate governance in the Netherlands over the course of the 20th century can be analysed using the varieties of capitalism literature. We take this approach from the perspective of shareholders because these investors interact with the other stakeholders in the firm and they play different roles in the ideal types: liberal market economy (LME) and coordinated market economy (CME). Our descriptions lead to the conclusion that early in the 20th century, the Dutch shareholders' role is characteristic of an LME environment, but that after the Second World War the system moves towards a CME. Finally, the most recent developments since the 1980s reveal a tendency back towards an LME system.

We do, however, wish to make this broad interpretation more nuanced in three ways.

First, the VoC literature has specific ideal-type characteristics of shareholders in mind, while in reality we find a multitude of types of shareholders, each with different influence on firms. Over time, we observe changes in the roles of insiders versus outsiders, as well as in the concentration of ownership and the presence of large blockholders. Finally, there is variation in the importance of various groups of shareholders, such as families, minority shareholders, institutional investors, etc. Therefore, rather than focusing on the LME versus CME distinction, it is more useful to distinguish three regimes over the 20th century, based on the dominant players in the corporate world. In the first decades, insider owner-managers—to a large extent, families—are in control, since most stock is owned by the inside shareholders who keep control rights tightly limited within a small circle. After the Second World War, managers monopolise control, as ownership and management become separated. Shareholder rights are increasingly circumscribed as they became more dispersed. In the most recent decades, international and institutional investors become much more important and dispute the powers of the management with limited success.

A second nuance we would like to introduce is that the way in which shareholders exert influence on firms also varies over time. Shareholders' meetings are in many instances rituals where preordained decisions by insiders are rubber stamped. However, we also observe occasions where management proposals are denied approval. We would like to indicate that a limitation of our study is that one-on-one meetings between shareholders and managers typically remain undocumented. An analysis of the minutes of the supervisory board was outside the scope of this chapter, but it might offer an interesting perspective for further research.

A third nuance is that we observe a constant characteristic over the course of the long century, which is the power of firms' top management. We find that initially the power of outside shareholders has generally been very limited, and that real authority rested with management and supervisory board insiders in collaboration with large shareholders. Attempts to give employees a voice seem to have mainly shifted power to the board and management, further curtailing shareholder influence. It is clear that if companies are to have the autonomy needed to take a broader, 'stakeholder' viewpoint of their goals, they need to have in place some defensive measures to protect them from the threat of hostile takeovers. That is, shareholder rights need to be curtailed, and this ultimately gives more power to the management. In recent decades, we observe increased activity by institutional investors, in particular Dutch pension funds, and in general we find that recently shareholders have become increasingly well organised. However, during the entire period considered, small investors were never very powerful—they simply received what was left after more powerful actors had taken their share.

NOTES

1. Hall and Soskice, eds. *Varieties of Capitalism*.
2. Strätling, 'General meetings: A dispensable tool', 74–82.
3. Westerhuis, 'The Dutch corporate network: Considering its persistence'.
4. See Sluyterman, *Dutch Enterprise*.
5. Westerhuis and De Jong, *Over geld en macht*, chapter 2. We do not refer to page numbers for this source because the text has not yet been published; instead we refer to chapters.
6. Zeff, Van der Wel, and Camfferman, *Company Financial Reporting*, 33.
7. See Cheffins, Koustas, and Chambers, 'Ownership dispersion', Table 1, for an analysis of the prospectuses of domestic UK IPOs in 1900–1911, showing that 103 of 128 companies that become officially listed issue preference shares, and in 69 of those cases, the ordinary shares are kept by the vendors and only the preference shares are issued to the general public.
8. Townsend, 'Optimal contracts and competitive markets', 265–293; Gale and Hellwig, 'Incentive-compatible debt contracts', 647–663.
9. However, there was a corporate tax on profit distributed to shareholders and founders at a low rate of 2½ to 2¾ per cent, replaced in 1914 by an income tax of 6.65 per cent withheld on the net payout to shareholders, rising to 12.05 per cent in 1938.
10. Koert, 'Winstverdeeling bij Nederlandsche Naamlooze Vennootschappen', 110–123.
11. Stadsarchief Amsterdam, access no. 1520, inv.no. 231, Statuten der Naamlooze Vennootschap Stoombierbrouwerij "'t Haantje', Hoofdstuk VII. Winst, 1910, 13–14.
12. Westerhuis and De Jong, *Over geld en macht*, chapter 2.
13. Tekenbroek, *De verhouding tusschen de aandeelhouders en bestuurders*, 51.
14. Westerhuis and De Jong, *Over geld en macht*, chapter 3.
15. Zeff, Van der Wel, and Camfferman, *Company Financial Reporting*, 56–62.
16. Stadsarchief Amsterdam, access no. 869, inv.no.16, minutes of the shareholder meeting of 26 March 1927.

17. For a detailed account of the situation of the company in the interwar period, see Dankers and Van der Linden, *Samensmeltend glas*, 33–63.
18. We have collected information for 1942, the last relatively normal year in the Second World War and therefore preferred to 1943.
19. Westerhuis and De Jong, *Over geld en macht*, chapter 4.
20. Westerhuis and De Jong, *Over geld en macht*, chapter 4.
21. *Vereniging Effectenbescherming*. Its precursor, founded in 1924, was the *Vereeniging van Fondsenhouders*.
22. Editorial, *Beleggers Belangen*, 1–20 (28 September 1957).
23. Introduction to trial issue *Beleggers Belangen* (December 1956).
24. The text in this section is adapted from Westerhuis and De Jong, *Over geld en macht*, chapter 4.
25. W. C. Posthumus Meyjes, 'Wilton-Fijenoord', *Beleggers Belangen* 111, 1957, 9.
26. Th.E.M., 'Aandelhouders Scholten-Honig met een kluit in het riet gestuurd', *Beleggers Belangen* 14 June, 1970, 140–141.
27. *Limburgs Nieuwsblad*, 21 June 1969.
28. Voogd, *Statutaire Beschermingsmiddelen*, 221.
29. The discussion of motives for takeover defences is adapted from Westerhuis and De Jong, *Over geld en macht*, chapter 4.
30. Both studies are described in Stichting Maatschappij en Onderneming, *Machtsverdeling in de naamlooze vennootschap*.
31. Stichting Maatschappij en Onderneming, *Machtsverdeling in de naamlooze vennootschap*, 20.
32. Hoge Raad 1 April 1949, NJ, 1949, 465.
33. Hoge Raad 21 January 1955, NJ, 1959, 43.
34. De Jong, Mertens, and Roosenboom, 'Shareholders' voting at general meetings', 353–380.
35. Westerhuis and De Jong, *Over geld en macht*, chapter 4.
36. Author's interview with Enterprise Chamber judge, 2007.
37. W. C. Posthumus Meyjes, 'Jaarvergadering Groninger Rijwielenfabriek A. Fongers N.V.: Verslaggeving laat te wensen', *Beleggers Belangen* 118, 9–11.
38. In the meeting, 1,410 votes were cast against approval. The chairman of the management board was absent due to illness, and a supervisory board member abstained from voting his 1,000 shares because he felt he had insufficient information, so that the six voters in favour could only muster 1,142 votes. The shareholder who had voted against discharge argued that the company had an uncertain future due to English competition in the cultivation of sisal in Tanzania, insisting on a broadening of the production base or a merger. The management was willing to sell the company but considered the current price to be unattractive. In a subsequent meeting in December, the annual accounts were approved without further changes after the dissenting shareholders had talked to management, which was finally able to persuade them of the good prospects of the Tanzanian activities. See 'Cultuurmij Ngombez', *Financieel Archief Systemen Keesing* 56 (14 September 1966), 556 and 101 (30 December 1966), 825.
39. Posthumus Meyjes, *Jaarvergadering en Jaarverslag*.
40. Posthumus Meyjes, *Jaarvergadering en Jaarverslag*, 20.
41. Posthumus Meyjes, *Jaarvergadering en Jaarverslag*, 17.
42. Posthumus Meyjes, *Jaarvergadering en Jaarverslag*, 20.
43. Posthumus Meyjes, *Jaarvergadering en Jaarverslag*, 28.
44. See also Westerhuis, 'The Dutch corporate network'.
45. De Jong, Röell, and Westerhuis, 'Changing national business systems', 773–798.
46. Westerhuis and De Jong, *Over geld en macht*, chapter 5.

47. Vereniging voor de Effectenhandel, *Annual Report* (1985).
48. De Jong, Röell, and Westerhuis, 'Changing national business systems'.
49. See van der Grinten, 'Overname en beschermingsconstructies', 835; Boot, 'Corporate Governance: hoe verder?', 533–544.
50. Van der Elst, De Jong, and Raaijmakers, 'Een overzicht van juridische en economische dimensies'.
51. Abma and Munster, 'De rol en positie van de aandeelhouders'.
52. De Jong, Röell, and Westerhuis, 'Changing national business systems', 791–792.
53. Von Eije and Megginson, 'Dividends and share repurchases'.
54. Committee on Corporate Governance, *Corporate Governance in the Netherlands*, Secretariat Committee on Corporate Governance, Amsterdam (1997).
55. In 2006, it expanded to include other institutions and changed its name into Eumedion; see http://www.eumedion.nl/nl/overeumedion.
56. 'Onderonsjes tasten jaarvergadering aan', *Het Financieele Dagblad*, 24 January 2006.
57. Speech of Mr. H. Hoogervorst, 18 December 2002.
58. Committee on Corporate Governance, *Dutch Corporate Governance Code* (2003).
59. See 'Nederlandse aandeelhouder het slechtste af', *Het Financieele Dagblad*, 9 October 1996.
60. 'Wouter wikt, de stemadviseur beschikt' and 'Stemmingmakerij', *FEM Business*, 5 April, 2008, 6 and 14–15.
61. Van der Elst, De Jong, and Raaijmakers, 'Overzicht van juridische en economische dimensies', Table 39.
62. Westerhuis, 'The Dutch corporate network'.
63. De Jong, Mertens, and Roosenboom, *Aandeelhoudersvergaderingen in Nederland, 1998–2002* (2003) and *Activiteiten van aandeelhouders 2005* (2005); Klaasen, Molenbroek, and Out, *Algemene vergadering van aandeelhouders, van eindstation naar tussenstation* (2006).
64. De Jong, Mertens, and Roosenboom, 'Shareholders' voting', 361.
65. Typically, firms present the abolition of the structured regime as an improvement of their governance structure. However, the timing of their exit suggests that unwillingness to allow labour representation on the board is a more likely motive. See for example: 'ABN Amro beperkt rechten van ondernemingsraad', *Het Financieele Dagblad*, 19 February 2003, where the CEO argues that giving shareholders a say is the motivation for the removal of the voluntary structured regime.

REFERENCES

Abma, R. and R. Munster, 'De rol en positie van de aandeelhouders', in: S.C. Peij, ed., *Handboek Corporate Governance* (Amsterdam: Kluwer, 2007): 85–112.
Boot, A.W.A., 'Corporate governance: hoe verder?', *Maandblad voor Accountancy en Bedrijfseconomie (MAB)*, Oktober (1999): 533–544.
Cheffins, B.R., D.K. Koustas, and D. Chambers, 'Ownership Dispersion and the London Stock Exchange's 'Two-Thirds Rule': An Empirical Test', University of Cambridge Faculty of Law Research Paper No. 17/2012 (2012). Available at SSRN: http://ssrn.com/abstract=2094538
Dankers, J. and J. van der Linden, *Samensmeltend glas. Honderd jaar N.V. Vereenigde Glasfabrieken 1899–1999* (Amsterdam: Boom, 2001).
Elst, C. van der, A. de Jong, and T. Raaijmakers, 'Een overzicht van juridische en economische dimensies van de kwetsbaarheid van Nederlandse beursvennootschappen',

in: Sociaal-Economische Raad, *Evenwichtig ondernemingsbestuur: Externe consultatie en (onderzoeks) rapportages* (Den Haag: SER, 2008).

Gale, D. and Hellwig, M., 'Incentive-compatible debt contracts: The one-period problem', *The Review of Economic Studies*, 52 (1985): 647–663.

Grinten, W.C.L. van der, 'Overname en beschermingsconstructies', *Economisch-Statistische Berichten (ESB)*, September 14, 1988.

Hall, P.A. and Soskice, D., eds. *Varieties of Capitalism. The Institutional Foundations of Comparative Advantage* (Oxford: Oxford University Press, 2001).

Jong, A. de, G.M.H. Mertens, and P.G.J. Roosenboom, *Aandeelhoudersvergaderingen in Nederland 1998–2002*. Report to Minister of Finance, 2003.

Jong, A. de, G.M.H. Mertens, and P.G.J. Roosenboom, *Activiteiten van aandeelhouders 2005*. Monitoring Committee Corporate Governance (Frijns Committee), 2005.

Jong, A. de, G.M.H. Mertens, and P.G.J. Roosenboom, 'Shareholders' voting at general meetings: Evidence from the Netherlands', *Journal of Management and Governance*, 10 (2006): 353–380.

Jong, A. de, A. Röell, and G. Westerhuis, 'Changing national business systems: Corporate governance and financing in the Netherlands, 1945–2005', *Business History Review*, 84, Winter (2010): 773–798.

Klaasen, A., M. Molenbroek, and B. Out, *Algemene vergadering van aandeelhouders: van eindstation naar tussenstation*. Monitoring Committee Corporate Governance (Frijns Committee), 2006.

Koert, J.A. 'Winstverdeeling bij Nederlandsche Naamlooze Vennootschappen' (PhD dissertation, Nederlandsche Handels-Hoogeschool Rotterdam, 1934).

Posthumus Meyjes, W.C. *Jaarvergadering en Jaarverslag* (Laren: Andries Blitz, 1960).

Sluyterman, K.E., *Dutch Enterprise in the Twentieth Century: Business Strategies in a Small Open Economy* (London and New York: Routledge, 2005).

Stichting Maatschappij en Onderneming, *Machtsverdeling in de naamlooze vennootschap* (Den Haag: SMO, 1971).

Strätling, R., 'General meetings: A dispensable tool for corporate governance of listed companies', *Corporate Governance: An International Review*, 11 (2003): 74–82.

Tekenbroek, E., 'De verhouding tusschen de aandeelhouders en bestuurders bij de publieke naamlooze vennootschap in Nederland' (PhD thesis, Nederlandsche Handelshoogeschool Rotterdam. Delft: Universiteits-Boekencentrale, 1923).

Townsend, R.M., 'Optimal contracts and competitive markets with costly state verification', *Journal of Economic Theory*, 22 (1979): 265–293.

Von Eije, H., and W.L. Megginson, 'Dividends and share repurchases in the European Union', *Journal of Financial Economics*, 89 (2008): 347–374.

Voogd, R.P., *Statutaire Beschermingsmiddelen bij Beursvennootschappen* (PhD dissertation University of Nijmegen, 1989).

Westerhuis, G., 'The Dutch corporate network: Considering its persistence', in T. David and G. Westerhuis, eds., *The Power of Corporate Networks. A Comparative and Historical Perspective* (London: Routledge, 2014).

Westerhuis, G., and A. de Jong, *Over geld en macht. De financiering en corporate governance van het Nederlands bedrijfsleven* (Amsterdam: Boom Publishers, forthcoming).

Zeff, S.A., F. van der Wel, and K. Camfferman, *Company Financial Reporting. A Historical and Comparative Study of the Dutch Regulatory Process* (Amsterdam: North-Holland Elsevier, 1992).

4 An Entrepreneurial Perspective
Varieties of Capitalism and Entrepreneurs in the 20th Century

Jacques van Gerwen and Ferry de Goey

INTRODUCTION

In this chapter the focus is on the development of entrepreneurs and enterprises in liberal market economies (LMEs) and coordinated market economies (CMEs) during the 20th century and especially the concept of homogenisation. We will argue that instead of homogenisation our research reveals a large variety of entrepreneurs and enterprises in LMEs and CMEs. In the last decades of the 20th century, this variety has not become less but has increased even further. The explanation for this is the hybrid character of LMEs and CMEs that increased after the 1980s in response to the economic crisis of the late 1970s and the changing economic policy of western states. Because of the hybrid character, institutional complementarity remains weak, and the pressure on entrepreneurs and enterprises to homogenate is equally low. This allows for a great variety of entrepreneurs and enterprises.[1]

According to the theory of Varieties of Capitalism (VoC), as developed by Peter A. Hall and David Soskice, firms need to coordinate their requirements related to capital, labour, and competition. In LMEs coordination occurs mainly through market exchanges and in CMEs via cooperation and regulation. The institutions in both Varieties of Capitalism are attuned to this, resulting in institutional complementarity. Following this theoretical logic, other scholars, like Jens Beckert, argue that because of the institutional complementarity, a dominant type of firm for each type of capitalism will emerge.[2] The VoC approach results in an increasing homogenisation of enterprises or isomorphism: over time they will become more alike, through coercion, emulation, and competition. In LMEs the dominant type may be called the shareholder-based managerial enterprise, while in CMEs it is the bank-monitored alliance-centred firm.

In the VoC approach, the Netherlands and Germany are considered CMEs, while the United States and Great Britain are labelled as LMEs. This dichotomy seems to be related to diverging attitudes towards entrepreneurship.[3] Available empirical research demonstrates that Americans are indeed more positively inclined towards an entrepreneurial career than people from the Netherlands and Germany. Whether this has been the case for the whole 20th century we do not know. Sociological research from the 1980s confirmed the greater interest of Americans in becoming self-employed compared to other western countries.[4] The earliest available research of the European Commission (EC) from the year 2000 showed that Americans favoured self-employment more than wage labour, while in the EU the preference for self-employment was generally lower than in the United States. A similar survey of the EC from 2007 demonstrated that 61 per cent of the US population preferred being self-employed, while only 50 per cent of Europeans preferred self-employment above wage labour.[5] The greater number of people in the United States wanting to become entrepreneurs is often linked to the high social status of entrepreneurs and greater social mobility. The social mobility of American citizens is likewise assumed not be determined by the social background of individuals but mainly by their own ability and motivation. In 1993 President Bill Clinton said, 'The American Dream that we were all raised on is a simple but powerful one—if you work hard and play by the rules you should be given a chance to go as far as your God-given ability will take you'.[6] In his victory speech on December 7, 2012, President Obama repeated this in almost the same words.[7]

Based on the VoC literature, we assume that there are differences between entrepreneurs and enterprises in LMEs and CMEs because otherwise the whole idea of a dichotomy becomes meaningless. Our general hypothesis, based on the previous discussion about entrepreneurial attitudes, is that LMEs are more entrepreneurial than CMEs. We will limit our research to a number of qualitative and quantitative variables. The qualitative variables include social status background, schooling, and competencies, while the quantitative variables focus on the number of entrepreneurs and enterprises, the size distribution of enterprises, and the number of self-employed and employed directors (i.e. professional managers). Based on our general hypothesis, we have formulated four postulates:

(1) in LMEs entrepreneurs enjoy a higher social status than in CMEs;
(2) in LMEs less value is attached to the social background of entrepreneurs than in CMEs;
(3) in LMEs entrepreneurs receive dedicated educational programs and schooling more often than in CMEs; and
(4) in LMEs the share of entrepreneurs in the working population is higher than in CMEs.

These postulates will be investigated by comparing two CMEs (the Netherlands and Germany) and two LMEs (the United States and Great Britain). The classification of these countries in LME or CME is based on the existing VoC literature. There is, however, some debate about this classification. Capitalism is constantly changing, and this affects the classification of countries. Although Hall and Soskice presented a mostly static image of LMEs and CMEs, it has become clear that countries change. The longer the period, the more change we can observe. We will return to this problem in the third section. For our analysis, we will maintain the Hall and Soskice classification to compare entrepreneurs in LMEs and CMEs. The point of departure for our analysis is the development of the Dutch business system during the 20th century. In the third section of this chapter, the results of our analysis are used to evaluate the VoC approach, with special attention for the Dutch case. This is followed by some concluding remarks.

ENTREPRENEURS IN LMES AND CMES

Before we start our analyses, we want to stress that in the VoC approach, although presented as actor based, entrepreneurs hardly play a role, and as far as they are discussed, the focus is mainly on the CEOs of large industrial enterprises. Entrepreneurs used to be the heroes of business historians, but since the late 1980s they have been neglected.[8] Entrepreneurs are, however, studied by other scholars (e.g. economists and business administration) using different methods, theories, and definitions. While some researchers are primarily interested in the self-employed managing a small business, others are mainly focusing on the professional managers of big corporations or the chief executive officers (CEOs).[9] This gives a distorted view of the role of entrepreneurs, and therefore we will include all types of entrepreneurs (self-employed and managers) in all types of enterprises because this gives a more comprehensive view of the business system in a country.[10]

Attitudes, Status, and Competencies

The first two hypotheses state that in LMEs entrepreneurs enjoy a higher status and the social background of entrepreneurs is less important than in CMEs. In our third hypothesis we assume LMEs develop dedicated schooling programs and attach more value to specific education for entrepreneurs than in CMEs. We may therefore expect that more people aspire to become entrepreneurs in LMEs than in CMEs. LMEs furthermore develop educational programmes sooner and more extensively than CMEs. International comparative research on the status and competencies of entrepreneurs is scarce. This is certainly true for historical research that is mostly qualitative in nature. Given these limitations, we will first present an overview of the status and competencies of Dutch entrepreneurs before we compare these with the United States, Great Britain, and Germany. We will make a distinction between the elite (i.e. the directors of large companies) and the small businessmen.

The Dutch Business Elite

During the 20th century, the status of Dutch entrepreneurs varied between groups of businessmen and changed over time. In the first decades of the

20th century, there was a gap in status between the directors of large companies on the one hand and the small business owners on the other hand.[11] While the former often circulated in the higher echelons of society, frequently through family connections, the latter struggled to distinguish themselves from the growing number of skilled labourers. Yet even within the business elite, there was a difference in status between directors of banks and large trading houses from respected families and the growing number of captains of industry. In 1930, the ten largest businesses (measured by their stock value) included many well-respected banks and international trading companies, while there were only a few large industrial firms. In 1950, however, the large industrial firms (e.g. Royal Dutch Shell, Unilever, and Philips) had replaced the banks and trading firms and now occupied the top five positions.[12]

There existed close ties between the large companies: personal relations (family ties), business relations, and financial ties (e.g. occupying seats on the supervisory boards). The elite of Dutch entrepreneurs were a very close-knit community, and outsiders (including foreigners) had difficulty becoming part of this group. Political scientists have demonstrated that during the 20th century, these features hardly changed despite the growing internationalisation of Dutch business.[13] The elite of entrepreneurs asserted a certain amount of economic and political power. Precisely how influential and powerful they were, let alone whether they were dominant in society, is almost impossible to determine because it very much depended on the criteria and the historical circumstances. During the Second World War, the exiled Dutch government asked several directors of large industrial companies and banks as advisors on policy matters. After the liberation in May 1945, the establishment of the Stichting van de Arbeid (The Labour Foundation) united representatives of employers and labourers, and their collaboration was further enhanced by the governmental advisory board: Sociaal Economische Raad (The Social and Economic Council of the Netherlands) founded in 1950.[14] In these organisations the business elite was well represented.

The elite entrepreneurs received better training and education than most small businessmen. Although a few universities have offered courses in business economics since the 1920s, only a very small number of business leaders actually attended these classes. Before the 1940s, a minority of business leaders went to university, and in most cases they studied law and not economics.[15] This did not really prepare them for a business career, but their education often included several years of training on the job in the family business or with an acquaintance abroad. One example is Henri Deterding (1866–1939), director of Royal Dutch Shell between 1900 and 1936, who received no academic education because of family circumstances. As in most other western countries, the elite entrepreneurs usually came from an entrepreneurial background. Until the second half of the 20th century, many companies, although incorporated and perhaps even listed on the Amsterdam stock exchange, remained in fact family businesses. The career pattern of the business elite was therefore to a large extent shaped by managing the family and the family business.

From the 1950s, the level of education of the business elite steadily improved as more business leaders went to university studying technology and business economics, besides their traditional preference for law. Prospective business leaders could not study business administration because there were no business schools in the Netherlands in the 1950s. For this they had to go to America, but only a few did.[16] In the 1960s, the first business schools started to offer courses attracting small numbers of students. This changed dramatically in the 1980s and 1990s, when business schools became really popular. Because of their late development in the Netherlands, the business schools did not play a major role in educating and forming the business elite during the 20th century.[17]

The Business Elite in the United States, Great Britain, and Germany

When comparing the Dutch business elite with those of the United States, Great Britain, and Germany, it is obvious that, while each country had its own peculiarities, there were many similarities.[18] The variety in the status of entrepreneurs was certainly not smaller than in the Netherlands. In each country a small group of big entrepreneurs enjoyed the highest status. In the beginning of the 20th century, they managed their family businesses and often tried to build long-lasting dynasties (e.g. Ford, Rockefeller, Morgan, Vanderbilt, Lever, Harrod, Rowntree Cadbury, Krupp, Thyssen, and Siemens).[19] Most business leaders in the United States, Great Britain, and Germany came from the existing elite and were raised in wealthy business families. About 70 per cent of the American business elite born between 1891 and 1920 came from a business family.[20] This background provided them with the necessary attitude, skills, and financial means. The careers of most directors started and ended in their family businesses, whether private firms or joint-stock companies. Beginning in the 1920s, professional managers trained at business schools became more important, especially in the United States.[21] Although they usually had no family connections with the original founders, many behaved like their predecessors.

Through extensive interlocking of corporate boards (of private firms and banks), the largest corporations formed a network that remained in place for most of the 20th century. Occasionally new businessmen entered the business elite; from the 1980s this included the founders of new businesses in the ICT sector.[22] Social mobility between the working class and the business elite was and remained exceptional: the popular American rags-to-riches stories were a myth. Walter A. Friedman and Richard S. Tedlow demonstrate that in the 20th century most business leaders came from the white and Protestant elite, with a northern European ancestry, and 'the closing decades have shown some limited changes in the circumstance'.[23]

Interestingly, in Great Britain there were more business leaders coming from the lower levels of society (e.g. manual workers or employees) in the late 1980s than in the United States or Germany.[24] This greater social mobility is perhaps related to changes in British society following Prime Minister Margaret Thatcher. The Thatcherite Revolution has certainly created better opportunities for start-ups in Great Britain, although it may well be that important differences existed between the level of social mobility of old and new types of industries and large and small cities.[25] The relatively small geographical size and the high concentration of economic activities in the large cities in the western part of the Netherlands may have contributed to the formation of a more close-knit community of business leaders than in much larger countries like the United States, Great Britain, and Germany.[26]

While the level of formal education increased in most western countries, future business leaders continued to receive on-the-job training. This is particularly true for Great Britain, while in Germany and the United States a college or university degree became essential for a business career.[27] Although the United States already had business schools since the 1880s, it wasn't until the 1970s that the first professional managers entered the business elite. The Managerial Revolution in the United States was important mainly for the growing number of middle managers, and only a few reached the level of CEO.[28] Business leaders really gained in status and importance during the 1950s and 1960s, when big business was *en vogue*. In the 1990s, professional managers even became celebrities, featured on television shows, in newspapers, and in business journals. Their status reached a high point during the economic boom of the late 1990s, but it rapidly declined after the burst of the ICT-Bubble in 2001. In the United States the status of professional managers in 2007, before the financial crisis, was rather low compared to most EU countries, perhaps because they are not viewed as real entrepreneurs but primarily as employees.[29]

Like the Netherlands, Great Britain and Germany did not establish business schools until the 1960s and 1970s. In the case of Great Britain, this is surprising because the VoC approach considers it to be a LME like the United States. The impact of business schools on the business community in these countries therefore remained small. As far as Germany is concerned, Youssef Cassis concludes, 'Up to the generation active in the late 1980s, less than 5 per cent of the top German businessmen had been trained in one of these colleges'.[30] In the last decades, acquisitions and mergers influenced the careers of the business elite, particularly in the United States and Germany. In these two countries the legal and organisational structure of companies offered more opportunities to pursue a business career than in Great Britain, where family firms remained important. From the 1980s, most company directors stayed for only a few years before moving to another company. This career pattern is usually attributed to the rising pressure of institutional shareholders on top managers and the advent of shareholder value capitalism following the poor performance of many joint-stock corporations in the 1970s.

Small Business in the Netherlands

Although the elite of entrepreneurs may have had a dominant influence on the business community, the overwhelming majority were the small businessmen.[31] Until the 1960s, they were known as the Middenstand in the Netherlands. The name not only referred to the specific type of business with no or a small number of employees, but it was also used to refer to a specific societal category or class and related norms and values. While the expression 'Middenstand' was replaced by Midden en Kleinbedrijf (MKB, or small and medium-sized enterprises: SMEs), it is still often used in Germany (Mittelstand).

Most SME-entrepreneurs were self-employed and sole proprietors: the majority had no employees or only occasionally, often family members. The overwhelming majority of these small businessmen managed a family firm. The Organisation for Economic Co-operation and Development (OECD) calls them micro-enterprises.

The Dutch Middenstand before the 1950s was far from uniform and included a great variety of entrepreneurs, each with a different social status. At the very bottom were numerous petty traders who sold their produce on local markets. The largest group, however, consisted of shopkeepers, while the large retailers and apothecaries belonged to the elite of the Middenstand. Most small businessmen came from an entrepreneurial family: in 1950, almost 50 per cent.[32] Social mobility remained limited for most of the 20th century. Even in the middle of the century it was fairly uncommon for manual labourers to become small businessmen. Small businessmen could rise within their own group or class, but hardly ever became part of the elite of big entrepreneurs. Although the financial position of many of these small business owners was often precarious, lacking financial reserves and adequate administrative and organisational skills, the lifespan of some of these businesses was surprisingly long. Craftsman (e.g. silversmiths, blacksmiths, or butchers), for instance, frequently operated their businesses for thirty or forty years. When they were succeeded by one of their sons, the business could reach the age of one hundred years or older. But the most striking feature was perhaps the large number of start-ups that exited within the first five or ten years, because of bankruptcy or, more often, because of a change in occupation or interest. It appears that, despite better education, this high percentage of business exits (between 40 and 50 per cent) in the first five years has remained rather constant for most of the 20th century.[33]

Small business owners were proud of being self-employed and independent, although they often worked longer hours and earned less money than some of the skilled labourers. Even in the 1990s, this was the case. The greatest fear of small businessmen before the 1950s was slipping down the social ladder. This led them to found numerous political and nonpolitical organisations to represent their interests. The high level of organisation of different social groups, including entrepreneurs, is considered a typical feature of the Dutch business system.[34] Already before 1914 this resulted in the first national employer organisations, and by the end of the 20th century, large businesses were members of NCW-VNO, while small enterprises were represented by MKB-Nederland.

The social and economic position of small businessmen was particularly threatened during the severe economic crisis of the 1930s, when large numbers of unemployed workers tried to escape poverty and started their own business. The various organisations of small businessmen petitioned political parties to stop the influx of these marginal entrepreneurs. Their lobby was successful: in 1937, a new law (Vestigingswet Kleinbedrijf) required certain minimum qualifications of new businessmen, including administrative skills and sufficient start-up capital. This is an example of the agency of entrepreneurs to change existing institutions.[35] The law, amended in 1954, remained in force until 2007 in an effort of the Dutch government to reduce the red tape for start-ups as part of the deregulation and liberalisation of the economy.[36]

For the majority of small businessmen, the level of education until the 1960s was and remained low. Most had completed grammar school, and only a small percentage high school. In the 1950s and 1960s, the level of education improved, but the social status of small businessmen declined.[37] They were increasingly seen as remnants of the early 20th century and considered unable to compete with the more efficient large enterprises and provide sufficient jobs for the growing population. The negative attitude of politicians and public opinion towards SMEs and family businesses in general changed during the economic crisis of the late 1970s, when many big businesses were forced to lay off large numbers of workers. Inspired by American and British examples, the Dutch government changed its policy and began to stimulate entrepreneurship and SMEs.

Small Business in the United States, Great Britain, and Germany

Entrepreneurs managing a small business never attracted the same amount of interest from business historians as the big business leaders.[38] The available literature, however, demonstrates that entrepreneurs in small businesses in the United States, Great Britain, and Germany operated in quite similar conditions and their status and competencies were comparable to Dutch small businessmen.[39] There are of course differences between countries and periods. In Germany the Mittelstand was in general viewed more positively during most of the 20th century, than in the United States and Great Britain.[40] At the beginning of the 20th century, the level of formal education of most small businessmen in the United States, Great Britain, and Germany was low. This improved before the 1950s, but their most important training occurred on the job.

Until the Second World War, SMEs were regarded as the backbone of society, offering opportunities for enterprising individuals. They could rely on the support from conservative and liberal politicians.[41] The rise of big business in the first decades of the 20th century did not go unnoticed by existing lobby organisations for small businessmen, particularly their practices of unfair competition and market domination through economic concentration. Neither did it escape the attention of politicians and governments (e.g. Sherman Antitrust Act of 1890 and subsequent laws in the United States). However, national considerations concerning the competitive strength of states, especially during economic crises and wars, meant that governments stimulated big business while trying to look after the interests of SMEs.

During the Second World War, the United States government increasingly turned to big business to supply the army. This was also apparent in Great Britain and Germany. After the war, the status of SMEs had declined noticeably and would continue to do so until the economic crisis of the late 1970s. Between 1945 and 1970, generally regarded as the heyday of Company Man and Fordism, SMEs were seen as inefficient, uncompetitive, and incapable of generating sufficient jobs for a growing population.[42] This negative attitude towards SMEs changed in the 1980s, starting in the United States and Great Britain. President Ronald Reagan announced the Age of the Entrepreneur in 1988.[43] Politicians believed that having a large number of SMEs offered national competitive advantages, particularly during the rapid economic globalisation of the 1980s and 1990s. They were considered to be more flexible, innovative, and productive than big businesses, and important for creating new jobs.[44] In an attempt to counter the economic crisis and the huge unemployment problem, governments thus began to stimulate SMEs through a series of special programs. These programs were meant to foster an enterprise culture: people aspiring to become self-employed should be able to start their own businesses.[45] In all western countries, governments tried to cut the number of laws, rules, and regulations frustrating start-ups. As a result of this policy change, the status of small business owners and SMEs in general increased.

In sum we conclude that, when looking at the status, social background, and competencies, there was a large variety of entrepreneurs in the two LMEs and the two CMEs. During the 20th century, the variety has not become less, and there are thus no indications of homogenisation or isomorphism of entrepreneurs in LMEs and CMEs. The hypothetical differences between LME and CME (our hypotheses one, two, and three) are not supported by the available evidence on these qualitative variables. This will be become even clearer when we look at some quantitative variables.

The Number of Small and Large Businesses, Self-Employed, and Managers

During the 20th century, the number of entrepreneurs and enterprises increased in the Netherlands (see Table 4.1).[46] The number of registered enterprises increased from 395,000 in 1930, to 334,000 in 1947 and 534,000 in 2000. The total number of entrepreneurs rose from about 322,000 in 1899, to 553,000 in 1947, to 590,000 in 1981, and c. 1 million in 2000. The majority of entrepreneurs were the self-employed: owners managing their small or medium-sized family businesses. The number of professional managers increased markedly from the 1980s, although their share in the working population remained modest during the whole century: between 0.5 and 1.7 per cent. During the 20th century, the share of entrepreneurs in the working population declined: more and more people were working as employees. This downward trend was stopped in the last years of the 20th century and even reversed. A similar development occurred in other countries.[47]

Our fourth hypothesis states that because of the higher status of entrepreneurs, the relatively unimportant social background, and the availability of dedicated educational programmes, the share of entrepreneurs (including self-employed and professional managers) in the working population will be higher in LMEs than in CMEs. OECD statistics, however, demonstrate that, at least between 1986 and 2000, the share of entrepreneurs in the United States was actually lower than in the Netherlands (see Table 4.2).[48]

Table 4.1 Entrepreneurs in the Netherlands: Numbers and share in working population, 1899–2000

	Total number of entrepreneurs (x 1,000)	Self-employed (x 1,000)	Self-employed in working population (%)	Professional managers (x 1,000)	Professional managers in working population (%)
1899	322	311	15.3	11	0.5
1930	406	390	12.3	16	0.5
1947	553	538	13.9	15	0.4
1963	493 (1960)	466	10.9	27	0.5
1981	590	525	10.2	65	1.3
2000	1,006	882	11.9	124	1.7

Source: Jacques van Gerwen en Ferry de Goey, *Ondernemers in Nederland. Variaties in ondernemen in de twintigste eeuw* (Amsterdam: Boom, 2008) 72–74, 116–117, 171–173, 218–222.

Table 4.2 Self-employment as percentage of civilian employment

	Netherlands	Germany	United Kingdom	United States
1986	11.3	n.a.	13.2	8.9
1988	11.8	n.a.	14.7	9.0
1990	11.6	n.a.	15.1	8.8
1992	11.0	10.1	15.7	8.7
1994	12.3	10.6	15.7	8.8
1996	12.5	10.8	14.9	8.4
1998	11.8	11.0	13.7	7.9
2000	11.2	11.0	12.8	7.4

Source: OECD, *Labour Force Statistics 2010* (Paris: OECD Publishing, 2011).

Using a Dutch database covering the period 1972 until 2006 presents a somewhat different picture. For most years, the Dutch share of entrepreneurs was lower than the United States and Great Britain, while the British share was higher than the American share since 1986. However, from 1998 the Dutch share exceeded the United States and converged on the British share.[49]

Whatever dataset is used, we again must conclude that the hypothetical difference between LME and CME, as formulated in hypothesis four, is not borne out by these statistics. Looking more closely at the type of entrepreneurs in LMEs and CMEs, it is evident that the largest group is the self-employed, not the professional managers that are the focus of the VoC approach. The dominance of the self-employed is directly related to the type of enterprises in LMEs and CMEs. If entrepreneurs in LMEs have a higher status and social background is less important with ample opportunities to enrol in dedicated educational programmes for entrepreneurship, the result would be a higher share of small businesses in a LME than in a CME. But is this also confirmed by the available statistics? Most self-employed operated a small or medium-sized enterprise, and therefore the majority of enterprises in both LMEs and CMEs are in fact SMEs (see Table 4.3). Interestingly, this feature has remained fairly constant during the 20th century. Obviously, only a few per cent of the enterprises have the potential and opportunities to become large (measured by number of employees). But there are no marked differences in this between LMEs and CMEs.

According to Table 4.3, covering the last two decades of the 20th century, the overwhelming majority of enterprises in the two LMEs and two CMEs were small. The number of small businesses in all western countries is in fact so large that using a different criterion than the number of employees (e.g. value added), has little effect on the conclusions drawn. Small businesses were particularly dominant in retailing and other services (restaurants,

Table 4.3   Size distribution of enterprises (%)

	Small business (fewer than 100 employees) (% of all businesses, excl. primary sector)
Netherlands	1985: 99
	2000: 99
Germany	1997: 99.8*
United States	1983: 98.1
	2002: 99.6
Great Britain	1979: 98.6
	1997: 99.5

* Based on annual turnover.
Source: Jacques van Gerwen en Ferry de Goey, *Ondernemers in Nederland. Variaties in ondernemen in de twintigste eeuw* (Amsterdam: Boom, 2008), 218, 250–251, 256, 264.

hotels) but also in manufacturing, including the construction industry. The large group of small business was far from homogenies, but it was a mixture of new and old, fast growing and stagnating or declining firms; some were innovative, but most were not. Some businessmen set out to create a large company from the beginning, while others were content with a certain level of income to support a family. The latter group saw entrepreneurship more as a lifestyle than a profession. In general, most small businesses will remain small during their existence, and this is the same for LMEs and CMEs.[50] These observations on the type of entrepreneurs and the related size distribution of enterprises have important implications for the VoC approach. Clearly the majority of businesses in LMEs and CMEs do not experience the coordinating issues like the large managerial enterprises regarding labour, capital, and competition, which is the main concern of the VoC approach.

During the 20th century, big business, using Dutch criteria, certainly became more important, as an employer and contributor to GDP, particularly the large manufacturing plants that were common in shipbuilding, textiles, petrochemicals, chemicals, and electronics. But the large factories were not dominant as far as their share in national employment or GDP is concerned before the 1950s or the 1980s. Furthermore, most of these large enterprises were still owned and operated by entrepreneurial families. A well-known example is Heineken. Family firms remained dominant throughout the 20th century. A Managerial Revolution, comparable to the United States, did not occur in the Netherlands until the late 1960s and early 1970s.[51]

Gender and Nationality

Our second hypothesis states that given the more entrepreneurial nature of LMEs, the social background of entrepreneurs is less important than in

CMEs. We expect that this stimulates minorities or other socially marginalised or discriminated groups to pursue careers as entrepreneurs, resulting in a higher share of female entrepreneurs and migrants in LMEs than in CMEs. Unfortunately, international comparative statistics on gender and nationality or ethnicity are sparse and rather unreliable. What is apparent, however, is the growth in absolute numbers of entrepreneurship amongst females and migrants, particularly from the 1960s and even more so after the 1980s. Dutch statistics record a rise in the number of self-employed female entrepreneurs from about 50,000 in 1979 to almost 300,000 in the year 2000 and 348,000 in 2009. The share of female entrepreneurs in the total number of entrepreneurs reached almost 32 per cent in 2000, up from 10 per cent in 1979.[52] However, because of the even faster growth of male self-employment after the 1980s, the share of woman self-employment in the working population did not increase that much.

Female entrepreneurship in the United States showed a similar increase, but started earlier. In 1970, about 5 per cent of all American SMEs were owned by women, while in 1997 this had increased to 38 per cent. However, the share of female self-employed in the United States was a modest 5.4 per cent of the working population in 1980. According to OECD statistics, the self-employment rate of females, as a percentage of female civilian employment, in the Netherlands in 1996 was 10.6 and in 2000 declined to 9.4, before rising again to 10.5 in 2009. In Germany the rate was 8.1 in 1992 and 7.9 in 2000, but increased to 8.5 in 2009. The rates for the United States were lower: 6.5 in 1986, 6.1 in 2000, and 5.7 in 2009. Great Britain, however, clearly deviated from the United States: the rate of self-employment of females was 8.0 in 1986, 8.3 in 2000, and 8.5 in 2009.[53] Note that according to these statistics, the Netherlands had the highest rate of female self-employment in 2000. (See Table 4.4)

Table 4.4   Self-employment as percentage of female civilian employment

	Netherlands	Germany	United Kingdom	United States
1986	n.a.	n.a.	8.0	6.5
1988	n.a.	n.a.	9.1	6.8
1990	n.a.	n.a.	8.9	6.7
1992	n.a.	8.1	10.1	6.4
1994	n.a.	8.3	9.8	7.1
1996	10.6	8.1	9.3	6.9
1998	9.8	8.2	8.7	6.4
2000	9.4	7.9	8.3	6.1

Source: OECD, *Labour Force Statistics 2010* (Paris: OECD Publishing, 2011).

The second important change besides the growing number of female entrepreneurs was the increase in the number of migrant entrepreneurs. In 2009, the share of self-employment of migrants in most OECD countries was higher than the native born.[54]

There were migrant entrepreneurs in the Netherlands at the start of the 20th century (mainly from Germany and Belgium), but their numbers and share remained modest: about 2 per cent of the working population.[55] After the economic crisis of the 1970s and early 1980s, many former guest-workers from Mediterranean countries started their own businesses. At the same time, former colonials from Surinam and to a lesser extent the Dutch Antilles also started their own businesses. In the year 2000, there were about 114,000 migrant entrepreneurs and in 2007 almost 152,000, or 14 per cent of all entrepreneurs.[56] Migrant entrepreneurship has become a vital element of Dutch business since the 1980s. Some migrant groups showed more entrepreneurial spirit than others. Migrants from Surinam or former guest-workers from Turkey and Morocco are less frequently self-employed than Italians or Greeks. Even within these groups of migrants there existed differences. Migrants from Surinam originating from the former Dutch East Indies (Indonesia) are more inclined to become self-employed than those descending from former slaves.

In comparison to most West-European countries, the United States has had a more liberal policy on immigration since the Immigration Act of 1965 that ended restrictions imposed in the 1920s. The number of immigrants entering the United States in the 1990s was equal to the mass migration of the first decade of the 20th century: about 9 million. Migrant entrepreneurs played an important role in the American economy. Between 1980 and 1998, Chinese and Indian migrants accounted for about 24 per cent of all new business technology start-ups in Silicon Valley. Other migrant groups specialised in certain industries: the Cubans in construction, the Chinese in retailing, and the Vietnamese in restaurants.[57]

The decolonisation from the late 1940s led to increasing numbers of immigrants from all parts of the erstwhile British empire. This immigration, reaching really large numbers in the late 1950s, was stopped by the Commonwealth Immigrants Acts (1962 and 1968) followed by the Immigration Act (1971). From the 1980s, many immigrants started their own businesses to escape unemployment and discrimination. According to Barrett et al., migrant entrepreneurship in Great Britain shows more similarity to the United States than to continental Europe.[58] However, on closer examination, it seems that migrant entrepreneurs in Great Britain display many similarities with other European migrant entrepreneurs with respect to the type of business, the size of their businesses, the marketing, and the location in major urban centres. In 1991, the share of migrant entrepreneurs in Great Britain was 15.1 per cent, while the native or white population's share was 12.8 per cent. Like in other countries, certain migrant groups display a greater interest in self-employment in Great Britain than others:

South Asians are 20.8 per cent self-employed, but blacks (Africans) only 6.7 per cent.

German immigration was heavily influenced by political and military events in the 20th century. During the Second World War, forced labour (in German: *Zwangsarbeit*) was introduced, and this caused an influx of workers from most Nazi-occupied countries. After the war, West Germany was flooded by refugees, often ethnic Germans, from Eastern Europe. During the economic boom of the 1950s and 1960s, West Germany recruited guest-workers from Spain, Greece, Turkey, Morocco, Portugal, and Yugoslavia. Legal regulations did not allow these guest-workers to start their own businesses, in contrast to migrants from other EU countries. These different phases are reflected in the share of self-employment of migrants. In 1998, about 9.5 per cent of foreigners in Germany were self-employed. This was only slightly lower than the share of native Germans: 10 per cent. As in the other countries, there are marked differences in the rate of self-employment between groups of migrants. In 2008, only 8.2 per cent of employed Turks were self-employed, in contrast to 16.2 per cent Greeks or 12.3 per cent Italians.[59]

DISCUSSION AND CRITIQUE

Our research has focused on a number of characteristics of entrepreneurs and enterprises in the Netherlands, Germany, the United States, and Great Britain during the 20th century. These fall into two groups: qualitative (status, social mobility, education, and competencies) and quantitative (the number of entrepreneurs, self-employed and managers, large and small businesses, woman and migrant entrepreneurs). In LMEs people do have a more positive attitude towards entrepreneurs than in CMEs, and Americans in general prefer self-employment much more than Germans or Dutch do. Whether this has been the case for the whole 20th century is unknown. There was, however, little difference in the status LMEs and CMEs attach to being an entrepreneur. The main distinction, as revealed by our research, was between the business elite and the small business owners and even between subgroups in these two categories. Businessmen usually came from a business family; few labourers managed to eventually reach the business elite. The social background of entrepreneurs became less important for a business career in LMEs and CMEs, while formal education increased in importance. During the 20th century, LMEs as well as CMEs developed into meritocratic societies.

To these more qualitative features of entrepreneurs we added quantitative characteristics. The overwhelming majority of entrepreneurs in our sample of countries are the self-employed. The majority of self-employed operated a small or medium-sized enterprise. In absolute numbers the SMEs dominate the business community. The number of professional managers increased, but their share in the working population or total number of entrepreneurs remained rather small. During the 20th century, the small number of large firms has become more important as employers and in terms of productivity or added value. The importance of SMEs should, however, not be disregarded. In LMEs and CMEs the number and share of businesses owned by women and migrants increased. They have become an important part in the business community.

To recapitulate: our research demonstrates that the populace of entrepreneurs and enterprises in LMEs and CMEs was not dominated by one type. From the beginning of the 20th century, there was a great variety and in the last two decades of the 20th century this has increased even further. We therefore agree with Richard Deeg that the idea of a representative firm for each type of capitalism, however attractive in theory and logically following from the VoC approach, is problematic. Heterogeneity is a much more common feature of business systems than homogenisation.[60] The variety at the micro level may increase even further with the inclusion of non-western countries, particularly given the more recent rise of Asian and Latin American economies.[61]

How to explain the similarities (i.e. the large variety of entrepreneurs and enterprises) of LMEs and CMEs? We believe that the answer lies in the hybrid character of the countries fitting somewhere between LME and CME. As Hodgson and Crouch have argued, the chance of finding pure types is small given the 'impurity principle' or 'mongrel elements'.[62] As a consequence of the impurity, institutional complementarity is weak or even absent. There is little institutional pressure on entrepreneurs and enterprises to homogenise. The differences between countries in the degree of business regulation are, for instance, small: on a scale of seven points it is only one point between typical market-based countries (on average 0.98: United States, Great Britain, Canada, and Australia) and Mediterranean countries (on average 1.95: Spain, Portugal, Italy, and Greece).[63] The dichotomy of Hall and Soskice is now considered to be inadequate and too simple.[64] In more recent publications the number of capitalist models has increased to four: besides CME and LME, VoC scholars now distinguish Étatisme (e.g. France before 1990s) and compensating states (e.g. emerging markets and transition economies in Eastern Europe).[65] By adding more types, the VoC approach confirms the great variety of entrepreneurs and enterprises as demonstrated in our research. Perhaps even more important in recent research is the recognition that institutions in countries are not static but change over time and thus the need for a more historical perspective.[66] This revision of the original model of the VoC approach provides a more historical and evolutionary perspective on the varieties of capitalism. Most research is, however, still focused on the big western economies and rather biased towards the large firms in the manufacturing sector.

We believe that the changes that have occurred in our sample of countries during the 20th century indicate that these are primarily the result of global developments, including capitalism (e.g. Americanisation after 1945, post-Fordism, and a global shift to Asia), technology, migration, decolonisation, emancipation, and political internationalisation. Entrepreneurs respond to societal changes, but some are more willing and inclined to do so because the changes and their potential consequences are not always readily apparent and they do not always affect all entrepreneurs in the same manner. Countries develop institutions to soften the impact of exogenous and endogenous influences and shocks. If entrepreneurs believe that it is in their interest, they will try to change these institutions. If this is too difficult, too costly or time consuming, or if they are unsuccessful, they may develop alternatives, as Michael Carney et al. have demonstrated for Asian entrepreneurs.[67] However, because entrepreneurs in a country do not constitute a homogeneous group, having different attitudes, interests, and motives, not all of these institutional alternatives will be available or acceptable. We must furthermore recognise that there are some factors that governments and entrepreneurs cannot change such as geography: the available natural resources, climate, and geographical location.

Changing Business Systems and the VoC Approach

To what extent do our results shed light on the discussion on changes in business systems or types of capitalism? More specifically: has the Netherlands changed from being a CME to a more LME type of capitalism after the 1980s? These questions point towards a major problem for historians when they apply a static theory like VoC. As mentioned before, the classification of countries in LME and CME by Hall and Soskice is primarily based on the conditions in the late 1990s. When we investigate a whole century, it immediately becomes clear that business systems change: alternating between more LME and more CME. Although the Netherlands is considered a typical CME in the existing literature on VoC, in 1900, this was certainly not so obvious. The same problem applies to the classification of other countries, like Great Britain, the United States, or Germany.[68]

Like most other West-European countries, the Netherlands pursued a policy of economic liberalism during the last quarter of the 19th century. Government involvement in the economy was rather limited, and entrepreneurs therefore had a large degree of managerial and economic freedom. This would imply that in c. 1900 the Netherlands was more a LME than a CME. Given the openness of the Dutch economy, depending on imports and exports, this is understandable. The openness of the Dutch economy has been a persistent factor in its history. According to Andeweg and Irwin, the Netherlands is 'the largest open economy in the world'.[69] Peter Katzenstein argues that small countries with an open economy are forced to make swift institutional changes in response to developments in world markets.[70] This would mean that a configuration of institutions as found in a LME would best suit the Netherlands.[71] However, while the Netherlands was more like a LME in 1900, during the First World War and particularly the economic crisis of the 1930s, the government increasingly intervened in the economy, and this trend continued after the Second World War, reaching its apogee in the welfare state of the late 1970s. By then the Dutch economy had clearly shifted towards a CME.

According to Hall and Soskice, the Netherlands was still a CME in the 1990s. Is this classification correct? Has the Netherlands become more of a LME since the 1980s, or is it indeed still predominantly a CME? As we have already mentioned, the Dutch business system has seen several changes during the 20th century. In response to the economic downturn of the late 1970s, the system again changed.[72] Most of these changes must be understood as a move towards a more LME type of capitalism. However, such a move has occurred in most western countries.[73] Countries already oriented stronger towards a LME, like the United States, became even more LME after the 1980s, while those with more CME characteristics, like Germany and the Netherlands, have moved more towards a LME. However, the policy measures following the financial crisis since 2008 and the new regulation imposed on banks, insurance companies, and financial institutions may well result in a much stronger government involvement in the economy and a return towards a more CME type of capitalism in western countries.

As far as entrepreneurs and enterprises are concerned, the changes in business systems are less visible: the similarities between LME and CME remain more striking than the differences. The changes have certainly not led to a convergence on one model because all countries started from different institutional settings and have different histories.

CONCLUDING REMARKS

The VoC approach offers a challenging theory for business historians because it places the firm at the centre of its research. However, this actor approach remains rather underdeveloped and entrepreneurs especially are sorely missing. As Crouch argues, despite presenting itself as a firm-centred theory, the VoC approach is mainly concerned with the macro level of the economy.[74] The strong focus on large managerial enterprises has led to a partisan image of entrepreneurs and businesses in LMEs and CMEs.[75] The micro level or agency is hardly considered because individuals at firm level are treated as simply adhering or adjusting to existing institutions, with no inclination to pursue their own goals or strategy, including the possibility to change existing institutions.[76] None of our four hypotheses were confirmed in the research. Instead of a growing homogenisation of entrepreneurs and enterprises in LMEs and CMEs, which would lend support to the dichotomy of the VoC approach, we discovered a great variety, and in the last decades of the 20th century this has increased even further, at least as far as entrepreneurs and enterprises are concerned. It may well be that the quantitative and qualitative variables we have included in the research on entrepreneurs and enterprises do not respond or relate to changes in business systems, but that still leaves the lack of homogenisation unanswered. Our research also clearly reveals that business systems are not static. Capitalistic systems change, but not always in the same direction, at the same time or the same pace.

NOTES

1. Jackson and Deeg, 'Comparing capitalisms: Understanding institutional diversity', 555–556.
2. Beckert, 'Institutional isomorphism revisited', 153–162; Boyer, 'How and why capitalisms differ', 546.
3. Bloom, Calori, and De Woot, *Euromanagement*, 76.
4. Steinmetz and Wright, 'The fall of the petty bourgeoisie', 973–1018.
5. EC Flash Eurobarometer 83: Entrepreneurship (September 2000). There were, however, important differences between EU countries. In the Netherlands, Belgium, Luxembourg, and the Nordic countries, being employed was clearly preferred above self-employment, while in the southern European countries the preference for self-employment was higher. EC Flash Eurobarometer 192, Entrepreneurship Survey of the EU (25 Member States), United States, Iceland and Norway (April 2007).
6. Quoted in Huntington, *Who Are We?*, 70.
7. See http://politicalticker.blogs.cnn.com/2012/11/07/transcript-obamas-victory-speech/: 'I believe we can keep the promise of our founders, the idea that if you're willing to work hard, it doesn't matter who you are or where you come from or what you look like or where you love. It doesn't matter whether you're black or white or Hispanic or Asian or Native American or young or old or rich or poor, able, disabled, gay or straight, you can make it here in America if you're willing to try'.
8. Jones and Wadhwani, 'Entrepreneurship', 501–528; Cassis and Pepelasis Minoglou, eds., *Entrepreneurship*, 9.
9. Carlsson et al., 'The Evolving Domain of Entrepreneurship Research'.
10. We exclude the primary sector (agriculture, fisheries, and forestry). The main publications for this research are: Van Gerwen and De Goey, *Ondernemers in Nederland*; Van Gerwen and De Goey, 'Ondernemers in Nederland', 223–259; De Goey, Van Gerwen, and Van Driel, 'De veerkracht', 53–82.
11. Van Gerwen and De Goey, *Ondernemers in Nederland*, 51–56, 100–105.
12. Van Gerwen and De Goey, *Ondernemers in Nederland*, 100.
13. Heemskerk, *Decline of the Corporate Community*; Fennema and Schijf, eds., *Nederlandse elites in de twintigste eeuw*.
14. Van Gerwen and De Goey, *Ondernemers in Nederland*, 95–100.
15. Van Gerwen and De Goey, *Ondernemers in Nederland*, 55, 103–104.
16. Van Gerwen and De Goey, *Ondernemers in Nederland*, 155–157.
17. Van Gerwen and De Goey, *Ondernemers in Nederland*, 202–205.
18. Van Gerwen and De Goey, *Ondernemers in Nederland*, 246–249, 255–256, 262–263; Cassis, *Big Business*; Cassis, ed., *Business Elites*. Overviews of the history of entrepreneurship in various countries including Great Britain,

Germany, and the United States in: Landes, Mokyr and Baumol, eds., *The Invention of Entrepreneurship*.

19. Landes, *Dynasties*.
20. Kaeble, 'Long-term changes in the recruitment of the business elite', 404–423; Newcomer, *The Big Business Executive*.
21. Van Driel, De Goey, and Jacques van Gerwen. 'Testing the Chandler thesis', 439–463.
22. Mizruchi, 'Berle and Means Revisited', 579–617.
23. Friedman and Tedlow, 'Statistical Portraits', 106.
24. Kaelbe, 'Long-term changes', 409.
25. Haveman, Habinek, and Goodman, 'Who Are the Entrepreneurs'.
26. See Gregory and Neu, 'The American industrial elite', 53–72.
27. Van Gerwen and De Goey, *Ondernemers in Nederland*, 247–248, 255–256, 262–263.
28. Van Driel, De Goey, and Van Gerwen, 'Testing the Chandler thesis', 439–463.
29. EC Flash Eurobarometer 192, Entrepreneurship Survey of the EU (25 Member States), United States, Iceland and Norway (April 2007).
30. Cassis, *Big Business*, 138.
31. We use the term 'small businessmen' to cover the owners of small and medium-sized enterprises. These include self-employed (with no employees) or sole proprietors and self-employed with employees.
32. Van Gerwen and De Goey, *Ondernemers in Nederland*, 102.
33. Van Gerwen and De Goey, *Ondernemers in Nederland*, 118; Blauw, 'Starten in crisistijd', 304–325.
34. Andeweg and Irwin, *Governance*, 1–49.
35. Van Gerwen and De Goey, *Ondernemers in Nederland*, 107.
36. Van Gerwen and De Goey, *Ondernemers in Nederland*, 199–200.
37. Van Gerwen and De Goey, *Ondernemers in Nederland*, 51.
38. Walton, 'New directions in business history', 1–16.
39. For the United States: Blackford, *A History of Small Business*; Brock, Evans, and Phillips, *The Economics of Small Business*; Bruchey, ed., *Small Business in American Life*; Phillips, *Little Business in the American Economy*. For Great Britain: Brooksbank, 'Self-employment and small firms', 7–31. For Germany: Berghoff, 'The end of family business', 263–295; Fritsch, 'The role of small firms in West Germany', 38–55. A general overview with country studies can be found in: Odaka and Sawai, *Small Firms, Large Concerns*.
40. Frenkel and Fendel, 'How important is the Mittelstand for the German economy?', 1–27.
41. De Goey, Van Gerwen, and Van Driel, 'De veerkracht', 53–82.
42. Micklethwait and Wooldridge, *The Company*, 119.
43. Reagan, 'Why is this an entrepreneurial age?', 3.
44. Sundin, 'Small businesses', 209–226.
45. Burrows, *Deciphering the Enterprise Culture*.
46. To investigate our hypotheses, we will use national and international statistics. Using these statistics over a period of one hundred years presents major difficulties in classification and continuity of time series. Nevertheless, we feel that this exercise is worthwhile to discover major trends and shifts over time.
47. Wennekers, *Entrepreneurship at Country Level*.
48. OECD, 'Self-employment', in: *Labour Force Statistics 2010*.
49. De Goey, Van Gerwen, and Van Driel, 'De veerkracht', 66–68; Wennekers et al., 'The relationship between entrepreneurship and economic growth', 186.
50. Bridge, O'Neill, and Cromie, *Understanding Enterprise*; Gill, *Factors Affecting the Survival and Growth*; Dale, 'Self-employment and entrepreneurship', 35–53.
51. Van Driel, De Goey, and Van Gerwen, 'Testing the Chandler thesis', 456.

52. EIM, *Monitor vrouwelijk en etnisch ondernemerschap.*
53. OECD, *Labour Force Statistics 2010.*
54. OECD, *Entrepreneurship and Migrants.*
55. Rath and Kloosterman, 'The Netherlands: A Dutch treat', 123–147.
56. Van Gerwen and De Goey, *Ondernemers in Nederland*, 77–78, 120–121, 174, 222–224.
57. Gap Min and Bozorgmehr, 'United States: The entrepreneurial cutting edge', 17–38. For the Silicon Valley, see Saxenian, *Regional Advantage.*
58. Barrett, Jones, and McEvoy, 'United Kingdom: Severely constrained entrepreneurialism', 101–123; Panayi, *An Immigration History of Britain.*
59. Wilpert, 'Germany: From workers to entrepreneurs', 233–260; OECD, *Entrepreneurship and Migrants.*
60. Deeg, 'The rise of internal capitalist diversity?', 553.
61. Dore, 'Will global capitalism be Anglo-Saxon capitalism?', 9–18.
62. Hodgson, 'The evolution of capitalism from the perspective of institutional and evolutionary economics', 72–74; Crouch, *Capitalist Diversity and Change*, 19–20.
63. Dannreuther and Petit, 'Contemporary capitalism and internationlisation', 77–102.
64. Deeg and Jackson, 'The state of the art', 149–79.
65. Hancké, Rhodes, and Thatcher, 'Introduction: Beyond Varieties of Capitalism', 3–39.
66. An overview is provided by Scott, 'Approaching adulthood', 427–42; Hall, 'The evolution of Varieties of Capitalism in Europe', 39–86.
67. Carney et al., 'Varieties of Asian capitalism', 361–380.
68. According to Lazonick, the United States should not be classified as a LME. William Lazonick, 'Innovative business models and Varieties of Capitalism', 675–702. Shonfield argues that the business system of the United States only acquired its capitalistic characteristics at the end of the 19th century with the rise of big business: Shonfield, *Modern Capitalism*, 301. For most of the 20th century, Great Britain must be classified as a CME and not a LME: Booth, *The British Economy in the Twentieth Century*, chapter 6.
69. Andeweg and Irwin, *Governance and Politics of the Netherlands*, 208.
70. Katzenstein, *Small States in World Markets*, 39–80.
71. Kesting and Nielsen reached the same conclusion after studying two other small countries: New Zealand and Denmark. Kesting and Nielsen, 'Varieties of Capitalism', 23–52. See also Campbell and Pedersen, 'The Varieties of Capitalism and hybrid success', 307–333.
72. On the impact of international and transnational developments, particularly the European Union with respect to the Netherlands, see Ian Bruff, 'European varieties of capitalism', 615–638; Spithoven, 'The Third Way: The Dutch experience', 333–368.
73. Panuescu and Schneider, 'Wettbewerbsfähigkeit und Dynamik', 31–59.
74. Crouch, *Capitalist Diversity*, 44.
75. This critique applies more to the VoC approach than the theory on business systems developed by Richard Whitley. For this see Morgan, Whitley, and Moen, eds., *Changing Capitalisms?*, 190–234. However, as Casson and Lundan remark, even Whitley does embrace the idea of the 'typical industry or firm'. Mark Casson and Lundan, 'Explaining international differences in economic institutions', 25–42.
76. Jackson and Deeg, 'Comparing capitalisms', 555–556.

REFERENCES

Andeweg, Rudy B. and Galen A. Irwin, *Governance and Politics of the Netherlands* (Houndmills: Palgrave Macmillan, 2009).

Barrett, Giles A., Trevor P. Jones, and David McEvoy, 'United Kingdom: Severely constrained entrepreneurialism', In Robert Kloosterman and Jan Rath, eds., *Immigrant Entrepreneurs. Venturing Abroad in the Age of Globalization* (Oxford and New York: Berg, 2003) 101–123.

Beckert, Jens, 'Institutional isomorphism revisited: Convergence and divergence in institutional change', *Sociological Theory*, 28 (2010): 153–162.

Berghoff, H., 'The end of family business. The Mittelstand and German capitalism in transition 1949–2000', *Business History Review*, 80 (2006): 263–295.

Blackford, Mansel G., *A History of Small Business in America* (New York: Twayne Publishers, 1991).

Blauw, M.J.E., 'Starten in crisistijd. Het wel en wee van beginnende ondernemingen in de jaren dertig in het gebied van de Kamer van Koophandel en Fabrieken te Veendam', *Economisch-en Sociaal-Historisch Jaarboek*, 52 (1989): 304–325.

Bloom, H., R. Calori, and P. de Woot, *Euromanagement. A New Style for the Global Market. Insights from Europe's Business Leaders* (London: Kogan Page, 1994).

Booth, Alan, *The British Economy in the Twentieth Century* (Basingstoke: Palgrave, 2001).

Boyer, Robert, 'How and why capitalisms differ', *Economy and Society*, 34 (2005): 509–557.

Bridge, Simon, Ken O'Neill, and Stan Cromie, *Understanding Enterprise. Entrepreneurship and Small Business* (Basingstoke: Palgrave Macmillan, 2003).

Brock, William A., David S. Evans, and Bruce Dalton Phillips, *The Economics of Small Business. Their Role and Regulation in the U.S. Economy* (New York: Holmes & Meier, 1986).

Brooksbank, D., 'Self-employment and small firms', In: S. Carter and D. Jones-Evans, eds., *Enterprise and Small Business. Principles, Practice and Policy* (Essex: Pearson Education Limited, 2000) 7–31.

Bruchey, Stuart W., ed., *Small Business in American Life* (New York: Columbia University Press, 1980).

Bruff, Ian, 'European varieties of capitalism and the international', *European Journal of International Relations*, 16 (2010): 615–638.

Burrows, Roger, *Deciphering the Enterprise Culture. Entrepreneurship, Petty Capitalism and the Restructuring of Britain* (London: Routledge, 1991).

Campbell, John L., and Pedersen, Ove K., 'The Varieties of Capitalism and hybrid success: Denmark in the global economy', *Comparative Political Studies*, 40 (2007): 307–333.

Carlsson, Bo, Pontus Braunerhjelm, Maureen McKelvey, Christer Olofsson, Lars Persson, and Håkan Ylinenpää, 'The Evolving Domain of Entrepreneurship Research'. Paper presented at the 14th International Joseph A. Schumpeter Conference, Brisbane, Australia, July 2–5, 2012.

Carney, Michael, Eric Gedajlovic, and Xiaohua Yang, 'Varieties of Asian capitalism: Toward an institutional theory of Asian enterprise', *Asian Pacific Journal of Management*, 26 (2009): 361–380.

Cassis, Youssef, *Big Business. The European Experience in the Twentieth Century* (Oxford: Oxford University Press, 1997).

Cassis, Youssef, ed., *Business Elites* (Aldershot: Edward Elgar Publishing, 1994).

Cassis, Youssef and Ioanna Pepelasis Minoglou, eds., *Entrepreneurship in Theory and History* (Basingstoke: Palgrave Macmillan, 2005).

Casson, Mark and Lundan, Sarianna M., 'Explaining international differences in economic institutions', *International Studies of Management and Organization*, 29 (1999): 25–42.

Crouch, Colin, *Capitalist Diversity and Change. Recombinant Governance and Institutional Entrepreneurs* (Oxford: Oxford University Press, 2005).

Dale, Angela, 'Self-employment and entrepreneurship: Notes on two problematic concepts', In: Roger Burrows, ed., *Deciphering the Enterprise Culture. Entrepreneurship, Petty Capitalism and the Restructuring of Britain* (London: Routledge, 1991) 35–53.

Dannreuther, Charlie and Pascal Petit, 'Contemporary capitalism and internationlisation: From one diversity to another', In: Wolfram Elsner and Hardy Hanappi, eds., *Varieties of Capitalism and New Institutional Deals. Regulation, Welfare and the New Economy* (Cheltenham: Edward Elgar Publishing Ltd., 2008) 77–102.

Deeg, Richard, 'The rise of internal capitalist diversity? Changing patterns of finance and corporate governance', *Economy and Society*, 38 (2009): 552–579.

Deeg, Richard, and Gregory Jackson, 'The state of the art. Towards a more dynamic theory of capitalist variety', *Socio-Economic Review*, 5 (2007): 149–179.

Dore, Ronald, 'Will global capitalism be Anglo-Saxon capitalism?', *Asian Business & Management*, 1 (2002): 9–18.

Driel, Hugo van, de Goey, Ferry, and Gerwen, Jacques van, 'Testing the Chandler thesis: Comparing middle management and administrative intensity in Dutch and US industries, 1900–1950', *Business History*, 49 (2007): 439–463.

EC Flash Eurobarometer 83: Entrepreneurship (September 2000).

EC Flash Eurobarometer 192: Entrepreneurship Survey of the EU (25 Member States), United States, Iceland, and Norway (April 2007).

EIM, *Monitor vrouwelijk en etnisch ondernemerschap 2010* (Zoetermeer: EIM, 2010).

Fennema, Meindert and Huibert Schijf, eds., *Nederlandse elites in de twintigste eeuw: continuïteit en verandering* (Amsterdam: Amsterdam University Press 2004).

Frenkel, Michael and Ralf Fendel, 'How important is the Mittelstand for the German economy?', In: Christian Homburg, ed., *Structure and Dynamics of the German Mittelstand* (Heidelberg: Physica Verlag, 1999) 1–27.

Friedman, Walter A., and Tedlow, Richard S, 'Statistical portraits of American business elites: A review essay', *Business History*, 45 (2003): 89–113.

Fritsch, M., 'The role of small firms in West Germany', In: Z.J. Acs and D.B. Audretsch, eds., *Small Firms and Entrepreneurship: An East-West Perspective* (Cambridge: University of Cambridge, 1993) 38–55.

Gap Min, Pyong, and Mehdi Bozorgmehr, 'United States: The entrepreneurial cutting edge', In: Robert Kloosterman and Jan Rath, eds., *Immigrant Entrepreneurs. Venturing Abroad in the Age of Globalization* (Oxford and New York: Berg, 2003) 17–38.

Gerwen, Jacques van, and Ferry de Goey, 'Ondernemers in Nederland. De dynamiek in de ondernemerspopulatie in de twintigste eeuw', In Onno Boonstra, Peter Doorn, René van Horik, Jacques van Maarseveen, and Ko Oudhof, eds., *Twee eeuwen geteld. Onderzoek met de digitale volks-, beroeps-en woningtellingen, 1795–2001* (CBS/DANS: Den Haag, 2007) 223–250.

Gerwen, Jacques van, and Ferry de Goey, *Ondernemers in Nederland. Variaties in ondernemen in de twintigste eeuw* (Boom: Amsterdam, 2008).

Gill, John, *Factors Affecting the Survival and Growth of the Smaller Company* (Aldershot: Gower, 1985).

Goey, Ferry de, Gerwen, Jacques van, and Driel, Hugo van, 'De veerkracht van de zelfstandige ondernemer. Ondernemers en midden-en kleinbedrijf in Nederland, de Verenigde Staten en Groot-Brittannië vanaf 1950', *Tijdschrift voor Sociale en Economische Geschiedenis*, 6 (2009): 53–82.

Gregory, Frances W., and Irene D. Neu, 'The American industrial elite in the 1870s: Their social origins', In: Youssef Cassis, ed., *Business Elites* (Aldershot: Edward Elgar Publishing, 1994) 53–72.

Hall, Peter A., 'The evolution of Varieties of Capitalism in Europe', In: Bob Hancké, Martin Rhodes, and Mark Thatcher, eds., *Beyond Varieties of Capitalism. Conflict, Contradictions, and Complementarities in the European Economy* (Oxford: Oxford University Press, 2007) 39–86.

Hancké, Bob, Martin Rhodes, and Mark Thatcher, 'Introduction: Beyond Varieties of Capitalism', In: Bob Hancké, Martin Rhodes, and Mark Thatcher, eds., *Beyond Varieties of Capitalism. Conflict, Contradictions, and Complementarities in the European Economy* (Oxford: Oxford University Press, 2007) 3–39.

Haveman, Heather A., Jacob Habinek, and Leo A. Goodman. 'Who Are the Entrepreneurs: The Elite or Everyman?', Working Paper Series, Institute for Research on Labor and Employment, UC Berkeley, 2011.

Heemskerk, Eelke, *Decline of the Corporate Community. Network Dynamics of the Dutch Business Elite* (Amsterdam: Amsterdam University Press, 2007).

Hodgson, G.M., 'The evolution of Capitalism from the perspective of institutional and evolutionary economics', In: Geoffrey M. Hodgson, Makoto Itoh, and Nobuharu Yokokawa, eds., *Capitalism in Evolution: Global Contentions—East and West* (Cheltenham: Elward Elgar Publishing Ltd., 2001) 63–83.

Huntington, Samuel P., *Who Are We? America's Great Debate* (London: Free Press, 2005).

Jackson, Gregory and Deeg, Richard, 'Comparing capitalisms: Understanding institutional diversity and its implications for international business', *Journal of International Business Studies*, 39 (2008): 540–561.

Jones, Geoffrey and R. Daniel Wadhwani, 'Entrepreneurship', In: Geoffrey Jones and Jonathan Zeitlin, eds., *The Oxford Handbook of Business History* (Oxford: Oxford University Press, 2008) 501–528.

Kaeble, Hartmut, 'Long-term changes in the recruitment of the business elite: Germany compared to the U.S., Great Britain, and France since the Industrial Revolution', *Journal of Social History*, 13 (1980): 404–423.

Katzenstein, Peter J., *Small States in World Markets: Industrial Policy in Europe* (Ithaca: Cornell University Press, 1985).

Kesting, Stefan, and Klaus Nielsen, 'Varieties of Capitalism: Theoretical critique and empirical observations', In: Wolfram Elsner and Hardy Hanappi, eds., *Varieties of Capitalism and New Institutional Deals. Regulation, Welfare and the New Economy* (Cheltenham: Edward Elgar, 2008) 23–52.

Landes, David S., *Dynasties. Fortunes and Misfortunes of the World's Great Family Businesses* (New York: Penguin Books, 2006).

Landes, David S., Joel Mokyr, and William J. Baumol, eds., *The Invention of Entrepreneurship.* (Princeton: Princeton University Press, 2010).

Lazonick, William, 'Innovative business models and Varieties of Capitalism: Financialization of the U.S. corporation', *Business History Review*, 84 (2010): 675–702.

Micklethwait, John, and Adrian Wooldridge, *The Company. A Short History of a Revolutionary Idea* (New York: Modern Library, 2003).

Mizruchi, Mark S., 'Berle and means revisited: The governance and power of large U.S. corporations', *Theory and Society*, 33 (2004): 579–617.

Morgan, G., R. Whitley, and E. Moen, eds., *Changing Capitalisms? Internationalization, Institutional Change, and Systems of Economic Organization* (Oxford: Oxford University Press, 2005).

Newcomer, Mabel, *The Big Business Executive. The Factors That Made Him 1900–1950* (New York: Columbia University Press, 1955).

Odaka, K., and M. Sawai, *Small Firms, Large Concerns. The Development of Small Business in Comparative Perspective* (Oxford: Oxford University Press, 1999).

OECD, *Entrepreneurship and Migrants, Report by the OECD Working Party on SMEs and Entrepreneurship* (Paris: OECD Publishing, 2010).

OECD, *Labour Force Statistics 2010* (Paris: OECD Publishing, 2011).

Panayi, Panikos, *An Immigration History of Britain. Multicultural Racism since 1800* (Harlow: Longman Publishing Group, 2010).

Panuescu, Mihai, and Schneider, Martin, 'Wettbewerbsfähigkeit und Dynamik institutioneller Standortbedingungen: Ein empirischer Test des, Varieties-of-Capitalism'-Ansatzes', *Schmöllers Jahrbuch (Journal of Applied Social Science Studies)*, 124 (2004): 31–59.

Phillips, Joseph D., *Little Business in the American Economy* (Urbana: University of Illinois Press, 1958).

Rath, Jan and Robert Kloosterman, 'The Netherlands: A Dutch treat', In: Robert Kloosterman and Jan Rath, eds., *Immigrant Entrepreneurs. Venturing Abroad in the Age of Globalization* (Oxford and New York: Berg, 2003) 123–147.

Reagan, Ronald, 'Why is this an entrepreneurial age?', *Journal of Business Venturing*, 1 (1985): 1–5.

Saxenian, Anna Lee, *Regional Advantage: Culture and Competition in Silicon Valley and Route 128* (Cambridge: Harvard University Press, 1994).

Scott, W. Richard, 'Approaching adulthood: The maturing of institutional theory', *Theory and Society*, 37 (2008): 427–442.

Shonfield, Andrew, *Modern Capitalism. The Changing Balance of Public and Private Power* (London: Oxford University Press, 1969).

Spithoven, A.H.G.M, 'The Third Way: the Dutch experience', *Economy and Society*, 31 (2002): 333–368.

Steinmetz, G., and Wright, E.O., 'The fall of the petty bourgeoisie: Changing patterns of self-employment in the postwar United States', *American Journal of Sociology*, 94 (1989): 973–1018.

Sundin, Elisabeth, 'Small businesses: The solution for what and for whom?', In: Wolfram Elsner and Hardy Hanappi, eds., *Varieties of Capitalism and New Institutional Deals. Regulation, Welfare and the New Economy* (Cheltenham: Edward Elgar, 2008) 209–226.

'Transcript of President Obama's Election Night Speech'. http://www.nytimes.com/2012/11/07/us/politics/transcript-of-president-obamas-election-night-speech.html?_r=0 (accessed November 21, 2013).

Walton, John K., 'New directions in business history: Themes, approaches and opportunities', *Business History*, 52 (2010): 1–16.

Wennekers, S., *Entrepreneurship at Country Level. Economic and Non-Economic Determinants* (Rotterdam: Erasmus Research Institute of Management, 2006).

Wennekers, Sander, Stel, André van, Carree, Martin, and Thurik, Roy, 'The relationship between entrepreneurship and economic growth: Is it U-shaped?,' *Foundations and Trends in Entrepreneurship*, 6 (2010): 167–237.

Wilpert, Czarina, 'Germany: From workers to entrepreneurs', In Robert Kloosterman and Jan Rath, eds., *Immigrant Entrepreneurs. Venturing Abroad in the Age of Globalization* (Oxford and New York: Berg, 2003) 233–260.

5 Competition and Varieties of Coordination

Bram Bouwens and Joost Dankers

INTRODUCTION

In their seminal work, *Varieties of Capitalism*, Hall and Soskice define the broad field of interfirm relations as one of their five 'spheres' of study. This sphere is defined as 'the relationships a company forms with other enterprises and notably its suppliers or clients, with a view to secure a stable demand for its products, appropriate supplies of inputs, and access to technology'.[1] In fact it covers all forms of competitive and anticompetitive behaviour of firms in all stages of the value chain. Hall and Soskice do not, however, pay much attention to competition between firms as such. In their view the relations between firms and their resulting strategies are highly dependent on the institutional setting in which these firms operate. The formal and informal rules of the game are important conditions for the behaviour of firms on the market: 'strategy follows structure', they summarise.[2]

Within the Varieties of Capitalism approach two ideal types are distinguished: the liberal market economy (LME) and the coordinated market economy (CME). Both systems are different in the way firms organise their interfirm relations and resolve coordination problems, either through market relations or through strategic interaction. LMEs are characterised by competitive market conditions that are often enforced by severe antitrust regulations. These regulations should prevent firms from collusive activities such as price fixing, manipulation of total industry output, division of market shares, and allocation of territories. Markets are fluid and encourage firms to make the best use of their skills and opportunities. On the other hand, firms in CMEs are also stimulated to create value, but they work within a framework that is characterised by close relationships between companies. Firms are connected by all kinds of networks, and the exchange of information is crucial for the functioning of the market economy. Risks and uncertainties are predominantly countered through negotiation.[3]

In CMEs business associations, trade unions, and other semi-public organisations often have a strong role in the implementation of coordinating policies. By entering into 'implicit contracts', these organisations can support and even administer governmental policies and at the same time draw benefits of their own from this cooperation. These coordinating policies are more difficult to implement in LMEs because the organisations lack the convening power required to enforce them. At the same time associations of producers are less willing to enter into such cooperative policies when they do not trust the government nor have the power to sanction the government when it breaches the 'implicit contracts'.[4] Thus, while networks, associations, and cartels are characteristic for the way interfirm relations are shaped in a CME, these anticompetitive instruments do not fit a LME.

The general picture of the Netherlands shows a highly coordinated market economy for most of the 20th century. Nevertheless this was not the case during the entire century. At the beginning of the 20th century, the Netherlands was a typical LME in which interfirm relations were dominated by the market. This changed fundamentally with the Depression of the 1930s and the Second World War. These crises forced the government to abandon its liberal policy. Hence the Netherlands became the typical CME, which it continued to be for several decades after the war. It was only as a result of the economic crisis of the late 1970s and early 1980s that this changed. Under the pressure of European integration and globalisation, the coordinating system from the 1980s onwards gradually changed into a more liberal market economy.[5]

In this chapter we want to analyse how the instruments that regulate interfirm relations correspond to the changes in Dutch business system. What does the competitive behaviour of firms tell us about the organisation of the Dutch market economy? According to the Varieties of Capitalism literature, business interest associations and cartel agreements play a crucial role in a CME. To what extent does this prove to be the case in the Netherlands, and what does this tell us about these instruments? Mergers and acquisitions are not a distinctive feature of either a CME or LME. Nevertheless we also want to include them in the picture because they offer an efficient, alternative way of organising interfirm relations. Though competition is not necessarily reduced by concentration, it is certainly affected by the sheer fact that the number of competitors diminishes. For that reason mergers and acquisitions, like cartels, have an effect on market relations and are also monitored and regulated by public authorities. In a CME mergers and acquisitions are normally related to long-term bank lending and ongoing business relations. Hostile takeovers are an exception in this situation. In a LME, on the other hand, mergers and acquisitions, and especially hostile takeovers, can be seen as a phenomenon representing a market mechanism for corporate governance. So the ways mergers and acquisitions are effectuated are different, and this tells us something about the evolution of the business system.[6]

This chapter will follow the evolution of the Dutch business system by studying the competitive behaviour of firms and especially the use of business interest associations, cartels, and mergers and acquisitions as strategic instruments in interfirm relations during the past century. We will conclude this chapter by comparing the developments in the Netherlands with those in the United States as the ultimate example of a LME on the one hand and in Germany as a typical CME on the other hand.

CHANGING FUNCTIONS OF BUSINESS INTEREST ASSOCIATIONS

Business Interest Associations (BIA) typically perform activities to advance or defend the interests of business collectively. A BIA is an organisation of employers or companies, working for the common interests of its members.[7] Thus BIAs have a clear and strong coordinating function. Nevertheless BIAs can be found in market economies varying from liberal to coordinated.

Figure 5.1 shows the emergence of BIAs in the Netherlands during the first half of the century. Most associations were founded during World War I and its direct aftermath and during the economic crisis of the 1930s. BIAs were apparently very popular during years of economic depression. It could be argued that most of these associations were founded to eliminate risks, to protect existing business interests, and to control the circumstances of increasing competition. The peak of the late 1940s can be explained by the re-formation of BIAs that were outlawed by the German occupiers during World War II.[8] After 1960, no consistent data on the number of associations are available, but there is no doubt that the degree of organisation was high. In 1980, the Dutch Social Economic Council counted 894 alliances, while social scientists reviewed these figures and made an estimation

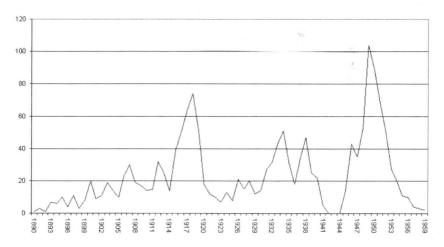

Figure 5.1   Number of new business interest associations in the Netherlands, established each year, 1890–1959

Source: Verslagen en mededelingen (1936); Van Waarden, 'Emergence', 521–562.

of 1,660 BIAs.[9] Measured in total numbers, Dutch entrepreneurs belonged to the most coordinated and cooperating businesspeople in Europe, together with their colleagues in Germany, Austria, Belgium, and Sweden.[10]

Whether or not the BIA contributes to the coordinated nature of the market economy, however, depends on the functions it performs. For instance, while in the United States, BIAs concentrate on lobbying and providing service for their members, in Germany the main task is to negotiate with trade unions. During the second half of the 20th century, Dutch BIAs played a key role in the organisation of the famous 'Polder Model'. The way social relations are regulated by BIAs and trade unions is seen as a decisive factor in Dutch economic success by most economists. In this respect these associations clearly contributed to the coordinated nature of the Dutch system. But this feature of the BIA in the Netherlands has not always been so prominent.

During the 20th century, BIAs adopted different functions determined by changing social, political, and economic conditions. To analyse the changes over time, we used the model presented by VNO-NCW, the largest Dutch federation of employers, together with the management consultant Berenschot in 2003. They distinguished five different functions of the BIA.[11] Here we will use this model to analyse the changing functions of BIAs over time.[12] Many associations started as a *society*, promoting common values and offering a network and platform for discussion. Entrepreneurs in the same industry discuss common problems and issues. The BIA organises conferences, lectures, and other societal activities that bring together these members and give them a common identity. A second function evolves from this: the BIA acts as a *diplomat*, working on behalf of its members and trying to influence political decisions through lobbying. The function of the BIA as a *guild* also develops logically from the societal role. The BIA can force its members to accept internally binding agreements on, for example, the quality of their products, screening, codification, professionalism, or codes of conduct. Membership of the BIA in this case is seen as a hallmark for quality. The line with collusive practices is blurred because these agreements can also cover prices, production, and markets in order to suppress competition. In that case the BIA becomes a cartel organisation. Parallel to this, many BIAs function as a *negotiator*. They make deals and agreements with other parties outside the BIA, especially trade unions and governments, but also organisations of consumers. As we shall see, these external binding agreements are sometimes even considered to be the origin of the BIA. The fifth and last function is that of *service provider*. BIAs can have an important role in providing information and services for their members—for example, regarding social and fiscal regulations. Not all of these functions have the same effect on the organisation of the market economy. Lobbying, providing services to members, or offering a network as a society does not necessarily interfere with the ideal type of the liberal market economy, where markets are expected to be fluid. On the other hand, acting as a guild, forcing agreements on its members, or as a negotiator, concluding agreements with the government or trade unions, definitely makes the BIAs into instruments that support firms in dealing with an imperfect market. To determine to what extent BIAs contributed to the coordinated nature of the Dutch economy, we will have to take a closer look at their changing functions during the 20th century.

Table 5.1 shows the various functions of business interest associations and their main focal points during the 20th century. In the 19th century, associations mainly functioned as lobbyists and societies. BIAs already existed before the 1880s. Very often they brought together businesspeople from different industries in a rather informal way. In most cases these associations were regionally organised, and they promoted shared interests on matters such as infrastructure, taxes, trade policy, or education of employees. Nevertheless, the degree of association was still low. Family and social networks were of greater importance for daily business.[13] Around the turn of the century, however, the number of BIAs boomed, and a horizontal concentration of associations took place. The nature of joint actions changed. Businesspeople from the same crafts or industries tried to incorporate their individual perspectives into organisations of a more economic homogeneity. Their organisations developed into more formal institutes with offices and employees. This partly was a reaction to the growing power of trade unions in this period.[14]

During the 1910s, trade unions increased remarkably, and in 1920, about 40 per cent of the employees belonged to one of the trade unions.[15] In response, the number of BIAs increased rapidly during the first decades of the 20th century. Between 1907 and 1920, the Ministry of Economic Affairs counted an increase from 342 to 1,666.[16] Representing employers in negotiating with the unions became an essential function of the BIA in this period. Organisations of both employers and workers became more intensively involved with negotiations on wages and conditions. Collective agreements on wages were partly recognised by law in 1927 and became fully sanctioned in 1937. If a firm wanted to have influence on the wages that they were going to pay, it had to become a member of the BIA to

Table 5.1   Main functions of Dutch business interest associations, 1900–2000

	Society	Diplomat	Guild	Negotiator	Service provider
1900	X	X			
1930			X		
1950			X	X	
1980				X	X
2000				X	X

Source: Bouwens and Dankers, *Concurrentie en concentratie*, passim.

voice its opinion.[17] Making both internally and externally binding agreements was on the agenda of the various organisations prominently. Self-regulation with minimum interference of government characterised the organisation of business around the turn of the 19th century. This would hardly change during the first three decades of the 20th century As BIAs got a more coordinated function, almost every industry and every profession had to have its own organisation. Especially in the years around World War I, numerous BIAs were founded. At the same time, these organisations became more formal. They proposed specific requirements for membership, and the members were bound by regulations. Local and regional organisations joined together to form national associations, and the resulting organisational structures received a professional constitution. As a result, these national associations during the 1920s found a willing ear in government and also put more clout in their negotiations with the trade unions. The function of the Dutch BIAs thus contributed to the creation of a coordinated market.

The crisis of the 1930s and the subsequent war had far-reaching consequences for the position of BIAs in the Netherlands, as in most countries. Their function as negotiators and lobbyists became even more significant, while their guild function also gained importance. The economic crisis stimulated collaboration and joint action of entrepreneurs, and numerous new organisations were founded. In 1936, the Ministry of Economic Affairs counted 748 associations of shopkeepers, craftsmen, manufacturers, and traders.[18] The position of the BIA became stronger because the opposition to government intervention amongst firms dwindled. Laws increasingly replaced the traditional self-regulation. At the same time, the implementation of these laws was often based on close cooperation between government and industry. This gave the BIAs a function in the crisis management and the regulation of markets deemed necessary because of the crisis. Many associations developed into negotiators and guilds with a coordinating function in the market and were instrumental in price and production agreements.

During the German occupation, BIAs were superseded by a new structure in line with the German national-socialist model. After the Second World War, this structure was gradually dissolved, and the BIAs recovered their traditional position and functions. But the government also tried to set up a new public-private organisation, built on corporatist ideas dating from the crisis. The Labour Foundation established immediately after the liberation and the Social and Economic Council founded in 1950 were the outstanding symbols of this policy.[19] It resulted in a strong coordination of wages and prices in which BIAs, together with the government and the trade unions, had a key role. This collective effort was first and foremost directed at the common interest and prosperity of the population, but clearly it was also to the benefit of Dutch business.[20] The strong position the BIAs acquired in the prewar period of crisis would be retained in the postwar decades of reconstruction and of economic boom.

After World War II, many BIAs—both general and industry specific—joined forces and abolished denominational, geographic, and technical boundaries that traditionally divided the associations in the same industry. The increasing complexity of laws and regulations in the field of social security stimulated not only concentration of BIAs but also participation.[21] As a result of integration and growing membership, the position of the BIA as negotiator and guild, but also as a lobbyist, was strengthened. The function of the BIA gradually shifted towards a professional service provider including marketing and communication issues and towards consultation on, for example, environmental questions or complicated tax problems. The BIA also continued to exert control on quality and reliability. This guild function implied that the member companies adhered to the rules in exchange for collective support and security. As a result of the public debate on cartels, companies became more secretive on their activities in this respect. To what extent agreements on prices and production were made within the framework of the BIA is less visible. Nevertheless it is clear that apart from its continued function as guild, the BIA continued to have a strong coordinated position as negotiator and powerful lobbyist during the 1950s and 1960s.

From the 1980s, deregulation and liberalisation led to a new appeal on the BIA in its role as negotiator, lobbyist, and consultant. The organisational degree of Dutch business was still high, and the position of employers' organisations in the consultative political economy strengthened after the crisis of the 1970s.[22] In 1982, the leaders of the trade unions and the employers' organisations concluded the Wassenaar Agreement. In this agreement they proclaimed cooperation between employees, employers, and the government essential for economic recovery. The pact encouraged wage moderation in exchange for a reduction in working hours to fight unemployment and increase profitability of industry. This resulted in renewed economic growth. The success of the Dutch 'Polder Model' attracted much international attention.[23] In 1993, employers' associations and trade unions agreed on a decentralisation of collective bargaining, which again raised the importance of the BIA as negotiator. This decentralisation was a consequence of the deregulation that got momentum in the 1990s, not only in the Netherlands but all over the western world. The policy, based on 'more market and less government', resulted in new tasks and responsibilities for BIAs. In the field of environment, sustainability, and security, BIAs increasingly made agreements on behalf of the affiliated members. These covenants between the government and the BIA as representative of an industry or trade were an attractive alternative to legislation. They also appealed to the tradition of self-regulation. BIAs thus renewed their function as negotiators and diplomats. Despite deregulation, the increased complexity of laws and regulations required more specialist knowledge, which the BIA could offer. As a result, the BIAs also played an increasingly important role as service providers for their members.

Globalisation and European integration placed new demands on business and hence on their organisations, which became more professional with, for example, a salaried president. European integration made lobbying more international and promoted cross-border cooperation of national associations. BIAs felt the need to be present in Brussels, where 80 per cent of the rules with relation to business were made.[24] Large sectorial organisations enabled them to operate at international level. Cooperation with other associations to reach a common goal and cooperation with partners that operated in the same value chain occurred frequently.[25] Thus the BIA retained its position as a lobbyist and negotiator on behalf of the internationally oriented companies. At the same time, national BIAs lost part of their coordinating function. Along with the internationalisation of industries, the focus shifted from a national to an international level. The pressure to liberalise the market mounted. The European Union stimulated competition and started a fierce prosecution of all sorts of collusive practices. Dutch government formulated a law to retaliate this kind of collusion in 1998. It definitely changed the internal binding function of the BIA. Cartel agreements on prices, production, and markets became a taboo. As a consequence the BIAs lost its function as a platform for creating mutual agreements.[26]

Throughout the 20th century, BIAs have been vital for the functioning of the Dutch market economy. The high degree of organisation is one of the characteristics of the coordinated market economy. However, apart from this continuity, there were major shifts in organisation and function. The extent to which entrepreneurs organised themselves and were willing to grant power to their association depended strongly on the economic situation, the structure of the industry, and the institutional setting. During crises the need to coordinate and to cooperate was felt stronger than in times of economic prosperity. When the economy was going down badly or if their interests were at risk, entrepreneurs tended to organise themselves. In these periods the role of the BIA as a guild and as a negotiator making external and mutual agreements to curb competition became more pronounced. When the economic tide was favourable, the BIA more frequently acted as a consultant and lobbyist, and the organisation had a more informal function as a society. The political context also determined the functions that BIAs could perform, most markedly in the case of the guild function and the anticompetitive performance of many associations. The possibility to influence the market through mutual agreements became legally based during the crisis of the 1930s. The legal base completely disappeared with the strong emphasis on free markets at the end of the 20th century. As a result, the BIA, as far as can be seen from the outside, lost one of its strong coordinating functions. As a service provider and diplomat, BIAs still have an important function—they inform their members and represent them in the political arena.

THE DOUBLE FACE OF CARTELS

BIAs and cartels are in a sense complementary. On the one hand, a certain degree of organisation of individual entrepreneurs is a precondition for making cartel agreements. On the other hand, these agreements were a motivation for entrepreneurs to organise themselves into BIAs during most of the 20th century. These associations were an ideal platform to exchange information on products, prices, and markets. The privacy BIAs offered made it easier to arrange cartel agreements. Especially successful were organisations with a high participation rate, whose members produced a relatively homogeneous product.[27] However, cartels were not synonymous with BIAs. Associations did not necessarily have to be involved in cartels, and also cartels could be, and frequently were, concluded outside the BIA.

Cartels can be defined as a voluntary written or oral agreement among financially and personally independent, private, entrepreneurial sellers or buyers fixing or influencing the values of their parameters of action, or allocating territories, products, or quotas, for a future period of time.[28] They are generally seen as an instrument in market coordination and for that reason a clear indicator of a coordinated market economy. Cartels are often associated with unfair market practices and seen as disruptive to competition. As such they are considered detrimental to consumers, innovation, and economic growth. For that reason the United States, as the champion of the liberal market economy, already at the end of the 19th century strictly prohibited any kind of agreement regarding the internal market, including price fixing and customer allocation.[29] In Europe there was a long and heated discussion on the effects of cartels. Not everyone thought these agreements had a negative impact on economic growth and prosperity. Proponents argued that cartels could have a positive effect on standardisation and rationalisation, which ultimately would be to the consumers' profit. Also cartels in times of economic crises could safeguard employment. Opponents stressed that cartel agreements are mostly motivated by maximising profits and result in higher prices.[30] Dutch government for a long time refrained from legal action against cartels because this would interfere with the freedom of action of the entrepreneur. This attitude gave room to further coordination of Dutch business. If any company thought it more profitable to cooperate with its competitors, it was, in the liberal view of policymakers, free to do so. Apart from the economic conditions, the institutional setting was critical to the coordination function of cartels. Law and regulation, but also public opinion and values and standards within the industry, defined the scope of the cartel. Although they were finally banned in the Netherlands in 1998, cartels had been discussed from the beginning of the century.[31]

As in most countries, there is much uncertainty on the range and significance of cartels in Dutch business.[32] This has to do with the secrecy entrepreneurs kept and still keep in relation to this subject, which makes it difficult to estimate the number of cartels and even more their economic impact. This silence was related partly to the nature of the agreements themselves, which in many cases depended on the discreteness of the participating parties. When competitors or consumers would become informed of these agreements, they would lose much effect or would even provoke resistance. The political ambivalence towards cartels also motivated entrepreneurs to keep their agreements out the limelight. During much of the 20th century, cartels were surrounded by a veil of secrecy. Apart from this secretiveness, the lacking of a coherent and accessible database from which numbers and scope of cartels could be derived, for much of the 20th century, hampers the study of this phenomenon. In the Netherlands, the government only occasionally published data from the Cartel register that was set up in 1941 by order of the Germans and that was kept until the 1980s. The exact number and significance of cartels, their impact on the industry, and the extent to which companies took advantage, thus is difficult to assess.

At the end of the 19th century, the openness of the Dutch economy put a brake on cartels. The Dutch domestic market was hardly shielded from foreign competition by import tariffs. This made it hard to conclude cartel agreements. Successful agreements were only possible if foreign competitors were involved or when the agreements were confined to a somewhat shielded local market. Apart from the openness of the Dutch economy, the coexistence of larger, modern enterprises and small companies, hindered stable agreements. In contrast, big business in Germany was already highly cartelised at the beginning of the 20th century, and even a journal on cartel issues existed.[33] In this respect German firms had a first mover advantage in their knowledge of how to organise cartel agreements, which turned out to be very profitable in creating international agreements during the interwar period.[34] Though cartels were at that time not characteristic of the Dutch economy, nevertheless a number of larger cartels existed alongside the widespread local pricing agreements. In 1903, the socialist Wibaut counted at least fifteen nationally organised cartels related to primary goods like salt, sugar, and peat.[35]

During the First World War, the Netherlands were cut off from supply lines by unilateral actions of the belligerents and imports, and exports came largely to halt. These years marked a closer cooperation among businesspeople that was supported by the government. Agreements on prices and production became widespread. Participating firms discovered that these agreements could be very profitable. They were continued after the war and in some cases expanded to foreign partners. International cartels became prevalent in the 1920s, especially on raw materials and on finished, more or less uniform, products. The Dutch, in terms of participation in international cartels, belonged to the average. Mainly large multinationals were involved in the international agreements in their market. It was estimated that about a third of the hundred largest industrial companies in the Netherlands in 1930 were connected with an international cartel or involved in domestic agreements on prices, production, or market allocation.[36]

The economic depression of the 1930s made cartels even more important for the domestic market. Not only in the Netherlands, but in all western economies, this was the heyday of the cartel, the archetypal period of cartels as *Kinder der Not*. The crisis and the sharp fall in prices fuelled competition and unemployment increased rapidly. To defend employment the government abandoned its permissive policy with regard to anticompetitive strategies of firms. Tariffs and import restrictions had to limit competition from abroad. For companies it became imperative to agree on prices and production in order to protect themselves against murderous competition. There are no hard figures on the numbers of cartels, but from documentation of the Ministry of Economic Affairs it can be deduced that approximately 60 per cent of companies with employees were linked by agreements, joint ventures, or were working in an industry that was controlled by cartels.[37] Some cartels were even established at the insistence of the government to prevent further decline in employment. To make governmental intervention possible, in 1935, the Business Agreements Act was passed. This law empowered the government to declare mutual agreements binding for all companies in a particular industry. Although the direct impact of the law was limited, it constituted a fundamental break with the liberal market ideology of the previous period.

During the German occupation of the Netherlands, the coordinated economy was reinforced by a new regulation on cartel agreements, which gave the government power to impose cartels. Due to this measure the veil of secrecy surrounding cartels was lifted because for the first time cartels had to be registered. At the same time, war and occupation marginalised the role of cartels. In a market dominated by shortages and governmental distribution systems, mutual agreements had hardly any significance. This would soon change after the liberation in May 1945. The tight government regulation that accompanied economic recovery opened opportunities for numerous price and production agreements. Despite the anti-cartel crusade that the Americans initiated after the war, the Dutch government encouraged and sanctioned these agreements, in order to increase productivity and rationalise production. Cartels in this period had a strong influence on the market, and almost all industries were regulated. In 1958, the government adopted the Economic Competition Act that made it possible to break up cartels when companies involved abused their market position, tried to seize monopolistic power, and, more generally, harmed the public interest. The Act was the beginning of a long and slow process in which competition was increasingly seen as the motor for economic growth and cartels gradually became taboo.

During the 1950s and 1960s, the new law did not induce major policy changes. A general ban on cartels, which was strongly advocated by the United States, was held off. The Economic Competition Act left room for many agreements. The government could not easily intervene, since no well-defined definition of the term 'public interest' was given. As a result Dutch companies continued the use of mutual understandings and agreements as a method to restrict competition, keep prices high, and keep markets allocated. From the late 1960s onward, the cartel as a strategic tool gradually lost importance due to a changing economic environment. The pursuit for larger scale, driven by innovation and internationalisation, stimulated further concentration by mergers and acquisitions. The cartel by its defensive nature was no longer appropriate to restrict competition and coordinate markets. As can be seen in Figure 5.2, cartels for this period show a gradual downward trend.[38]

While there were still hundreds of cartels active on the Dutch market, it is clear that the number of cartels declined. This might be the result of the European debates and the fear of many firms that cartels would be prohibited and prosecuted in all European countries. However, under the influence of the economic crisis, the pursuit of harmonisation with European legislation regarding cartels shifted to the background in the Netherlands and in Europe as a whole. During the economic crisis of the 1970s and early 1980s, mergers and acquisitions of companies in economic distress and acquisitions by foreign companies drew more public and political attention than the tacit agreements between entrepreneurs. Only in the 1980s did the focal point shift back to cartels. Liberalisation and deregulation put a greater emphasis on competition. The Dutch tradition of cooperation and mutual agreements was increasingly criticised, and cartels got a strong negative connotation. The classical objections against economic cooperation became more imperative.[39] The increasing economic integration within the European Community also forced the Dutch government to adjust to

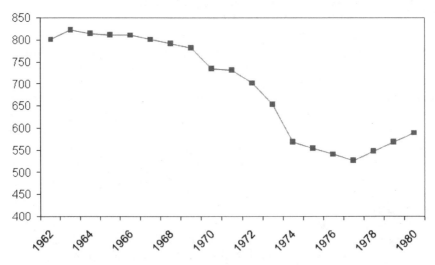

Figure 5.2   Total number of cartel agreements in the Netherlands, 1962–1980

Source: Bouwens and Dankers, 'Invisible handshake', 751–771.

the European rules. As in many other countries—for example, Finland and Sweden—Dutch politicians already in the early 1980s formulated the first proposals for a modification of the existing law on economic competition. Yet it took nearly twenty years before a law was passed under which cartels were prohibited and severe prosecution became reality. Mainly because of this lenient policy towards cartels and the slow progress in adapting new legislation, the Netherlands were typified as the 'cartel paradise' of Europe.

The Competition Act, which eventually came into force in 1998, inferred a definitive ban on cartels. It also constituted the Dutch Competition Authority (NMa), which would monitor compliance with the new rules. The Dutch 1998 law and the supervision it provided for was a belated, but fundamental break with the traditional policy that allowed mutual agreements between entrepreneurs. It was an essential change by which the Netherlands lost a typical feature of its coordinated market economy, converged with other European economies, and moved towards a more liberal market economy. Yet cartels did not disappear completely. Frequently national but also European authorities found new and often widespread agreements on daily products like beer, shrimp, or flour.

MERGERS AND ACQUISITIONS

With the Competition Act of 1998 that banned cartels, also the control on mergers and acquisitions was strengthened. Besides monitoring compliance with the new law on cartels, the NMa had to assess the effect of mergers, acquisitions, and joint ventures on the market. This suggests a link between these different forms of cooperation that affect competition. Both cartels and mergers and acquisitions can be seen as a possibility for external growth, and they are in this sense substitutes.[40] There are many reasons why mergers and acquisitions make coordination more likely. Among these is that concentration lowers the number of competing firms and reduces the organisational tasks for the remaining companies to reach an agreement or understanding about prices, output, or market allocation.[41]

In fact cartels on the one side, and mergers and acquisitions on the other, can be considered as communicating vessels. This is not a recently gained insight. When the 1890 Sherman Act prohibited cartels in the United States, the number of mergers and acquisitions increased dramatically.[42] The same happened in the 1990s and 2000s. Hüschelrath and Smuda constructed a database on merger activity after EC-cartel cases during the first decade of the 21st century. They calculated that, comparing the three years before the cartel breakdowns with the three years afterwards, the average number of all merger activity increased by up to 51 per cent. For the subset of horizontal mergers, the activity was even higher, by up to 83 per cent.[43] Curtailing cartels apparently encouraged companies to turn to other forms of concentration to enhance their competitiveness. Authorities for that reason considered mergers and acquisitions to have the same kind of negative impact on market allocation, shareholder value, R&D investment, and output as cartels.[44] Hence control was deemed necessary. What does the alternation of cartels and mergers and acquisitions tell us about the Dutch market economy? One method to explore this is by comparing the Dutch evolution of mergers and acquisitions in the 20th century with the merger waves that characterised the liberal American market (see Figure 5.3). Internationally five merger waves are discerned, all occurring during periods of economic upswing.[45] Can these fluctuations in merger activity also be seen in the Netherlands, and what does this tell us about the Dutch business system?

At the turn of the 20th century, mergers and acquisitions were hardly significant for Dutch business. They were unfit for the small, artisanal family businesses that were so characteristic of that period. Family firms considered mergers, which often ended their autonomy, as unattractive. Mergers and acquisitions seemed to be typical for big businesses, with the 1907 Royal Dutch Shell agreement as the most striking example.[46] This situation changed rapidly as a result of World War I. The scarcity that resulted from the war in the neighbouring countries boosted modernisation, with an eminent role for the Dutch government. New technologies and increasing capital intensity led to further concentration. Mergers and acquisitions, also involving small and medium-sized companies, became more regular.[47] In the 1920s, the increased merger activity put the Netherlands in step with the

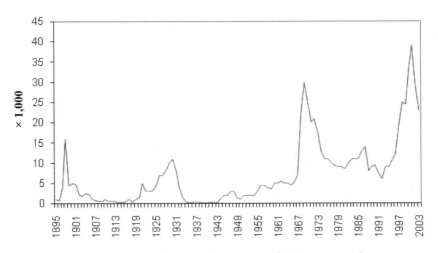

Figure 5.3　Merger waves in the United States, 1895–2000

Source: Nelson, *Merger Movements;* US Federal Trade Commission, Bureau of Economics (1981); Gugler, Mueller, and Yurtoglu, 'The determinants of merger waves'; Golbe and White, 'Catch a wave', 494.

international merger wave. Both horizontal and vertical mergers were seen, but cross-border mergers still were an exception until well into the 20th century. Like everywhere else the economic depression of the 1930s put a strong brake on merger activities of Dutch companies. The number of transactions on the Amsterdam stock market diminished. The shrinking market apparently offered little prospect for benefits of scale. On the other hand, new evidence shows that mergers and acquisitions of small and medium-sized firms—mostly family firms—belonged to the most important answers of many entrepreneurs to the crisis. These small companies that were not always able to eliminate competition through cartel agreements often were forced to amalgamate in order to survive.[48]

The extent to which Dutch companies engaged in mergers and acquisitions in the first postwar decades is unclear but can be estimated to be very low. The Netherlands was no exception compared to other economies. There are no consistent data on the numbers of transactions, but from the figures available a global trend emerges. Figure 5.4 shows the number of mergers and acquisition of companies with one hundred employees or more during the second half of the 20th century.[49]

In the second half of the 1960s, merger activity in the Netherlands increased, although the growth in number of mergers was less pronounced than in the United States. Dutch business community in these years seemed to be affected by the third international merger wave. These years were marked by the rise of conglomerates, and also in the Netherlands a few

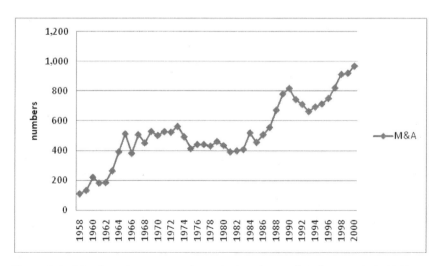

Figure 5.4 Number of mergers and acquisitions in Dutch industry, 1958–2000

Source: CBS (1958–1970); Hoyinck and Geeve, *Gelet op artikel 2; www.ser.nl.*

striking examples of these diversified companies such as OGEM and Bredero can be found. Vertical integration was generally seen as a way to reduce uncertainties of the market and stimulate coordination within the value chain. However, the number of horizontal mergers directed at concentration still prevailed in Netherlands. The search for economies of scale and scope turned out the most obvious response to market saturation and the narrowing of the margins, which was due to rising wages and the increasing costs for raw materials and capital in these years.

This higher merger activity caused societal uproar. Public and political attention did not focus on the reduction of competition and the consequences for consumers but rather stressed the effects on employment. People were afraid that concentration would result in massive redundancies. As long as the economy boomed and employment grew, this was not an imminent threat, but when the economy went down, the concerns about unemployment became more pressing. This, in 1970, resulted in a Merger Code that took the interests of both shareholders and employees into account. The employees had to be kept informed during the merger process, and hostile takeovers were considered inappropriate. However, this Code knew no penalties for violators and had no legal basis. It was based on a mutual agreement between BIAs and trade unions as part of their regular contacts with the government in the Social Economic Council.[50] This code was typical for the strongly coordinated Dutch economy. Dutch politicians and businesspeople strived after a coordinated way of concentration, with regard to all stakeholders. In the late 1960s and 1970s, the Dutch government even regarded concentration as an adequate solution for the near-collapse of many industries. Especially in labour-intensive sectors like shipbuilding, textiles, and cardboard, the government stimulated cooperation and further concentration. Cooperation and often complete amalgamation of deteriorating firms was a condition for governmental support. In retrospect this was an ill-fated strategy that could not return the fortunes of these sectors.[51]

With the economic recovery of the mid-1980s, a new phase in the concentration process started. In these years joint ventures became popular to share knowledge, allocate production, or make other agreements for a limited market or region. The joint venture was a less expensive and more flexible alternative to a merger or acquisition and sometimes a legal substitute for cartel-like forms of agreement that were increasingly prohibited by the EC and national governments.[52] The increased number of joint ventures foreshadowed the fourth merger wave in the second half of the 1980s. This wave fairly quickly collapsed with the onset of the recession after 1990. Characteristic was the horizontal concentration that could be seen as a modification of the third wave and matched the 'back to the core' strategy many firms followed. The number of cross-border transactions increased, reflecting the ongoing process of globalisation. Hostile takeovers became a new phenomenon in the Netherlands. Notwithstanding the Merger Code of 1970, Dutch business could no longer withstand the pressure of economic integration and competition. The placid, coordinated Dutch economy at the end of the 1980s was shaken by a series of hostile takeovers. Big publishing houses, like Elsevier and Kluwer, belonged to the first Dutch companies that were involved in a hostile takeover.[53]

As Figure 5.4 shows, after 1994, another merger wave unfolded. This wave, which peaked around the turn of the century, was characterised in the Netherlands as well as in the United States and most other western economies by an unprecedented number of transactions and record prices. In the coordinated German market economy, the merger activity increased as East German economy was integrated and industries rationalised.[54] Driven by high expectations of new technology in the field of ICT and logistics, companies fervently looked for expansion of production facilities and market shares, very often also in emerging markets. The risks entailed increased correspondingly with the skyrocketing prices for takeovers, and when confidence in ICT as a driver of economic growth began to fade at the end of 2001, the so-called Internet bubble burst. The stock market collapsed, and the merger wave came to an abrupt end in the Netherlands as well as the rest of the world.

Apart from cyclical fluctuations, institutional changes also explain the evolution of the merger movement and the consequent concentration at the end of the 20th century the Netherlands. In the 1980s, the European Community vigorously promoted a common market, which was actually created in 1993. The development of the single European market and the introduction of a common currency in the late 1990s put pressure on domestically oriented companies to reduce excess capacity and use mergers and acquisitions as a channel to consolidate in order to face regional competition. The ongoing European integration thus forced companies to reflect on their market position and on competition abroad. Economic integration stimulated cross-border mergers within Europe, but it also augmented interest of non-European companies for the expanding common market.[55] At the same time, in the Netherlands as well as in other western countries, liberalisation and privatisation were proliferating. Coordinated market economies gave more room to the forces of the free market to stimulate economic growth. The increased appreciation for the market also motivated companies to scale up and cooperate across borders. Concentration and specialisation were seen as a way to restrict competition. Horizontal concentration and the 'back to the core' strategy got an international dimension in the 1990s. However, it was not only Dutch companies that went abroad on an acquisition tour. Foreign multinationals acquired firms in the Netherlands. Several industries became almost completely dominated by owners from abroad. European integration and globalisation thus contributed to the intertwining of Dutch business and the Dutch market economy with Europe and the world.[56]

Looking at mergers and acquisitions, Dutch business by and large followed the international movement. From the 1980s until the first decade of the 21st century, Dutch merger activity resembled developments in other countries, both liberal and coordinated market economies. Dutch firms had their part in the third, but more clearly in the fourth and fifth, merger wave, both in the number of transactions and in terms of total deal value.[57] The drivers of these merger waves were different and varied from growth strategies in new industries, restructuring old industries or international market integration. Nevertheless, the way Dutch business amalgamated fitted the coordinated way, with the Merger Code of 1970 as a landmark. Hostile takeovers until the 1990s were an exception, and Dutch firms preferred negotiated acquisitions over tender offers. The institutional setting on mergers and acquisitions that was largely determined by European policymakers, forced business into a more liberal direction. Takeover defences, most of which dated from the 1930s, were restricted, and this made Dutch business more open to the concentration process.

COMPARING TO OTHER COUNTRIES

BIAs and mergers and acquisitions occur in both LMEs and CMEs, while cartels are characteristic for CMEs. As we have seen in the Dutch case, the features of these instruments differ in both systems, and their functions can change over time. Can we identify similar patterns in other nation states? As we saw, the Netherlands evolved into a CME during the first decades of the 20th century. In most European countries a comparable development took place. Everywhere BIAs played a crucial role in the organisation of the market economy and adopted several functions that made a high degree of coordination possible. Especially during periods of crisis, these associations were increasingly important in the organisation of the economy. The German market economy, for example, was widely seen as a system in which the role of the market was confined by state and social forces. BIAs had great influence and were able to look at long-term interests. They facilitated the interests of their members and increased their power in dealing with public authorities and trade unions. Recent studies on BIAs in Europe show that these associations gradually increased their services and progressively contributed to the control of the market mechanism during the first decades of the 20th century.[58]

Also the functions of these BIAs were more or less comparable to those of their Dutch counterparts. Making cartel agreements became one of the most important roles of BIAs before the war. This was generally supported by regulations in favour of cartels, like the *Gesetz über Errichtung von Zwangskartellen* in Germany.[59] All of these laws had the same message: cartel agreements were useful instruments to restore economic stability and create employment.[60] This coordinated European answer to the crisis stood in sharp contrast with the situation in the United States where severe antitrust legislation restricted the activities of BIAs. At the beginning of the 20th century, many associations developed from cartel organisations to service providers with cost accounting, benchmarking, and the improvement of productivity as their core activities.[61] During the inter-war years, American business leaders, however, urged the government to sanction cartels and indeed the Roosevelt administration temporarily suspended the enforcement of antitrust legislation. So, even the United States opened the gate for further coordination among firms in order to deal with economic depression. After World War II, American politicians, economists, and businesspeople returned to the view that competition would lead to a more efficient market order. This idea became crucial to American economic policy and fuelled the American anti-cartel crusade in Europe.[62]

The European Recovery Program that the United States initiated to help Europe recover from the war encouraged antitrust legislation. But this was not accepted all over Europe. The Scandinavian countries and Finland, like the Netherlands, introduced a legal system that in fact per-mitted cartels. On the other hand, countries like Germany, France, and the United Kingdom had a much stricter regime, which focused on prohi-bition. Germany, once the most cartelised nation of Europe, was the first European country that introduced strict anti-cartel laws in 1958.[63] The differences between these legal regimes clearly came to the surface with the formation of the EEC in 1957 and the ongoing European integration. The European treaties recommended competition as a precondition for economic growth on which restriction of the market was seen to have a negative impact. To obtain a comprehensive and generally approved com-petition policy would, however, take several decades. Only in the 1990s did all member states of the European Union introduce a competition policy in conformity with the general European rules on competition. This competition policy and the ensuing legal system forced the demise of cartels or at least tried to do so. Meanwhile cartels did not disappear, as many cases of national and European competition authorities prove. Data from the EC show that between 2005 and 2009 the European authorities imposed penalties for 9.7 billion euro on cartelising firms.[64] The transfor-mation from CME to LME thus in most nations was a lengthy process that only gradually made an end to cartels as an instrument to coordinate markets.

In most western countries merger waves that parallel the American ones can be distinguished. While the occurrence of merger waves turns out to be more or less similar, the rules of the game, however, differed widely. The market economy of the United States relied on central market-based mechanisms for corporate governance and the prevalence of shareholders. In LMEs hostile takeovers were the order of the day. In CMEs several struc-tural instruments—for example, bank-firm relations, cross-shareholders arrangements, or takeover defences—prevented such a practice.[65] German industry, like the Dutch, was confronted with a number of hostile acquisi-tions from the late 1980s onwards, which caused societal uproar. Neverthe-less the majority of mergers and acquisitions in these countries still were the result of consultation and negotiation. In this respect they continued to differ from LMEs.[66]

How exceptional is the Dutch evolution of coordination? The 1930s witnessed a global trend towards coordination between firms, trade unions, and governments. At the end of the 20th century and the beginning of the 21st century, coordinated market economies seem to develop in liberal direction. Global trends, however, do not necessarily guarantee convergence. Often national solutions that rely on traditions and unwritten rules of the game prevail. During most of the 20th century, the Dutch market economy followed a similar coordinated pattern as Germany and other continental economies. One major exception are the cartels, where Germany followed the American path of being stricter after the war. The existence and functioning of business interest associations in the Netherlands and the use of cartels clearly contrast the American situation. This is more difficult to conclude on mergers and acquisitions. Dutch industry in this respect followed the international trends, and dissimilarities can only be traced in the way these transactions were realised.

CONCLUSION: THE VARIETIES OF COORDINATION

Looking back at the development of the Dutch business system in the 20th century, it is clear that the interfirm relations during most of this period were dominated by a variety of coordinating instruments. The competitive behaviour of Dutch firms was shaped by the coordinating institutions that evolved during this century. In the Dutch business system, BIAs proved to be a lasting and important instrument in the anticompetitive strategies of firms. However, the function of these associations depended to a large extent on the political and economic conditions and thus changed over time. They started as local or regional societies uniting businesspeople often from different trades, lobbying for general purposes. BIAs gradually evolved into well-structured national organisations where businesspeople united forces as a reaction to the growing power of trade unions. In this process they created formal and informal rules that supported and structured their activities. During periods of crisis, most prominently during the 1930s, BIAs served as platforms for businesspeople to construct internal binding agreements. BIAs thus were important for interfirm relations, but they were also active in the political arena, negotiating with the government and the trade unions, mainly on labour-related issues. In this respect they were fundamental to the consensus-based Dutch economy. During the 1980s, there was a clear shift in the functions of BIAs, which reveals the transition of the Dutch market economy from coordinated to liberal. Internationalisation and EU market integration, accompanied by antitrust legislation, forced BIAs to reinvent themselves and to focus on activities adapted to the competitive principles of European and domestic regulations.

Cartels also were a quite persistent strategy of Dutch firms during most of the century, and in this respect the Dutch business system also can be characterised as a CME. Firms would try to manipulate the market by these kind of agreements whenever they saw a profitable opportunity. Though cartels were a continuous phenomenon in relations between firms, the use of this instrument also highly depended on the economic and political situation. It was essentially the changing policy of Dutch government and the resulting regulations that defined the scope and spread of cartels. In the first three decades, Dutch government ignored the existence of cartels and refused to take any action. Cartels were thought to be useless in a small open economy like the Netherlands. Yet they proved to have an important coordinating role in a number of industries. During the Depression of the 1930s and the recovery after World War II, cartels were seen as an important instrument to resolve the inefficiencies of the market and protect employment. Dutch government endorsed the use of this instrument, and firms in a wide variety of branches were actively engaged in concluding agreements on markets, prices, and production. Cartels continued to have an important role in interfirm relations for several decades because the Dutch government connived at these agreements. It resisted external pressure, mainly from the United States, to adopt anti-cartel legislation. As a result of European integration and ongoing internationalisation of the Dutch economy, this gradually changed during the 1980s. However, lobbying by BIAs and political resistance delayed formal legal action, and it was only in 1998 that anti-cartel legislation was passed.

Mergers and acquisitions occur in both liberal and coordinated market economies and thus are not distinctive to either system. Yet mergers and acquisitions are closely connected with economic cycles. When prospects for profitable business are growing, the number of transactions will increase. This is why mergers and acquisitions occur in waves. These waves can also be distinguished in the Dutch economy. In periods of economic downturn, like the 1930s, mergers and acquisitions were replaced with cartel agreements to reduce competition, and when cartels were criticised or banned in the 1980s and 1990s, firms fell back to acquisitions and joint ventures. In fact, as the Dutch example showed, these two instruments can be seen as communicating vessels. Finally, mergers and acquisitions in the Dutch business system typically were the result of consultation, negotiation, and careful planning with respect to all stakeholders. This, however, changed during the last decades of the 20th century. Takeover defences, which were widespread, were gradually torn down. Hostile takeovers, which were exceptional until the 1980s, became more general. Also in this respect the combination of internationalisation and changing legislation turned out to be decisive.

To sum up: a close study of business strategies with regard to interfirm relations confirms that the Dutch business system was a CME during most of the 20th century. It developed gradually from a LME at the beginning of the 20th century to a typical CME during the 1930s to the 1980s, and back again to a LME at the end of the century. The analysis of the different instruments allows us to specify this general picture. BIAs were characteristic of the Dutch business system since the start of the century, but their functions and subsequent coordinating power changed over time. Cartels were seen by Dutch business as an efficient way of structuring interfirm relations. Firms were reluctant to relinquish this instrument until the use of cartels at the end of the century finally was limited by legal force. The fact that takeover defences were widespread and hostile takeovers exceptional underlines that coordination prevailed during most of the 20th century in Dutch business. Coordination of interfirm relations proved to be fluid and flexible. Like the 'Varieties of Capitalism' label the differences between market economies, the different strategies regarding interfirm relations can be defined as 'varieties of coordination'.

NOTES

1. Hall and Soskice, *Varieties of Capitalism*, 6–7.
2. Hall and Soskice, *Varieties of Capitalism*, 15.
3. Hall and Soskice, *Varieties of Capitalism*, 21–33; Hall and Gingerich, *Varieties of Capitalism and institutional complementarities*, 453.
4. Hall and Soskice, *Varieties of Capitalism*, 47–48.
5. Sluyterman, *Dutch Enterprise*, passim; Gerwen and De Goey, *Ondernemers*; Sluyterman and Wubs, *Over grenzen*; Bouwens and Dankers, *Tussen concurrentie en concentratie*; Nijhof and Van den Berg, *Het menselijk kapitaal*; Davids, Lintsen, and Van Rooij, *Innovatie*.
6. Van Os, *Grensoverschrijdende fusies*, 22–23.
7. Lypczynski and Wilson, *Industrial Organization* 59–61; Schmiter and Streeck, *Organization of Business Interests*, 9; Fraboulet et al., *Historical and International*, 11–18; Rollings, 'Business Euro federations', 173.
8. *Verslagen en mededelingen* (1936); Van Waarden, 'Emergence', 521–562.
9. SER, *SER-Almanak* (1980); Vroom and Van Waarden, 'Ondernemersorganisaties', 667.
10. Van Waarden and Lehmbruch, *Renegotiating*, 78–79.
11. Schmidt, Van den Toren, and De Wal, *Ondernemende organisaties*, 29–31, 56–66.
12. Bouwens, and Dankers, 'Origins and shifting functions'.
13. Van Waarden, 'Regulering', 232–233.
14. Bouwens and Dankers, *Concurrentie en concentratie*, 54–59.
15. Windmuller, De Galan, and Van Zweeden, *Arbeidsverhoudingen*, 58–59.
16. 'National Archives The Hague, access number 2.06.001, inventory number 3924: *Handels-en Nijverheidsvereenigingen in Nederland* (1920).
17. Windmuller, De Galan, and Van Zweeden, *Arbeidsverhoudingen*, 72–73.
18. *Verslagen en mededelingen* (1936).
19. SER, *Met raad en daad*; De Haan, 'Parlementaire democratie', 32–37.
20. Sluyterman, *Dutch Enterprise*, 133–144.
21. De Vroom and Van Waarden, 'Ondernemersorganisaties', 664–670.
22. Bouwens and Dankers, *Concurrentie en concentratie*, 207–215.
23. Bos, Ebben, Te Velde, *Harmonie in Holland*.
24. Van Schendelen, *Machiavelli*.

25. Müller, Schmidt, and Tissot, eds., *Regulierte Märkte*, 19–20.
26. Müller, Schmidt, and Tissot, eds., *Regulierte Märkte*, 132–133.
27. Lewenstein and Suslow, 'What determines cartel success?', 43–95.
28. There are many definitions of a cartel; see, for example: J. Fear, 'Cartels', 271.
29. Berk and Schneiberg, 'Varieties in Capitalism'; Freyer, *Regulating Big Business*, Introduction.
30. Schröter, 'Cartelisation and decartelisation', 129–153.
31. Bouwens and Dankers, 'Invisible handshake', 751–771.
32. Barjot and Schröter, 'General introduction', 957–971.
33. Kleinwächter, *Die Kartelle*.
34. Schröter, 'Cartelisation and decartelisation', 133.
35. Wibaut, *Trusts*, 106–118.
36. Sluyterman and Winkelman, 'Dutch family firm', 152–183, 154–155; Societé des Nations, *Tableau provisoire* (1929).
37. National Archives, access number 2.06.001, inv.no. 8704.
38. Bouwens and Dankers, 'Invisible handshake', 751–771.
39. Goyder, *EC Competition Law*, 561–604; Craig and De Burca, *Regulating Cartels*, 140–142.
40. Schröter, 'Cartelisation', 989–1010.
41. Dick, 'Coordinated interaction', 66–67.
42. Bittlingmayer, 'Did anti-trust policy cause the great merger wave?'.
43. Hüschelrath and Schmuda, *Do Cartel Breakdowns Induce Mergers?*
44. Schenk, 'Fusies'.
45. Most studies use datasets of firms with a stock market quotation and ignore, for example, private limited companies. Scherer and Ross, *Industrial Market Structure*, 153–159; De Jong, 'De concentratiebeweging', 224–229; Tilly, 'Mergers', 629–658.
46. Jonker and Van Zanden, *From Challenger*, 81–89.
47. Sluyterman, *Dutch Enterprise*, 78–84.
48. Bouwens, 'Mergers and Acquisitions', 19–20; Bouwens and Dankers, *Concurrentie en concentratie*, 124–128.
49. CBS (1958–1970); Hoyinck and Geeve, *Gelet op artikel 2*; www.ser.nl.
50. Hoyink, 'Bescherming van werknemers', 277–301.
51. Bouwens, *Op papier gesteld*, 227–255; Bouwens and Dankers, *Concurrentie en concentratie*, 184–188.
52. Jagersma and Bell, 'International joint ventures'; Killing, *Strategies*, 1–8.
53. Van Os, *Grensoverschrijdende fusies*, 131–132; Johannes and Cohen de Lara, *Van Haarlem naar Manhattan*, 167–168.
54. Dietrich, 'National patterns', 149–165.
55. Jackson and Miyajima, 'Varieties of Capitalism', 6.
56. Bouwens and Dankers, *Concurrentie en concentratie*, 243–249.
57. Martynova and Renneboog, 'A century'.
58. Barjot, *International Cartels*; Müller, Schmidt, and Tissot, *Regulierte Märkte*.
59. Schröter, 'Cartelisation and decartelisation', 137; Alexander, 'The impact', 245–254; Alexander, 'Failed cooperation', 322–344; Freyer, *Regulating Big Business*, 202–206.
60. National Archives, access no. 2.06.001, inv.no. 8704.
61. Berk and Schneiberg, 46–87.
62. Freyer, 196–204.
63. Drahos, *Convergence*; Haucap, Heimeshoff, and Schultz, 'Legal and Illegal', 1–3.
64. Bouwens and Dankers, *Concurrentie en concentratie*, 224–225; www.ec.europa.eu/competition/cartels/statistics.

65. Jackson and Miyajima, 'Varieties of Capitalism', 4–11.
66. Ullrich, Wieseke, and Van Dick, 'Continuity and change', 1549–1569.

REFERENCES

Alexander, B.J., 'Failed cooperation in heterogeneous industries under the National Recovery Administration', *The Journal of Economic History*, 2 (1997): 322–344.
Alexander, B.J., 'The impact of the national recovery Act on Cartel Formation and Maintenance Costs', *The Review of Economics and Statistics*, 76, 2 (1994): 245–254.
Barjot, D., *International Cartels Revisited, 1880–1980* (Caen: Editions du Lys, 1994).
Barjot, D. and Schröter, H.G., 'General introduction', *Revue économique*, 64, 6 (2013): 957–971.
Berk, G. and Schneiberg, M., 'Varieties in capitalism, varieties of association: Collaborative learning in American industry', *Politics and Society*, 33, 1 (2005): 46–87.
Bittlingmayer, G., 'Did anti-trust policy cause the great merger wave?', *Journal of Law and Economics*, 28 (1985): 77–118.
Bos, D., M. Ebben, and H. te Velde, *Harmonie in Holland; het poldermodel van 1500 tot nu* (Amsterdam: Bert Bakker, 2007).
Bouwens, B., 'Mergers and Acquisitions in a Small and Open Economy; the Second Merger Wave in the Netherlands, 1920–1940', Paper presented at Fuji-conference 2008, vkc.library.uu.nl/vkc/seh/. . ./36/Bouwens%20MergersAcquisitions.pdf (Accessed January 3, 2014).
Bouwens, B., *Op papier gesteld; de geschiedenis van de Nederlandse papier en kartonindustrie in de twintigste eeuw* (Amsterdam: Boom, 2004).
Bouwens, B. and J. Dankers, 'Origins and shifting functions of Business Interest Associations; the Dutch case in the twentieth century', in: D. Fraboulet, A.M. Locatelli, and P. Tedeschi, eds., *Historical and International Comparison of Business Interest Associations; 19th–20th century* (Brussels: Peter Lang, 2013) 109–126.
Bouwens, B. and J. Dankers, *Tussen concurrentie en concentratie; belangenorganisaties, kartels, fusies en overnames* (Amsterdam: Boom, 2012).
Bouwens, B. and Dankers, J., 'The invisible handshake; cartelization in the Netherlands, 1930–1980', *Business History Review*, 84, Winter (2010): 751–771.
CBS, *Statistisch zakboek* (Den Haag: SDU 1958–1970)
Craig, P. and G. de Burca, *Regulating Cartels in Europe* (Oxford: OUP, 2003).
Davids, M., H. Lintsen, and A. van Rooij, *Innovatie en kennisinfrastructuur; vele wegen naar vernieuwing* (Amsterdam: Boom, 2014).
Dick, A.R., 'Coordinated interaction; pre-merger constraint and post-merger effects', *George Mason Law Review*, 12, 1 (2003–2004): 65–88.
Dietrich, M., 'National patterns of corporate restructuring; mergers and joint ventures in the European community', in: R. Delorme and K. Dopfer, eds., *The Political Economy of Diversity; Evolutionary Perspectives on Economic Order and Disorder* (London: Edward Elgar, 1994) 149–165.
Drahos, M., *Convergence of Competition Laws and Politics in the European Community—Germany, Austria and the Netherlands* (The Hague: Kluwer, 2001).
Fear, J., 'Cartels' in: G. Jones and J. Zeitlin, eds., *The Oxford Handbook of Business History* (Oxford: Oxford University Press, 2008) 268–292.
Fraboulet, D., A.M. Locatelli, and P. Tedeschi, eds., *Historical and International Comparison of Business Interest Associations; 19th–20th century* (Brussels: Peter Lang, 2013).

Freyer, T., *Regulating Big Business; Antitrust in Great Britain and America, 1880–1920* (New York: Cambridge University Press, 1992).

Gerwen, J. van, and F. de Goey, *Ondernemers in Nederland; Variaties in Ondernemen* (Amsterdam: Boom, 2008).

Golbe, D.L. and White, L.J., 'Catch a wave; the time series behavior of mergers', *The Review of Economics and Statistics*, 75, 3 (1994): 493–499.

Goyder, D.G., *EC Competition Law* (Oxford: Clarendon Press, 1998).

Gugler, K.P., D.C. Mueller, and B. Yurtoglu, 'The Determinants of Merger Waves', WZB-Markets and Politics working paper No. SP II 2006–01.

Haan, I. de, 'Parlementaire democratie en maatschappelijke organisatie; de politieke context van de Sociaal-Economische-Raad', in: T. Jaspers, B. van Bavel, and J. Peet, eds., *SER; zestig jaar denkwerk voor draagvlak* (Amsterdam: Boom, 2010) 23–48.

Hall, P. and D. Gingerich, 'Varieties of Capitalism and institutional complementarities in the political economy; an empirical analysis', *British Journal of Political Science*, 39, 3 (2009): 449–482.

Hall, P.A. and D. Soskice, *Varieties of Capitalism; the Institutional Foundations of Comparative Advantage* (Oxford: OUP, 2001).

Haucap, J., H. Heimeshoff, and L.M. Schultz, 'Legal and Illegal Cartels in Germany between 1958 and 2004', Düsseldorf: Heinrich Heine University discussion paper (2010).

Hoyinck, J.B.A., 'Bescherming van werknemers; de SER-fusiegedragregels 2000', in: J.C.K.W. Bartel, ed., *Fusies en acquisities; fundamentele aspecten van fusies en acquisities* (Dordrecht: Kluwer, 2002) 277–302.

Hoyinck, J.B.A. and A.J.C. Geeve, *Gelet op artikel 2; cijfers over fusies 1970–1996* (Den Haag: SER, 1997).

Hüschelrath, K. and F. Schmuda, 'Do Cartel Breakdowns Induce Mergers? Evidence from EC Cartel Cases', Mannheim: discussion paper ZEW (2013).

Jackson, G. and H. Miyajima, 'Varieties of Capitalism, Varieties of Markets; Mergers and Acquisitions in Japan, Germany, France, the UK and USA', Rieti Discussion Paper series 07-E-054 (2007).

Jagersma, P.K. and J. Bell, 'Internationale joint ventures; een empirische analyse', *ESB* (Vol. 77, November 4, 1992): 1064–1068.

Johannes, G.J. and M. Cohen de Lara, *Van Haarlem naar Manhattan; veertig jaar VNU* (Amsterdam: Boom, 2005).

Jong, H.W. de, 'De concentratiebeweging in de Europese economie', *ESB* (Vol. 73, March 2, 1988): 224–229.

Jonker, J. and J.L. van Zanden, *From Challenger to Joint Industry Leader, 1890–1939; a History of Royal Dutch Shell, volume 1* (Oxford: Oxford University Press, 2007).

Killing, P., *Strategies for Joint Venture Success* (London: Routledge, 1988).

Kleinwächter, F., *Die Kartelle. Ein Beitrag zur Frage der Organisation der Volkswirtschaft* (Innsbruck: Verlag der Wagnerischen Universitaets-Buchhandlung, 1883).

Lewenstein, M.C. and Suslow, V.Y., 'What determines cartel success', *Journal of Economic Literature*, 44, March (2006): 43–95.

Lypczynski, J. and J. Wilson, *Industrial Organisation; an Analysis of Competitive Markets* (Harlow England: Pearson Education, 2001).

Martynova, M. and L. Renneboog, 'Mergers and acquisitions in Europe', in: L. Renneboog, ed., *Advances in Corporate Finance and Asset Pricing* (Amsterdam: Elsevier, 2006) 15–71.

Martynova, M. and Renneboog, L., 'A century of corporate takeovers; what have we learned and where do we stand?', *Journal of Corporate Finance*, 14, 3 (2008): 2148–2177.

Müller, M., H.R. Schmidt, and L. Tissot, eds., *Regulierte Märkte: Zünfte und Kartelle* (Zürich: Chronis, 2011).

Nelson, R.L. *Merger Movements in American History 1895–1956* (Princeton: Princeton University Press, 1959).

Nijhof, E. and A. van den Berg, *Het menselijk kapitaal; sociaal ondernemersbeleid in Nederland* (Amsterdam: Boom, 2012).

Os, M. van, *Grensoverschrijdende fusies in de twintigste eeuw* (Amsterdam: Boom, 2009).

Rollings, N., 'Business Eurofederations and European integration from the Second World War to the 1970s', in: D. Fraboulet, A.M. Locatelli, and P. Tedeschi, eds., *Historical and International Comparison of Business Interest Associations; 19th–20th Century* (Brussels: Peter Lang, 2013) 173–190.

Schendelen, M.P.C.M. van, *Machiavelli in Brussels; the Art of Lobbying the EU* (Amsterdam: Amsterdam University Press, 2003).

Schenk, H., 'Fusies als economisch en strategisch verschijnsel; reële of ogenschijnlijke paradoxen?', in: J. Bartel, R. Frederikslust, H. Schenk, and M. Vijverberg, eds., *Fusies en Acquisities. Fundamentele aspecten van fusies en acquisities* (Amsterdam: Elsevier/LexisNexis, 2007) 67–139.

Scherer, F.M. and D. Ross, *Industrial Market Structure and Economic Performance* (Boston: Houghton Mifflin, 1990).

Schmidt, D., J.P. van den Toren, and M. de Wal, *Ondernemende organisaties; balanceren tussen belangen* (Assen: Van Gorcum, 2003).

Schmiter, Ph. C. and W. Streeck, *The Organization of Business Interests; Studying the Associative Action of Business in Advanced Industrial Societies* (Köln: Max-Planck-Institut, 1999).

Schröter, H.G., 'Cartelisation and decartelisation in Europe, 1870–1995: Rise and decline of an economic institution', *The Journal of European Economic History*, 129, 1 (1996): 129–153.

SER, *Met raad en daad; visies op de toekomst van de overlegeconomie op nationaal en sectoraal niveau* (Den Haag: SER, 2000).

SER, *SER-almanak voor Sociaal-Economisch Nederland* (The Hague: SER, 1980)

Sluyterman, K.E., *Dutch Enterprise in the Twentieth Century: Business Strategies in a Small Open Economy* (London: Routledge, 2005).

Sluyterman, K.E. and Winkelman, H.J.M., 'The Dutch family firm confronted with Chandler's dynamics of industrial capitalism, 1890–1940', *Business History*, 35 (1993): 152–183.

Sluyterman, K.E. and B. Wubs, *Over grenzen; multinationals en de Nederlandse markteconomie* (Amsterdam: Boom, 2009).

Societé des Nations, *Tableau provisoire des entents ind. et com. Internationals*, 26 April 1929: National Archive The Hague: inv. 2.06.001, number. 5585.

Tilly, R., 'Mergers, external growth and finance in the development of large scale enterprise in Germany 1880–1913', *The Journal of Economic History*, 42, 3 (1982): 629–658.

Ullrich, J., Wieseke, J., and Dick, R. van, 'Continuity and change in mergers and acquisitions; a societal identity case study of German merger', *Journal of Management Studies*, 42, 8 (2005): 1549–1569.

US Federal Trade Commission, Bureau of Economics, *Statistical Report on Mergers and Acquisitions* (Washington, DC: FTC, 1981).

Verslagen en mededelingen van de Afdeling Handel van het Departement van Landbouw, Nijverheid en Handel; Overzicht van de in Nederland bestaande patroonsverenigingen (Den Haag 1920 and 1936): National Archives The Hague, access no. 2.06.001, inv. no. 3986.

Vroom, B. de, and F. van Waarden, 'Ondernemersorganisaties als machtsmiddel (I)', *ESB* (Vol. 69, July 25, 1984): 664–670.

Waarden, F. van, 'Emergence and development of business interest associations; an example from the Netherlands', *Organization Studies*, 13, 4 (1992): 521–562.

Waarden, F. van, 'Regulering en belangenorganisaties van ondernemers', in: F.L. Holthoon, ed., *De Nederlandse samenleving sinds 1815; wording en samenhang* (Assen/Maastricht: Van Gorcum, 1985) 227–260.

Waarden, F. van, and G. Lehmbruch, *Renegotiating the Welfare State; Flexible Adjustment through Corporatist Concertation* (London, Routledge, 2003).

Wibaut, F.M., *Trusts en kartellen* (Middelburg: Soep, 1903).

Windmuller, J.P., C. de Galan, and A.F. van Zweeden, *Arbeidsverhoudingen in Nederland* (Utrecht: Spectrum, 1990, 7th edition).

6 The Dutch Knowledge Infrastructure and Institutional Change

Mila Davids and Harry Lintsen

INTRODUCTION

During their existence firms face various challenges, ranking from scientific discoveries, new technological inventions, and growing markets to increasing competition. To handle these constraints knowledge building is of prime importance. This includes in-house research as well as all knowledge-seeking and knowledge-acquiring activities. Interaction and relations with other organisations in an institutional setting is needed to gain, develop, and exchange various kinds of knowledge and information.[1] Therefore, a thorough analysis of relations between firms and various knowledge sources in the knowledge infrastructure can contribute to a better understanding of innovative capabilities of firms.

The Varieties of Capitalism (VoC) literature adopts also a relational view of the firm.[2] Engagement with others in the various spheres of the political economy is needed not only to get access to finance, to regulate wages and working conditions, and to guarantee the necessary skill level, but also to ensure access to technology. According to Hall and Soskice, effective coordination of those relations is considered the key to success.[3] They distinctly identify two modes of coordination. At one end of the spectrum (in LMEs), firms coordinate with other actors primarily through competitive markets, characterised by arms-length relations and formal contracting. 'At the other end stand CMEs where firms typically engage in more strategic interaction with trade unions, suppliers of finance, and other actors. Whether a firm coordinates its endeavors through market relations or strategic interaction is said to depend on the institutional setting'.[4]

Coordination of relations to acquire knowledge will therefore also vary. Hall and Soskice argue that in LMEs knowledge transfer will be accomplished primarily by licensing or taking on expert personnel. Firms in CMEs would work more closely together to exchange knowledge and technology and set up joined R&D projects. They also pose that in CMEs the government is more involved in investments in the knowledge infrastructure, while in LMEs the government is mostly absent.[5]

We argue that the relevant institutional setting for knowledge exchange is the knowledge infrastructure, which contains the constellation of actors and organisations established to develop and diffuse knowledge.

This brings us to the focal point of this chapter: an analysis of the knowledge infrastructure in the Netherlands from 1870 to the early 21st century. Leading are the following questions: How does the design of the knowledge infrastructure influence the transfer of knowledge? Does this change over time? And if so, how?

Starting with the VoC dichotomy between typical LME versus CME knowledge exchange mechanisms, we will focus on the question of whether the knowledge infrastructure stimulates knowledge exchange via licensing or formal contracting or by working together. However, to get a more thorough understanding of the working of the knowledge infrastructure, we should expand our analysis and explicitly integrate the accessibility of knowledge in our analysis.[6] For instance, the exclusivity is high when firms take a license or enter into a contract. When only members of a business interest organisation have access to the knowledge, the accessibility is also limited. But the knowledge reservoir can also be freely available for everyone interested. To gain an understanding of the role of the government vis-à-vis private and other stakeholders, we will pay attention to the character of the various knowledge organisations. Are they private, public, or a combination of the two?

This brings us to the dynamic part of our research question. The aim of this volume is to analyse how capitalism changes, why it changes, and how companies relate to those changes.[7] A starting point to link the historical question in this chapter to the VoC literature is the approach of Hall and Thelen. They distinguish three ways in which change can occur: by processes of reform, of defection, and of reinterpretation. Reform is 'at the initiative of the State, and its success depends crucially on the behavior of other agents, particularly firms'. Less common is their attention to the two other routes to institutional change. The term 'defection' is used 'for cases in which actors who have been following the practices prescribed by an institution stop doing so'. Hall and Thelen see 'reinterpretation' when 'actors associated with an institution gradually change their interpretation of its rules, and thus its practices, without defecting from or dismantling the formal institution itself'. They stress that 'in comparison with overt efforts to revise or abolish that institution, the process of reinterpretation shifts the existing practices in piecemeal fashion from below'.[8] We have used this perspective on institutional change as an analytical lens to study the changes in the knowledge infrastructure, striving to formulate conclusions over the most important agents of change and the three routes to change.

The analysis in this chapter will be presented chronologically, divided into three periods. In the first period from 1870 to around 1910, most knowledge came from foreign sources. Although still limited, the private knowledge institutes were most active in transferring knowledge, while a public knowledge infrastructure hardly existed. After 1910, the knowledge infrastructure started to expand, and a new patent law was passed. This occurred against a background in which scientifically grounded knowledge was increasingly valued. From 1970 onwards, the knowledge infrastructure changed considerably in character. In every period we will pay attention to the public as well as the private part of the knowledge infrastructure. In our conclusion we will come back to the most striking changes in the knowledge infrastructure and illustrate how those changes occurred. That will not only shed light on changes in the Dutch business system but also on the usefulness of the theoretical assumptions from Hall and Thelen.

FIRST SIGNS OF CHANGE (1870–1910)

In the 19th century, foreign knowledge was of prime importance for Dutch companies. It came in different ways. Via exhibitions the Dutch were informed of the latest developments and inventions. Dutch firms acquired knowledge and skills by recruiting foreign experts, taking out licenses on foreign products or processes, and by receiving training abroad.[9] At the turn of the century, the first signs of the expansion of the Dutch knowledge infrastructure became visible.

At the end of the 19th century, an increasing part of the workforce became schooled and had a *Dutch* certificate. This concerned lower, middle, as well as higher technical education. The number of students in technical education rose substantially, although the growth was not equal at all levels (see Appendix).[10] While for centuries most crafts were learned on the job, the 19th century saw the birth of more and more institutes for vocational training initiated by government, firms, and professionals. The basic technical schools offered practical and theoretical vocational training and were initially focused on building and metalwork, but increasingly also prepared students for industrial work.[11] Also the skills of the middle management had to be adjusted to industrialised production. For example, machinists were needed for operating steam engines. From 1878 onwards, they could be trained at the Training Facility for Engine Drivers (Kweekschool voor Machinisten) in Amsterdam. The founders came from various sectors using steam energy, like steam-shipping and sugar mills.[12] More intermediate technical schools were established, and the number of students increased (see Appendix).

Higher technical education was given at the Royal Military Academy (Koninklijke Militaire Academie) in Breda and the Royal Academy of Civil Engineers (Koninklijke Academie voor Burgerlijke Ingenieurs) in Delft, which became Polytechnic in 1863 and in 1904 Technical College (Technische Hogeschool). While in Breda military officers were trained, most engineers from Delft found work at the State Corps of Civil Engineers (Rijkswaterstaat). Government involvement in the teaching programmes was therefore not surprising. Towards the end of the 19th century, the focus broadened to industry-related studies like mechanical engineering and chemical technology. From 1905, students could also study electrical engineering. The broader orientation contributed to a growing number of students, which was not spectacular until 1900, but then accelerated. A lot of these engineers joined engineering societies, like the Royal Institute for Engineers (Koninklijk Instituut voor Ingenieurs, KIVI) that also organised lectures and published a general technical journal.[13] The growing numbers of engineers found their way into business.[14] From early 20th century, the increasing number of engineers, the growth of the engineering societies, and the growing percentage of engineers in the board rooms contributed to the growth of the knowledge infrastructure. Until 1905, the number of private and public institutes were limited, but not absent.

The Public Knowledge Infrastructure

At the end of the 19th century, the Dutch government became increasingly involved in working conditions, hygiene, and food safety, etc., which led to regulations. To support local, provincial, and national governments in performing their auditing tasks, inspection services were established by the national and local governments. To be able to examine food within the framework of the Food Safety Law (Warenwet), for instance, local and provincial agencies came into being, like in Rotterdam (1893).[15]

Until 1890, the government had only acted as customer of knowledge. With the support for an agricultural knowledge system, it took on another role and became responsible for public knowledge dissemination. The government acted in response to the agricultural crisis. Apart from the State Agricultural School (Rijkslandbouwschool) established in 1877, so-called experimental stations were founded where soil analyses, seed experiments, and research on issues such as soil fertility were done. An information service, instructors, and agricultural courses were meant to increase the application of new understandings in agricultural practice. Lower agricultural education received more subsidies. Initiatives from farmers and horticulturists were the essence of the further expansion of this system. Although they could freely make use of the knowledge system, farmers and horticulturists still relied to a large extent on their own knowledge-building and -acquiring activities for the development of new products and processes.[16] The design of the agricultural system with experimentation stations became a model for other public knowledge institutes that came into existence around 1910, such as the State Industrial Agency (Rijksnijverheidsdienst, RND). Public knowledge organisations aimed at knowledge diffusion for a large group of people, however, were limited to agriculture.

The Private Knowledge Infrastructure

In contrast to the public knowledge infrastructure, the private knowledge infrastructure was much more developed. Around 1900, the Netherlands embraced the first as well as the second Industrial Revolution. Industrialisation and mechanisation based on steam and coal and new key technologies, like electricity, the telephone, and the combustion engine, set new challenges for Dutch firms. To be able to apply new technologies properly or even to come up with new inventions, access to foreign knowledge alone was not enough. Firms needed an internal knowledge base. Knowledge could be acquired via books and periodicals. Entrepreneurs and engineers increasingly read the Dutch general technical journal, like the one published by the society of engineers. For specific engineering fields, like mechanical engineering, chemistry, and electrical engineering, international professional journals were more relevant.

Firms could also turn to independent commercial laboratories, like Boldingh en Van der Heide, who did sugar analyses. These commercial laboratories, which remained an important part of the Dutch private knowledge infrastructure until the 1920s, were established from the 1860s onwards. Increasing regulation and taxes had made more specifications about, for instance, the product content, more important. That stimulated the demand for physical and chemical analyses among trading companies and industry, health agencies, and governments.[17]

Also engineering firms were part of the private knowledge infrastructure. Their expertise lay in the field of development of production processes, constructions, and installations. They knew about the latest technology, machines, and equipment and could offer understanding of the conditions for, i.e. working with new equipment or building a new factory. They could give an overview of possible alternatives and calculate the various options. One of the first Dutch engineering firms, J. van Hasselt & De Koning, was established in 1881 by two young civil engineers and specialised in hydraulic projects.[18] Most engineering firms had a role as intermediary actor between firms (and governments) on the one hand and machine factories and construction workshops on the other, and formed an important link between knowledge sources and firms.

Besides hiring foreign technicians and engineers, studying or working abroad was another way to build a knowledge base. When education possibilities expanded, Dutch youngsters increasingly studied in the Netherlands. Problem solving became less 'trial-and-error' and more scientific grounded. Also experiments were done. This could lead to hiring more scientists and starting an industrial laboratory. An early example is the laboratory of the Netherlands Yeast and Spirit Factory (Nederlandsche Gist-en Spiritusfabriek, NSGF), founded in 1885. When the technologist from Delft engineering school and chemical expertise could solve the problem of the yeast's fluctuating quality, a microbiological research laboratory was formed, and a biologist with a PhD was hired. The research focused mainly on solving problems.[19] In the same year, Heineken, following the Danish brewer Carlsberg, established a laboratory to be able to improve the quality of its beer. The research efforts proved to be useful to improve the flavour and the shelf life.[20] Other early 20th-century Dutch companies followed, among which Royal Dutch Shell and Philips were the first to establish substantial research facilities.

In the interwar period, industrial research laboratories became an essential part of the private knowledge infrastructure. Also their role changed. Improving product quality and solving production problems had been the main task of the 19th-century industrial laboratories as well as of the laboratory of Royal Dutch Shell. The research efforts in Philips's industrial laboratory were also aiming to diversify and to build a patent position. While around 1880, German synthetic dyestuffs firms were the first to establish research laboratories, soon followed by German and American electrotechnical companies, Dutch companies were late with this kind of in-house technological knowledge development.[21]

The Dutch Patent Law

An important institutional factor that influenced knowledge transfer until 1912 was the abolishment of the patent law in 1869. The government, promoting a liberal market policy, had abolished the patent law hoping to increase the innovative performance of Dutch firms and to attract foreign firms. Without patent law Dutch firms could freely copy (foreign) inventions for the national market, although for export (international) patent filing would be necessary. Moreover, the general idea was that patent protection would stimulate monopoly positions for a few large companies and harm the large number of small firms in the Netherlands. Over time an increasing number of firms and other agents started to lobby for the reintroduction of a patent. Engineers, who wanted their inventions to be protected and rewarded and considered patent protection as a prerequisite for industrial progress, became increasingly influential within society. In the 1880s, the international patent situation was discussed internationally because American companies refused to attend the World Fair in Vienna in 1873 due to lack of patent protection. This led to the Treaty of Paris (1883) to protect industrial property, in which also the Netherlands, where in 1880 the Law on Factory and Trademarks was issued (*Wet op de Fabrieks-en Handelsmerken*), participated. Other countries, however, wanted to exclude the Netherlands from the treaty because no Dutch patent law existed. When Dutch factory and trademarks would no longer be protected, this would harm Dutch firms. From then onwards, the majority became convinced that a patent-free situation would actually harm the Dutch companies. In 1901, the Dutch government decided to install a new patent law, which was ready in 1910. From 1912 onwards, firms were able to file for a patent in the Netherlands to secure their inventions against infringements. Freely building on patented ideas from others was no longer possible.[22]

For SMEs producing for a local or regional market, it was more difficult to gain access to foreign knowledge. Sometimes equipment dealers enabled an apprenticeship in leading industrial clusters. For instance, Leicester and Nottingham, the centre of the British stocking industry, received a lot of youngsters from small Dutch stocking firms.[23] For most SMEs the activities of business interest associations were important. The local, regional, as well as national, associations often took a leading role in making (foreign) knowledge accessible for their members or even the whole sector. Butchers, tailors, carpenters, pharmacists, bakeries, and almost every shopkeeper joined a business interest association, the majority originated after 1880. Also industrialist formed associations. While local organisations acted more as 'guilds', trying to control mutual competition with price agreements and the formulation of quality standards, the national associations also lobbied the government. They also could see it as their task to supply their members with information, advice, and knowledge.[24]

THE EXPANSION OF THE KNOWLEDGE INFRASTRUCTURE (1910–1970)

From 1910 onwards, education expanded further. The number of technical students increased on all levels. (See Appendix) Gradually also the orientation was transformed—from basic technical training to elaborate technical schooling and from practice-oriented training to theory-oriented instruction.[25] This was closely related to the objectification of knowledge. Knowledge became less personal. To understand and use so-called codified knowledge recorded in books, articles, and technical drawings, formal education became more important. Although this trend started earlier, it increasingly had impact on education.

This went hand in hand with the increasing involvement of the national government, especially after the Technical Education Act was adopted in 1919. Legally obliged to subsidise the schools, the government wanted a say in the entry standards and content of the teaching programmes. In the 1930s, ministerial influence further increased with the consequence of more uniform and general intermediate technical training that was less focused on practice and more on theory. In 1957, the intermediate technical schools were changed into technical colleges (*HTS*). Higher technical education, concentrated in Delft, was expanded to Eindhoven in 1956 and to Enschede in 1961. Also new courses and departments were established, for which multinationals were sometimes responsible. Technical physics in Delft was established in 1929 thanks to the support of Philips and Royal Dutch Shell.[26]

The engineers increasingly found a job in business. In 1917, 13.5 per cent of the executives had an engineering grade from Delft. Alumni came also from general universities, like chemists. In 1918, about fifty general chemists had found a job in industry.[27] The education grade, however, varied substantially depending on the firm size and sector and could vary from attending an evening course to a university degree. In 1950, only 28 per cent of the entrepreneurs in medium and small companies had followed a kind of professional education. This was applicable for half of the electricians and butchers, while only 24 per cent of the grocers and 11 per cent of the greengrocers had professional training.[28]

The increasing number of educated employees and executives had an effect on the knowledge-acquiring possibilities of firms in various ways. A better-trained workforce facilitated the absorption of knowledge especially when knowledge became more formal. Engineers and scientists in the engineering departments and laboratories solved problems and came up with new ideas and inventions. This changed their position vis-à-vis foreign knowledge sources and facilitated issuing licenses and cross-licensing. The growing number of higher-educated executives stimulated a more scientific approach within the company, which enlarged their support for hiring higher-educated employees, investing in education, establishing in-house research facilities, or contributing to public knowledge institutes.

The Explosive Growth of the Public Knowledge Infrastructure

From 1910 onwards, the number of public knowledge institutes in the Netherlands increased substantially. In 1910, the State Industrial Agency (Rijksnijverheidsdienst, RND) was established as a state consultancy agency in line with the agricultural system. For advice and information, SMEs could appeal to so-called state industrial consultants. In 1910, the RND appointed its first, and soon two more consultants were hired. In 1913, also the State Industrial Laboratory was set up in Delft 'to gather technical data and address technical questions in order to support the state industrial consultants' that visited the companies. In the advisory board Delft professors were appointed.[29] Between 1919 and 1935, the RND received around 800 questions per year, after which it increased to 1,200 in 1939. In 1930, the Netherlands had 400,000 small firms. It's obvious that only a small proportion of the SMEs approached the RND, one out of four hundred, and in fact less because the requests also came from state organisations and larger firms. As is illustrated for 1930, the requests came from various sectors, although textile, metal, and food companies were overrepresented. (See Table 6.1.)

Most questions were technological, sometimes closely related to organisational issues or market possibilities. Until 1930, energy supply formed a key issue; while steam was often too expensive for small firms, they asked for advice in their choice between a gas and electric motor.[30]

While the advice of the RND to SMEs was free of charge, private consultants, especially those active in the energy sector were approached with the same kind of questions. To adjust the activities of the RND and the private consultants, the RND asked three consulting engineers to establish the

Table 6.1   Average firm size and requests for the State Industrial Agency from 1930 in various sectors

Firm type	Sector	Number of requests
Largest firms	Textile	69
	Paper	13
Around the median	Food	106
	Metal and shipbuilding	149
Smallest firms	Clothing and laundry	67
	Leather and rubber	43
Total requests		447

Sources: Gerwen and De Goey, *Ondernemers in Nederland,* Table 3.8; Annual Report State Industrial Agency 1930.

Association for Consulting Engineers (Orde van Nederlandsche Raadgevende Ingenieurs, ONRI). They would act as the RND's private counterparts in coming to agreements on the boundaries of each other's scope.[31]

During the first half of the 20th century, the number of business interest associations grew quickly, especially during the First World War and the economic depression of the 1930s. While in 1907, there existed 307 local and 35 national associations, after the war the numbers increased to 1,329 local and 337 national associations.[32] The growing number of business interest associations helped firms to meet changing requirements. One of their endeavours was to advise their members and to facilitate access to and dissemination and exchange of knowledge. To that purpose they organised (foreign) study trips, lectures, exhibitions, and courses; published relevant information in their journals; and took initiatives for joint research and sector-oriented knowledge institutes. To raise the quality of their products, business associations sometimes participated in standard setting and related activities.

The business interest associations were also responsible for the foundation of public knowledge institutes. The Organisation for Material Research (Organisatie van het Materiaalonderzoek) and the Experimental Station for the Laundry Industry (Proefstation voor de Waschindustrie), both begun in 1937, were both established by business interest associations.

The developments in the bakery sector can illustrate how efforts of business interest associations, the expansion of the knowledge infrastructure, and changes in legal environment interacted.[33] In reaction to the increasing state interference with food safety and quality, the bakery association pleaded for a research centre, where bakers could check their flour and yeast and customers the bread quality. This led to the establishment, in November 1909, of the Station for Milling and Baking (Station voor Maalderij en

Bakkerij). The existence of the Station for Milling and Baking was a decisive factor in the establishment of another knowledge institute in this sector. The increasing government involvement during World War I was accompanied by expansion of the activities of the association and the station. While the association made access to sources affordable, the Station helped bakeries to meet quality standards in war circumstances. Meanwhile the Station was asked to help the government to determine standards for wheat and to control four hundred milling companies. When supply decreased, the Station experimented with flour from rice, beans, corn, etc. The results were published in the association's journal. Public complaints about the bread quality remained. One of the Station's former teachers proposed to the minister of Agriculture, Industry, and Trade a training institute with bakery teachers because most bakers would lack the necessary knowledge and skills to bring the Station's advice into practice. The director of the Station successfully argued that a separate training institute wasn't preferable. The courses should be 'founded theoretically' and fall under the responsibility of the Station. A state subsidy was received to instruct ten teachers, who started in 1920. In five years almost 1,500 chief bakers followed a course. A decreasing craft-based attitude in which intangible knowledge was of prime importance made room for a more scientific one. This was a widely spread phenomenon.[34]

In these years the importance of science for trade and industry was more and more articulated, also by academics. In 1913, G. van Iterson Jr., professor in Delft, for example, took the initiative for the State Rubber Agency (Rijksrubberdienst). Good analyses were important for the rubber trade and industry. The research, among other things, into vulcanisation methods and latex applications, was located in the laboratory of van Iterson. The State Rubber Agency, the State Leather Agency (Rijkslederdienst) and, the State Fibre Agency (Rijksvezeldienst in 1919) fell under the Ministry of Trade and Industry, but they could act independently.[35]

The largest public knowledge organisation is TNO (Centrale Organisatie voor Toegepast Natuurwetenschappelijk Onderzoek [Central Organisation for Applied Scientific Research]). Its genesis goes back to World War I, when the Royal Netherlands Academy of Sciences pleaded to unite all existent 'scientific competence and experience' to solve the problem of scarcity. Finally, in 1932, TNO was founded. Subsidised by government, it felt under the Ministry of Education, Arts, and Sciences (Onderwijs, Kunsten en Wetenschappen, OK&W). By functioning as a 'mixed organisation' with representatives from business, government, and academia, the applied character of the organisation would be guaranteed. In fact TNO was based upon a linear perception of science; it should form a connection between science and practice. TNO's task to coordinate all the applied research of public knowledge organisations—which in fact was limited to those of the Ministry of Trade and Industry—led to a tug-of-war between TNO and the ministry, who was not eager to hand over its research agencies, like the Rubber

Institute and the State Leather Agency. That only happened during World War II on condition that ministerial representatives would become part of the board of the research institutes.[36]

The expansion of the public knowledge infrastructure with TNO was accompanied by a decline of knowledge transfer via market mechanisms. Access to knowledge was no longer exclusive because, according to the government, a subsidised TNO should serve the public interest. After the war, TNO grew substantially from 331 employees in 1946 to around 5,000 in 1970. It consisted of various research centres, around twenty-five in the 1960s. TNO maintained close relations with Dutch business. Of prime importance was the 'mixed organisation'. Firms and business interest associations were represented in the boards of the various TNO institutes. They contributed to the formulation generic research topics. Also so-called research associations, consisting of directors and managers, formulated research questions for TNO.[37] Although TNO sometimes received commissions from Shell and Philips, the relations with MNCs were not close. For most research questions, they had sufficient in-house knowledge. From the second decade of the century, most Dutch knowledge-intensive firms had established their own industrial laboratories.

The Private Knowledge Infrastructure: Expansion from the Inside

One of the most striking changes in the private knowledge infrastructure in this period was the birth of the industrial laboratories. While in 1900, there were only a handful of company laboratories, four decades later in almost every sector 'one could find companies . . . that structurally generated scientific and technological knowledge to improve or renew products and processes'.[38]

After the patent law was issued in 1910, commercialisation on illegal copied products was no longer an option, and firms had to invest in research capabilities. The electro-technical company Heemaf, which was accustomed to copying foreign products, developed a new engine in its own (small) research laboratory. In the Netherlands the number of patents increased substantially especially from the 1920s onwards.[39] The existence of a national patent law undoubtedly contributed to the increasing number of patents, especially in sectors where secrecy was difficult to keep. If (international) patent filing before 1912 was only necessary for products for foreign markets, it now became an essential step for all new products. Moreover, working on innovative products in a patent system increased the necessity to patent as many steps as possible. Also the existence of a patent office contributed to the increasing numbers of patents. The majority of the patents were filed by a select number of Dutch companies, large R&D intensive companies, which had started a research laboratory. The patent law, but also technological and commercial constraints, stimulated R&D investments.[40]

Forced by stiff competition from Standard Oil, Royal Dutch Shell needed to improve its product quality, for which it called upon a chemical-technologist from Delft. In 1906, he was hired full time, and a laboratory was established in Schiedam. In 1914, the laboratory moved to Amsterdam, after which the number of researchers grew substantially. With 1,350 employees, it was the largest laboratory in the Netherlands in 1940.[41] Philips—to be able to meet German competition—had started making the metal filament lamp and hired in 1908 a chemical technologist to know more about metals. Two years later, a chemical laboratory was founded. When in 1913 General Electric introduced the so-called half-watt lamp, Philips realised building up a good patent position would be crucial. In 1914, a physics laboratory, the NatLab, was founded. DSM, the coal company that expanded into chemicals, founded a research laboratory in 1938.[42]

The industrial research laboratories offered the growing number of Dutch university alumni ample job opportunities. In 1940, the NatLab had 516 employees, AKU 150, the Netherlands Yeast and Spirit Factory 90, and the central Laboratory of DSM 80. The laboratory of Unilever (in fact from the Unified Oilfactories Zwijndrecht, Vereenigde Oliefabrieken Zwijndrecht) had in 1937 only 30 employees.[43]

Especially after the Second World War, during the reconstruction and golden years of economic growth, the industrial laboratories were essential for the development of new products and processes. The inclusion of basic science, along more focused research, was considered important for devising future inventions. Another reason for the large investments in R&D, then, was the absence of some important research fields at the universities. For instance, solid-state physics and chemistry, physics and chemistry of synthetics, and catalysis.[44]

The growth pattern of the private knowledge infrastructure differed substantially from that of the public infrastructure. The multinationals took the initiative in the expansion of the private knowledge infrastructure that was characterised by the growth of the in-house research laboratories. The government was responsible for the various public knowledge institutes, together with individuals, societal agencies, business interest organisations, academics, and academic societies. The knowledge developed at the research laboratories was only for internal use. The output of the public knowledge institutes was mainly freely available, but sometimes it was 'for members only'. Part of the research was done on contract basis.

KNOWLEDGE INVESTMENTS DECLINE (1970S AND ONWARDS)

Industrial Research in Deep Water

After 1970, the role of industrial R&D changed. The confidence that fundamental research would automatically lead to marketable products declined, and R&D investments, especially in more fundamental research, decreased. The position of the industrial research laboratory became less self-evident. While in the 1950s and 1960s, they had been the initiators of most new products or processes, from the 1970s onwards, also other parts of the company took that function. The initiative for Philips's CD, for example, came from the business group Audio. They established a separate 'CD laboratory' where all the knowledge and expertise mainly from the NatLab was integrated.[45]

Philips's management became an advocate of a setup where the business departments initiated new products for which the central laboratory contributed the knowledge. R&D investments should lead to concrete products and processes by aiming at the commercial needs. An isolated position was not acceptable. This view, accompanied by other aspects like increasing competition and a worsening economic situation, led to budget cuts and reorganisations at most R&D intensive industries.[46] At the Central Laboratory of DSM, for example, between 1970 and 1985, the expenditure as percentage of total turnover diminished from more than 3.5 per cent to 1.7 per cent. Its personnel, which had been more than 1,500 in 1967 went to 1,100 in 1974. Until 1985, it never became more than 1,250.[47]

To stimulate more market-oriented research, R&D was restructured. Various measures were taken, like research coordinators, consulting committees, and conversion into a matrix or project organisation.[48] Shell rigorously dismantled the existing R&D organisation and established Shell Global Solution in 1995 and EP Technology a few years later. Both became commercial companies integrating research and technical service, charging market-conforming prices and offering their services to its affiliates and other firms.[49]

Changes in R&D strategy at the five large Dutch multinationals— sometimes accompanied by research investments abroad—contributed to a relative decline of their R&D investments in the total private investments. The majority of Dutch R&D investments had always come from large companies. In 1979, 80 per cent came from firms with more than 1,000 employees and 70 per cent from the Big Five, which number fell to 65 per cent in 1990 and to 53 per cent in 1999.[50] That drop was also due to the rise of other R&D intensive companies, like ASML (Advanced Semiconductor Materials Lithography) and NXP Semiconductors, which were both spinoffs of Philips. In 2011, ASML was, with 576 million Euro, the second largest R&D investor in the Netherlands after Philips. NXP Semiconductors was fifth, with 193 million Euro, after Shell and DSM.[51] Their high ranking and Philips's decrease in R&D investments are closely related, due to the process of disintegration. In the 1980s, most large integrated companies started to concentrate on their core business because of decreasing efficiency of internal supply and growing competition of specialised suppliers.

Philips started as early as the 1960s to outsource supply functions such as paper and cardboard manufacturing, later followed by more complex products. ASML had its origin in Philips. Its history illustrates that focusing on core business is not always the main argument for outsourcing. In the 1960s, Philips had started the in-house development of photolithographic machines for manufacturing integrated circuits to overcome production problems. When that became too expensive for internal supply only, Philips started to sell the machines externally. In 1982, IBM was the first customer. In 1984, ASM Lithography—later ASML—was founded. It was a joint venture between Philips and ASMI (Advanced Semiconductor Materials International) that since 1968 had made chip manufacturing equipment and brought experience and its customer network. Gradually Philips reduced its 50 per cent share to zero in 2004. A supplier-customer relation, where exchange of knowledge was crucial, remained.[52] Also with other firms, especially when vital supplies were outsourced, former interfirm knowledge transfer started to cross company borders. That could even lead to so-called co-makership relations with joint R&D endeavours.

In the 1970s, relations between R&D intensive firms and the public knowledge infrastructure also changed. Joint research programmes with universities and public knowledge institutes increased because the industrial laboratories had less financial funds and more need to offer short-term results. At the same time, governmental budgets for universities and public knowledge institutes decreased. For them, acquiring external money became an important lifeline and even a prerequisite on which they were evaluated.

Expansion of the Public Knowledge Infrastructure

The development of the public knowledge infrastructure saw on the one hand more public organisations with coordinating and subsidising roles and on the other diminishing funding for academic research and the existing public research institutes. The government invested less in R&D but increasingly wanted to have a greater say in the remaining expenditures. While public investments should serve society, another part of the explanation for the reduction lies in the economic situation. While during the 1970s, the export of natural gas backed the state finances, economising had become inevitable in the economic crisis of the early 1980s. Early 1970s total (private and public) R&D as percentage of GDP flattened at 2 per cent and declined slowly from then onwards, while public R&D varied between 0.85 per cent and 0.99 per cent until the early 1990s after it declined to around 0.65 per cent in the beginning of the 21st century.[53]

Universities were the first who felt the pain. From 1970 onwards, the state funding for academic research diminished and (technical) universities had to find additional funds. In addition to research grants from the Dutch Organisation for Pure Scientific Research (Nederlandse Organisatie voor Zuiver Wetenschappelijk Onderzoek, ZWO, since 1987 NWO) and the Society for Technical Science (Stichting Technische Wetenschappen, STW) contracts with industry became essential. For example, around 1980, the Ministry of

Education, Culture and Science financed 78 per cent of the capacity, which dropped to 40 per cent in 2004. The contribution of NWO and STW rose from around 10 per cent to 25 per cent. The percentage that was financed out of contract research for firms rose from 12 per cent to 35 per cent.[54] Especially at the technical universities, an increasing number of research projects were commissioned or joint projects with industrial researchers.[55]

This increasing state interference was rooted in a changing policy, which started in the early 1970s with the appointment of a minister for science policy. Science should serve the public interest. The innovation memorandum of 1979 focused on technology policy and innovation in business, and argued that science should contribute to innovation. Various programmes to stimulate innovation were set up, some to encourage cooperation between SMEs and public knowledge organisations and others for specific themes, like medical technology or information technology. The government launched more and more narrowly defined new subsidies and programmes. In the early 21st century, there were more than two hundred subsidy possibilities, all with programme committees, organisations, and consortia, for programming and dividing subsidies.[56]

The public knowledge infrastructure expanded with a growing number of enactments and supporting organisations and committees. Illustrative of the new approach are the research programmes and institutions in the energy sector. After the publication in 1972 of *Limits to Growth* by the Club of Rome and the first energy crisis in 1973, the Dutch government became concerned with the future energy supply. The call for research into sustainable energy rose, and the government asked the Reactor Centre Netherlands (Reactor Centrum Nederland, RCN) to broaden its research to other forms of energy. Subsequently the centre was renamed Energyresearch Centre Netherlands (Energieonderzoek Centrum Nederland, ECN). In the same year, 1976, a National Research Programme for Wind Energy (Nationaal Onderzoeksprogramma Windenergie, NOW) was established, followed by other national research programmes focusing on energy storage, solar energy, and coal. For every programme an expert committee had to formulate reference points and research themes. To lead the research programmes various organisations were established and placed under the umbrella of ECN. TNO also established an organisation to administer comparable research programmes focused on energy saving in the industry, building, and transport sectors. These various organisations later merged and became part of Senter-Novem (now Agentschap NL).[57]

The lowering of state revenues in the 1980s also hit the public knowledge institutes, such as ECN (former RCN) and TNO. The basic subsidies meant for generic research declined. In 1983, ECN, for example, had to cut back almost 20 per cent of its basic budget.[58] Apart from budget cuts, the relationship between public knowledge institutes and SMEs became a frequently discussed policy issue that continued into the 21st century. TNO, the largest public research organisation, was followed especially critically.

Its relationship with firms and business interest organisations changed considerably when the 'mixed form' of TNO was restructured in 1980. Only an advisory role remained. Moreover, TNO had to abandon the coordination of industrial research and focus on the market by offering contract research.[59] Research projects on the request of business interest organisations, who circulated the outcomes to their members or in the sector, could only be executed when paid for. Although TNO could serve SMEs via their business associations or contract research, the large R&D intensive companies and small high-tech companies became its main contract partners.[60]

From the 1970s onwards, the private and public knowledge infrastructure were confronted with decreasing funds and became more intertwined. The government, in contrast to the period before 1970, interfered more in the content. For the public knowledge institutes, contract research became more important, while delivering free knowledge became less important. Business interest associations still played an important role in disseminating research outcomes to their members, although more often generated by exclusive contracts with those public organisations.

THE DUTCH KNOWLEDGE INFRASTRUCTURE COMPARED WITH THE UNITED STATES

Focusing on the development of the knowledge infrastructure in the Netherlands—a CME according to Hall and Soskice—raises the question of whether this is unique to one country. Can the same mechanisms be observed in other countries with a comparable business system or even in a country with a LME? To answer these questions, we make a comparison with the knowledge infrastructure in the United States (labelled as a LME).

The Dutch knowledge infrastructure had a substantial number of LME characteristics in the period before 1910. Therefore, it is not surprising that there are various resemblances with the knowledge infrastructure in the United States. As in the Netherlands the involvement of the US federal government in the public knowledge infrastructure was limited. Both governments focused on the same kind of activities: higher education and agriculture. Besides a land-grant programme for state universities focusing on science and technology, the US federal government invested in locally based agricultural research organisations, the main purpose of which was the dissemination of knowledge and new discoveries.[61] The most important difference between the knowledge infrastructures of both countries was the larger number of industrial R&D laboratories in the United States. While around 1900 quality control and tests of raw materials and intermediate products were the main activities in the industrial laboratories in the Netherlands, R&D in US firms was aimed at diversification and expansion. Electro-technical and chemical companies in the United States had soon followed the example of German dyestuffs companies that were the first to start industrial research to improve existing and develop new products. In 1900, General Electric decided to follow the German example and start an in-house research facility.[62] Commercial and technological threats played a decisive role in starting research facilities. The American chemical company DuPont started R&D in 1902, and in 1903 in response to plans of its main customers, the army and navy, it began to produce explosives and gunpowder. Building an internal research laboratory and organising its activities and integrating it in the organisation, however, was not an easy task. The earlier practice of integrating inventions from independent inventors had to be adjusted to internal development and innovation.[63] There was one feature, the absence of a Dutch patent law, that was almost unique in this period. Switzerland was the only country that, from 1850 to 1907, also lacked a patent law.[64] The US patent system 'provided the first and true inventor of a device with an exclusive property right', and 'inventors had to be individuals'. Therefore obtaining patents on the markets was costly especially those from outside sources. The patent department of the American Bell Telephone company, for example, recommended in 1894 against purchasing most of the seventy-three patents from outside the company because the asking price was often thousands of dollars.[65] The growing international markets for patent protection illustrate that around 1900 not it was not only the Dutch knowledge infrastructure that was oriented towards international markets. This globalisation and resemblance of national knowledge infrastructure were interrelated developments.

An important feature of the Dutch knowledge infrastructure in the interwar period was the cooperation between private and public organisations resulting in 'mixed' knowledge organisations in which public as well as private actors participated. Some of these knowledge organisations were initiated by business interest associations. Although associations in the United States cooperated in R&D and educational projects, the federal government was less active, only in military R&D during the First World War.[66] If this endorses the assumption that in a LME the government involvement in the knowledge infrastructure is limited, this remains a question because in the United Kingdom (also labelled as a LME) the government had an active role.[67] Although the private knowledge infrastructure in the United States had also some CME characteristics, like cooperative R&D projects, knowledge exchange via the market, private funding, and exclusivity were dominant. The number as well as the size of private industrial laboratories grew. These R&D intensive firms, like chemical, electro-technical, and petroleum companies invested in their internal knowledge reservoir. R&D became more important when the US antitrust legislation made diversification by mergers and acquisition increasingly difficult. These industrial laboratories contributed to expansion by developing in-house inventions as well as acquiring external knowledge via patents or firms.[68]

After the Second World War, the US government got a more active role in the development of the knowledge infrastructure. This involvement, however, had another—more LME—characteristic than in the Netherlands. Of prime importance was the report from Vannevar Bush, entitled *Science: The Endless Frontier*. Bush had been director of the Office of Scientific Research and Development that had been established in 1941 to coordinate military research proposed to invest in more fundamental research. He argued that for the US military and technological advances, like radar, basic research from Europe had been of prime importance. A solid national knowledge base would be essential for further scientific and technical progress. He proposed to establish a National Research Foundation with a coordinating role between government departments, the military, universities, and industry. Moreover, federal funds should stimulate basic research in universities. The government decided only to take its financial role. The idea of a coordinating role was rejected.[69] This illustrates the more LME-like attitude of the US government that also delegated the research activities to universities instead of founding governmental research organisations. The public funding and public procurement that was stimulated by the concern for national security was positive for R&D of the US high-tech companies and affected the private knowledge infrastructure. The general attention for more fundamental research as well as the increase in academic efforts stimulated large industrial companies like DuPont, General Electric, and AT&T to expand their R&D, focusing more on scientific and fundamental research and taking a long-term perspective.[70]

In the period from the 1970s onwards, the knowledge infrastructure in the United States became more comparable with the Dutch. The large industrial research laboratories that had been dominant elements in the private knowledge infrastructure became less important. The period of strong faith in research came to an end. Firms cut their R&D budgets, especially on fundamental research. Market needs were playing a more directive role.[71] Like in the Netherlands, large diversified US firms started to focus on core tasks with disinvesting and outsourcing as a consequence. At the same time, the number of small high-tech firms increased due to upcoming sectors like ICT and biotechnology. An important difference between the United States and the Netherlands was the early expansion of venture capital since 1980 that contributed to the increase in start-ups in the United States.[72] The public knowledge infrastructure of both countries differed with regard to public funding, but converged in the direction of a more market-oriented public knowledge infrastructure. While in the United States, an explicit industrial or innovation policy was lacking, the federal government continued to support industrial R&D from the demand as well as supply side. The defence-related R&D investments and defence procurement continued and, at the end of the 20th century, also investments in health-related research increased substantially. These federal expenditures have stimulated the emergence of the US biotechnology sector.[73] Like in the Netherlands, knowledge transfer via the market relations gained in importance. During the 1980s, for example, private appropriation of government-sponsored research became acceptable, while initially the policy had been that results from public-funded research should be freely available. The Bahy-Dole Act of 1980 encouraged patenting by nonprofit organisations.[74] This convergence of these two knowledge infrastructures from two different countries—labelled as CME and LME—around 2000 is comparable to the picture of around 1900. Further research, however, is needed to prove if this conclusion also holds for knowledge infrastructures in other business systems.

CONCLUSION: CHANGES IN THE DUTCH KNOWLEDGE INFRASTRUCTURE

In the period from 1870 to the early 21st century, the Dutch knowledge infrastructure expanded enormously and made firms less dependent on foreign knowledge sources. Because knowledge exchange is in nature international in character, firms never focus on the national knowledge infrastructure alone, regardless of its strength. This is even less the case in a small country like the Netherlands. Nevertheless, the number of national knowledge institutes, private as well as public, had increased considerably during the 20th century.

From 1870 to 1910, the development of the private knowledge infrastructure differed from that of the public knowledge infrastructure. There were more private than public knowledge organisations. The main features were limited government involvement, the dominance of knowledge transfer via market contracts, and the absence of a patent law. The first two aspects are—in terms of Hall and Soskice—illustrative for a more liberal market economy. The legal environment, however, made licenses less important.

Seen in the light of the VoC approach, the knowledge infrastructure in the period from 1910 to 1970 gives a more nuanced picture. The increasing number of new public knowledge institutes was initiated by a variation of stakeholders, firms, and business interest associations, as well as the government. They often also contributed financially and/or were represented in the board of the new knowledge institutes. The public institutes were oriented towards a large part of Dutch business, including SMEs. Only contacts with the large R&D intensive companies were scarce. As a consequence of the 'mixed character' of the public knowledge institutes, part of the knowledge was exclusive—only available for, for example, association members. This started to change after World War II when more knowledge became publicly available, especially at TNO. During the whole period, firms were also able to get exclusive access to TNO knowledge by commissioned research. In the private knowledge infrastructure commercial laboratories disappeared, and R&D intensive firms, mainly the large multinationals, started their own research laboratories. After World War II, private R&D expanded enormously, and that knowledge was exclusive in character. For the R&D intensive firms, public knowledge institutes were less needed than for other parts of the economy.

To label the knowledge infrastructure in the period 1910–1970, we should make a distinction between the private and the public knowledge infrastructure. During the whole period, the LME features were dominant in the private knowledge infrastructure. For the industrial R&D laboratories licenses and market contracts were of prime importance, and the secrecy of most developments contributed to the exclusiveness of knowledge. R&D cooperation between these laboratories was uncommon. The public infrastructure was a combination of LME and CME characteristics: private as well as public funding, cooperation between various stakeholders to guide research as well as research contracts. After World War II, when the government involvement in the public knowledge infrastructure increased, it became more CME-like. While cooperation that is labelled as characteristic of CMEs could lead to limited access to knowledge, government involvement led to an increase in freely available knowledge.

From 1970 onwards, the character of the public and private knowledge infrastructure changed considerably. For public knowledge institutes, private contracts became increasingly important. They became more oriented towards the (large) R&D intensive companies, while government required that they should serve SMEs. In the private knowledge infrastructure, the importance of the industrial laboratories diminished and the decreasing size led to more external cooperation, stimulated by the mantra of open innovation. Since the end of the 20th century, the knowledge infrastructure is subject to returning changes that are closely related to the versatile technological and innovation policy. Due to the increasing importance of the market in the knowledge infrastructure in this period, it can be labelled as more LME-like. This, however, does not mean that there is no government involvement. On the contrary, its guidance only increased.

The major driving forces behind these changes varied over the course of time. The expansion of the education system had a large impact. The influx of engineers in business and society and the increasing importance attached to scientific knowledge contributed considerably to the expansion of the public and private knowledge infrastructure from 1910 onwards. After 1910, business interest organisations were important initiators of the public knowledge institutes. The role of the government increased during the century. Before 1970, the government mostly supported plans initiated by others; later it launched more initiatives. The private knowledge infrastructure was, of course, mainly initiated by entrepreneurs or private firms.

These initiators of change bring us back to Hall and Thelen's conclusions with regards to change. We can add that with regard to the development of the knowledge infrastructure, alongside firms and the government, also other actors are important, like academics, business interest associations, and the knowledge institutes themselves. The observation that also the business interest associations became important drivers of change illustrates that organisations that are typical features of a coordinated market economy contributed to the development of the knowledge infrastructure. When important features of the political economy are themselves important initiators of change, this raises the question of whether CMEs also change in another way than do LMEs.

Another assumption is that changes in one sphere of the economy are related to changes in other spheres of the economy. This is visible in the development of the Dutch knowledge infrastructure. Initiatives for new institutes were related to a more educated workforce, and the growth of business interest organisations led to new knowledge institutes. Especially two of the mechanisms of change from Hall and Thelen were visible: reform and reinterpretation. Reform, however, was the more obvious, although not only the government but also other actors played a role. More important than legal reform was reform of informal institutions. How people judged the relevance of (the type of) knowledge and knowledge sources. Reinterpretation was only visible in a few circumstances, shortly after new organisations were established. Defection was absent. This is not surprising because Hall and Thelen's mechanisms are more suitable for changes in more legally determined labour relations than for relations to acquire knowledge.

We have illustrated that the strength of a national public knowledge infrastructure increases firms' knowledge-building opportunities but also that their freedom to acquire knowledge from private and foreign sources is unlimited. The expectations of government investments in public knowledge institutes should therefore not be overestimated.

Appendix

Table 6.2   Number of students in technical daytime education

	Junior technical schools, craft schools	Extended junior technical schools or extended craft schools	Intermediate technical schools (after 1957, technical colleges)	Polytechnics (after 1905, technical universities)	Total	Evening or part-time courses
1870	422		175	171	768	2,692
1875	803		350	263	1,416	6,506
1880	757		700	224	1,681	6,625
1885	718		1,050	319	2,087	6,265
1890	1,145		1,400	255	2,800	7,116
1895	2,543		1,200	420	4,163	10,050
1900	3,218		1,245	784	5,247	13,772
1905	4,902		2,434	1,123	8,459	17,327

(Continued)

Table 6.2   (*Continued*)

	Junior technical schools, craft schools	Extended junior technical schools or extended craft schools	Intermediate technical schools (after 1957, technical colleges)	Polytechnics (after 1905, technical universities)	Total	Evening or part-time courses
1910	6,924		2,592	1,179	10,695	22,328
1915	10,506		3,496	1,371	15,373	25,171
1920	11,808		3,213	2,393	17,414	30,292
1925	17,791		2,511	1,675	21,977	34,273
1930	20,940		3,268	1,743	25,951	39,928
1935	29,699		3,188	1,842	34,729	33,238
1938	31,143		4,105	1,838	37,086	43,501
1945	36,722	600	7,442	4,072	48,836	31,280
1950	52,995	1,374	9,505	5,615	69,489	61,015
1955	63,693	3,636	11,003	5,062	83,394	67,985
1960	111,703	9,945	12,543	7,916	142,107	83,733
1964	129,297	16,394	15,082	9,803	170,576	103,338

Source: Baggen, Faber, and Homburg, 'The rise of a knowledge society', 277.

NOTES

1. Davids et al., 'Importance of networking activity', 184–185; Nonaka and Takeuchi, *Knowledge-Creating Company*.
2. See also chapter 1 in this volume.
3. Hall and Soskice, *Varieties of Capitalism*, 6–7, 18.
4. Hall and Gingerich, 'Varieties of capitalism'; Hall and Soskice, *Varieties of Capitalism*.
5. Hall and Soskice, *Varieties of Capitalism*, 48.
6. We thank Erik Nijhof for his suggestion to highlight this aspect.
7. See chapter 1 in this volume.
8. Hall and Thelen, 'Institutional change'; Streeck and Thelen, *Beyond Continuity*, 31.
9. Baggen, Faber, and Homburg, 'Knowledge society', 282; Faber, *Kennisverwerking*.
10. Baggen, Faber, and Homburg, 'Knowledge society', 256–257, 277–278.
11. Davids, Lintsen, and Van Rooij, *Innovatie en kennisinfrastructuur*.
12. Davids, Lintsen, and Van Rooij, *Innovatie en kennisinfrastructuur*, 37; Baggen, Faber, and Homburg, 'Knowledge society' 256–257.
13. Lintsen, *Ingenieur van beroep*.

14. Baggen, Faber, and Homburg, 'Knowledge society', 277; Davids, Lintsen, and Van Rooij, *Innovatie en kennisinfrastructuur*, 40–43; Van Hooff, *In het rijk van de Nederlandse vulcanus*, 117; Lintsen, *Ingenieur van beroep*, 55.
15. Davids, Lintsen, and Van Rooij, *Innovatie en kennisinfrastructuur*, 52.
16. Baggen, Faber, and Homburg, 'Knowledge society', 298; Davids, Lintsen, and Van Rooij, *Innovatie en kennisinfrastructuur*, 26.
17. Davids, Lintsen, and Van Rooij, *Innovatie en kennisinfrastructuur*, 45.
18. Davids, Lintsen, and Van Rooij, *Innovatie en kennisinfrastructuur*, 57.
19. Baggen, Faber, and Homburg, 'Knowledge society', 298; Homburg, *Speuren op de tast*.
20. Davids, Lintsen, and Van Rooij, *Innovatie en kennisinfrastructuur*, 50; Sluyterman and Bouwens, *Brewery, Brand and Family*, 89–92.
21. Baggen, Faber, and Homburg, 'Knowledge society', 283–285.
22. Davids, Lintsen, and Van Rooij, *Innovatie en kennisinfrastructuur*, 49; Gerzon, *Nederland, een volk van struikrovers?*; Sluyterman, *Dutch Enterprise*, 56–60.
23. Davids, Lintsen, and Van Rooij, *Innovatie en kennisinfrastructuur*, 90, 147.
24. Bouwens and Dankers, *Tussen concurrentie en concentratie*, 26–27; Davids, Lintsen, and Van Rooij, *Innovatie en kennisinfrastructuur*, 55.
25. Baggen, Faber, and Homburg, 'Knowledge society', 256–257.
26. Baggen, Faber, and Homburg, 'Knowledge society', 295.
27. Baggen, Faber, and Homburg, 'Knowledge society', 277; Davids, Lintsen, and Van Rooij, *Innovatie en kennisinfrastructuur*, 39–40; Van Hooff, *Rijk van de vulcanus*, 117.
28. Davids, Lintsen, and Van Rooij, *Innovatie en kennisinfrastructuur*, 85.
29. Davids, Lintsen, and Van Rooij, *Innovatie en kennisinfrastructuur*, 58–59.
30. Davids, Lintsen, and Van Rooij, *Innovatie en kennisinfrastructuur*, 79–81.
31. Tjong, 'De Rijksnijverheidsdienst'.
32. See also chapter 5 in this volume.
33. Tjong Tjin Tai, Davids, and Lintsen, 'Hoe moderniseerden bakkers'.
34. Davids, Lintsen, and Van Rooij, *Innovatie en kennisinfrastructuur*, 58; Tjong Tjin Tai, Davids, and Lintsen, 'Hoe moderniseerden bakkers'.
35. Davids, Lintsen, and Van Rooij, *Innovatie en kennisinfrastructuur*, 100–101; Lintsen, ed., *Tachtig jaar TNO*.
36. Davids, Lintsen, and Van Rooij, *Innovatie en kennisinfrastructuur*, 100–101; Lintsen, ed., *Tachtig jaar TNO*, 20–31.
37. Davids, Lintsen, and Van Rooij, *Innovatie en kennisinfrastructuur*, 122–123.
38. Baggen, Faber, and Homburg, 'Knowledge society', 284–286.
39. See Figure 8.4 in chapter 8 in this volume.
40. Baggen, Faber, and Homburg, 'Knowledge society'; Davids, Lintsen, and Van Rooij, *Innovaties en kennisinfrastructuur*; Sluyterman, *Dutch Enterprise*, 59–60.
41. Homburg, *Speuren op de tast*, 22.
42. Davids, Lintsen, and Van Rooij, *Innovatie en kennisinfrastructuur*, 127; Homburg, *Speuren op de tast*; Van Rooij, *The Company*.
43. Homburg, *Speuren op de tast*, 22.
44. Davids, Lintsen, and Van Rooij, *Innovatie en kennisinfrastructuur*, 135.
45. Davids, Lintsen, and Van Rooij, *Innovatie en kennisinfrastructuur*, 170–71; Van Rooij, 137.
46. Davids, Lintsen, and Van Rooij, *Innovaties en kennisinfrastructuur*, 171; De Vries, *80 Years of Research*.
47. Davids, Lintsen, and Van Rooij, *Innovaties en kennisinfrastructuur*, 171; Lintsen, ed., *Made in Holland*, 311; Van Rooij, *The Company*, 145, Graph A1, 281, Graph A2, 282; Sluyterman, *Dutch Enterprise*, 160.
48. Davids, Lintsen, and Van Rooij, *Innovaties en kennisinfrastructuur*, 172.

49. Davids, Lintsen, and Van Rooij, *Innovaties en kennisinfrastructuur*, 172; Sluyterman, *Keeping Competitive*, 431–432.
50. Commissie voor Ontwikkelingsproblematiek van Bedrijven, 38; Davids, Lintsen, and Van Rooij, *Innovaties en kennisinfrastructuur*, 174–175.
51. Davids, Lintsen, and Van Rooij, *Innovaties en kennisinfrastructuur*, 167 and Table 5.2, 175.
52. See http://www.newscenter.philips.com/nl_nl/standard/about/news/philips magazine/archive/december2006/article-15933.wpd, accessed 7-10-2013; http://www.philipsmuseumeindhoven.nl/phe/products/transistor.htm, accessed 7-10-2013.
53. As is illustrated in Figure 8.3 in chapter 8 in this volume.
54. Davids, Lintsen, and Van Rooij, *Innovaties en kennisinfrastructuur*, 178.
55. Davids, Lintsen, and Van Rooij, *Innovaties en kennisinfrastructuur*, 178.
56. Davids, Lintsen, and Van Rooij, *Innovaties en kennisinfrastructuur*, 178–179.
57. Verbong, Berkers, and Taanman, *Op weg naar de markt*.
58. The dependence on state funds, however, differed between the institutes. At ECN, for example, in 1986, the public subsidy formed 46 per cent of the revenues; the incomes from state contracts formed the largest part for the NLR, WL, and GD. MARIN, for which the private sector had been important from the start, received most of its income from firms, mostly international. Commissie voor Ontwikkelingsproblematiek van Bedrijven (COB/SER), Grote technologische instituten en kleinere ondernemingen).
59. Davids, Lintsen, and Van Rooij, *Innovaties en kennisinfrastructuur*, 178, 183–185.
60. Davids, Lintsen, and Van Rooij, *Innovaties en kennisinfrastructuur*, 178, 183–185.
61. Mowery and Rosenberg, 'The U.S. national innovation system', 37.
62. Boersma, *Inventing Structures*, 185–198.
63. Van Rooij, *The Company*; Hounshell, 'The evolution', 13–84; Mowery and Rosenberg, 'The U.S. national innovation system', 29–75; Lamoreaux and Sokoloff, 'Inventors'.
64. Moser, 'How Do Patent Laws Influence Innovation?'
65. Almost all of the twelve patents from its employees were filed, 'not apparently because the patent department found the ideas particularly valuable, but for moral reasons and because the cost of obtaining patents in this way was low (typically the company paid bonuses of $50 to employees whose inventions it patented)'. Lamoreaux and Sokoloff, 'Inventors', 19–60, 41.
66. Van Gerwen and De Goey, *Ondernemen in Nederland*, 245; Scranton, *Endless Novelty*.
67. Lintsen, ed., *Tachtig jaar TNO*, 37.
68. Bruland and Mowery, 'Innovation through time', 349–379; Van Rooij, *The Company*.
69. Bush, *Science: The Endless Frontier*.
70. Bruland and Mowery, 'Innovation through time', 349–379.
71. Van Rooij, *The Company*, 137.
72. Chesbrough, *Open Innovation*, 37–38.
73. Bruland and Mowery, 'Innovation through time', 349–379, 372.
74. Walsh and Le Roux, 'Contingency in innovation', 1307–1327.

REFERENCES

Baggen, Peter, Jasper Faber, and Ernst Homburg, 'The rise of a knowledge society', in: Johan Schot, Harry Lintsen, and Arie Rip, eds., *Technology and the Making of the Netherlands. The Age of Contested Modernization, 1890–1970* (Zuthpen: MIT/Walburg, 2010) 253–323.

Boersma, Kees, *Inventing Structures for Industrial Research. A History of the Philips Nat.Lab. 1914–1946.* (Amsterdam: Aksant, 2002).

Bouwens, Bram, and Joost Dankers. *Tussen concurrentie en concentratie. Belangenorganisaties, kartels, fusies en overnames* (Amsterdam: Boom, 2012).

Bruland, K. and D.C. Mowery, 'Innovation through time', in: J. Fagerberg, D.C. Mowery, and R.R. Nelson, eds., *Oxford Handbook of Innovation* (Oxford: Oxford University Press, 2004) 349–379.

Bush, Vannevar, 'Science—The Endless Frontier', *Transactions of the Kansas Academy of Science (1903–)*, 48, 3 (December 1945): 231–264.

Chesbrough, Henry, *Open Innovation. The New Imperative for Creating and Profiting from Technology* (Boston: Harvard Business School Publishing, 2003).

Commissie voor Ontwikkelingsproblematiek van Bedrijven (COB/SER), Grote technologische instituten en kleinere ondernemingen. Analyse naar de relatie tussen grote technologische onderzoekinstituten en middelgrote en kleine bedrijven uitgevoerd door Ikon Beleidskonsulenten B.V. 1987.

Davids, Mila, Eric Berkers, Harry Lintsen, Arjan van Rooij, and Frank Veraart, 'The importance of networking activity. Innovation and networks in The Netherlands', in: Paloma Fernandez Perez and Mary B. Rose, eds., *Innovation and Entrepreneurial Networks in Europe* (New York: Routledge, 2010) 184–204.

Davids, Mila, Harry Lintsen, and Arjan van Rooij, *Innovatie en kennisinfrastructuur. Vele wegen naar vernieuwing* (Amsterdam: Boom, 2013).

Faber, Jasper, *Kennisverwerving in de Nederlandse industrie 1870–1970* (Amsterdam: Aksant, 2001).

Gerwen, Jacques van, and Ferry de Goey, *Ondernemers in Nederland: Variaties in ondernemen* (Amsterdam: Boom, 2008).

Gerzon, F., *Nederland, een volk van struikrovers? De herinvoering van de Nederlandse octrooiwet (1869–1912)* (Den Haag: Orde van Octrooigemachtigden, 1986).

Hall, P.A., and D.W. Gingerich. 'Varieties of Capitalism and Institutional Complementarities in the Macroeconomy: An Empirical Analysis. Discussion paper 04/5, Cologne, Germany, Max Planck Institute for the Study of Societies (2004).

Hall, P., and D. Soskice, *Varieties of Capitalism: The Institutional Foundations of Comparative Advantage* (Oxford: Oxford University Press, 2001).

Hall, P.A., and Thelen, K., 'Institutional change in varieties of capitalism', *Socio-Economic Review*, 7 (2009): 7–34.

Homburg, Ernst, *Speuren op de tast. Een historische kijk op industriële en universitaire research* (Intreerede. Maastricht: Universiteit Maastricht, 2003).

Hooff, W.H.P.M van, *In het rijk van de Nederlandse vulcanus. De Nederlandse machinenijverheid 1825–1914* (Amsterdam: NEHA, 1990).

Hounshell, David A., 'The evolution of industrial research in the United States', in: R.S. Rosenbloom and W.J. Spencer, eds., *Engines of Innovation. U.S. Industrial Research at the End of an Era* (Boston: Harvard Business School Press, 1996) 13–84.

Lamoreaux, Naomi R. and Kenneth L. Sokoloff, 'Inventors, firms, and the market for technology in the late nineteenth and early twentieth centuries', in: Naomi R. Lamoreaux, Daniel M.G. Raff, and Peter Temin, eds., *Learning by Doing in Markets, Firms, and Countries* (Chicago and London: The University of Chicago Press, 1999) 19–60.

Lintsen, Harry, *Ingenieur van beroep. Historie, Praktijk, macht en opvattingen van ingenieurs in Nederland* (Den Haag: Ingenieurspers, 1985).

Lintsen, Harry, ed., *Made in Holland. Een techniekgeschiedenis van Nederland [1800–2000]* (Zutphen: Walburg Pers, 2005).

Lintsen, Harry, ed., *Tachtig jaar TNO, 1932–2012* (Delft: TNO/SHT, 2012).

Moser, Petra, 'How Do Patent Laws Influence Innovation? Evidence from Nineteenth-Century World Fairs', NBER working paper series (August 2003).

Mowery, David C. and Nathan Rosenberg, 'The U.S. national innovation system', in: Richard R. Nelson, ed., *National Innovation Systems. A Comparative Analysis* (New York and Oxford: Oxford University Press, 1993) 29–75.

Nonaka, I., and H. Takeuchi, *The Knowledge-Creating Company: How Japanese Companies Create the Dynamics of Innovation* (Oxford: Oxford University Press, 1995).

Rooij, Arjan van, *The Company That Changed Itself. R&D and the Transformations of DSM* (Amsterdam: Amsterdam University Press, 2007).

Scranton, Philip, *Endless Novelty. Specialty Production and American Industrialization, 1865–1925* (New Jersey: Princeton University Press, 1997).

Sluyterman, Keetie E., *Dutch Enterprise in the Twentieth Century. Business Strategies in a Small Open Economy* (London: Routledge, 2005).

Sluyterman, Keetie, *Keeping Competitive at Turbulent Markets, 1973–2007, a History of Royal Dutch Shell, volume 3* (Oxford: Oxford University Press, 2007).

Sluyterman, Keetie and Bram Bouwens, *Brewery, Brand and Family: 150 Years of Heineken* (Amsterdam: Boom, 2014).

Streeck, Wolfgang, and Kathleen Thelen, *Beyond Continuity: Institutional Change in Advanced Political Economies* (Oxford: Oxford University Press, 2005).

Tjong, Sue-Yen. 'De Rijksnijverheidsdienst in historisch perspectief'. Working document, Society of the History of Technology (2012).

Tjong Tjin Tai, S.Y.E., Davids, M., and Lintsen, H., 'Hoe moderniseerden bakkers aan het begin van de twintigste eeuw? De betekenis van de Nederlandse Bakkersbond en het Station voor Maalderij en Bakkerij', *Tijdschrift voor Sociale en Economische Geschiedenis*, 10, 3 (2013): 55–79.

Verbong, G, E. Berkers, and M. Taanman, *Op weg naar de markt. De geschiedenis van ECN 1976–2001* (Petten: ECN, 2001).

Vries, M. de, *80 Years of Research at the Philips Natuurkundig Laboratorium (1914–1994)*. (Amsterdam: Pallas Publications, 2005).

Walsh, Vivien and Le Roux, Muriel, 'Contingency in innovation and the role of national systems: Taxol and taxotere in the USA and France', *Research Policy*, 33 (2004): 1307–1327.

7 Multinationals as Agents of Change

Keetie Sluyterman and Ben Wubs

INTRODUCTION

In the introduction to this volume it was argued that national business systems differ between countries but are not static. They change over time, though that does not mean all systems converge to one point. This chapter analyses the role of multinational companies in supporting or changing national business systems. In the Varieties of Capitalism literature the role of multinational companies is perceived in different ways. In theory companies working in different institutional environments would be the logical instruments (intermediaries) in bringing countries and their institutions closer together. But is this indeed the role multinationals played? We addressed this question before on the basis of two multinationals (Royal Dutch Shell and the Dutch subsidiary of Sara Lee), but in this chapter we delve deeper into this issue and have included more companies.[1]

Multinational companies support globalisation of markets through internalising both production and services, but what is their influence on national business systems? In 2001, Glenn Morgan assumed that firms crossing institutional and national divides would not converge towards one single model of the 'global firm', but would continue to show diversity and divergence.[2] In order to have any impact on the national business systems of host or home country, multinationals would first have to develop strong global capabilities and organisational structure. Whitley argued that this would be possible in theory, but unlikely to happen in reality. Multinational companies from distinctive and cohesive business systems, such as the German or Japanese system, tend to seek collaboration abroad with companies from their own country, and as a consequence their interaction with the host country will be limited. On the other hand, companies from countries with arm's length coordination such as the United States will manage their overseas operations in the same arm's length way, limiting themselves to financial steering, and as a consequence have also little impact on the host economy, again according to Whitley. Following his arguments, in either case, the multinationals may become organisationally more complex, but are unlikely to develop new global institutions that subsequently will contribute to the change of national business systems.[3]

Eight years later, in 2009, Glenn Morgan returned to the question of whether multinationals reduce or increase diversity in national business systems. He wanted to move away from the convergence/divergence debate by focusing on the diversity within national business systems. Do multinationals create more diversity within national systems, do they reduce diversity, or do they have relatively little impact on diversity within the national systems? He came to the conclusion that the impact of multinational companies depended on the type of multinational and on the existing model of capitalism. In coordinated market economies such as Germany and the Scandinavian countries and in liberal market economies such as the United States, he expected more diversity as a consequence of multinational activity. In business systems in which the state and big business worked so closely together as in Japan, he expected less diversity but also less impact from multinationals. In the developmental states multinationals would have a larger impact and would therefore create more diversity. In most cases, therefore, multinationals would increase national diversity.[4] Once notion of diversity and change in capitalist systems is accepted, the question arises as to how change is created and who the relevant actors might be. Colin Crouch introduced the concept of the 'institutional entrepreneur', who departs from the familiar path by recombining exiting elements in a new way.[5] It is interesting to find out whether perhaps managers of multinationals acted as such 'institutional entrepreneurs'.

One aspect of this increasing diversity has caused particular concern in the Netherlands: the rising inequality in income and increased insecurity about jobs. While some of the senior executives pocketed large incomes and bonuses, for many others incomes remained stable and insecurity increased. Leo McCann, John Hassard, and Jonathan Morris compared the position of middle managers in five large companies in the United States, United Kingdom, and Japan in recent years. They concluded that in all three countries middle management became more skilled and accepted higher levels of responsibility and a larger span of control. As a consequence they faced an increased workload and greater work intensity. At the same time, their career expectations became less secure. These developments took place in both coordinated and liberal market economies, and the authors linked these to the growing complexities and interconnections of contemporary capitalism.[6]

In analysing developments during the 20th century, it is important to keep in mind that periods of globalisation and deglobalisation alternated. We use the term 'globalisation' in the way economists tend to interpret it, as a process in which commodity, labour, and capital markets as well as consumer markets and technology become integrated on a global scale.[7] The 19th century saw the rise of the first 'golden age of globalization', as Findlay and O'Rourke term it. They explain it as the culmination of the Industrial

Revolution, which brought technologies to speed up trade and increase the economic interaction between all the world's regions. Though at the end of the 19th century, they see the first signs of a backlash against globalisation in the form of tariffs and measures against immigration; these measures did not yet impact on the rapid growth of world trade and the integration of commodity markets.[8] Equally buoying were the capital markets, according to Obstfeld and Taylor. As more and more countries adopted the gold standard, a flourishing global capital market developed with London as its undisputed centre. No protectionist measures hindered the movement of capital from country to country.[9]

The First World War brought this global economic integration to an abrupt end. The attempt to recreate the prewar globalisation in the 1920s failed because of the disruptive consequence of the Depression of the 1930s and the subsequent Second World War. Protectionist trade measures abounded, and financial markets became closely regulated. While international trade between the OECD countries resumed after the Second World War, the world economy as a whole showed further disintegration as a consequence of the Cold War and the process of decolonisation. This was true for trade and even more for capital markets. Seeing unregulated capital markets as the cause of the 1930s Depression, governments restrained private capital movements.

The 1970s formed again a turning point. After the introduction of floating exchange rates in the industrial countries, governments reduced or lifted capital account restrictions. In the 1970s and 1980s, Latin America, Asia, and Africa started to open up to trade and investment from the rest of the world, and during the 1990s, this process accelerated. The 1990s ratio of world trade to GDP became higher than ever before, and the same was true for the ratio of foreign direct investment to GDP. A second age of globalisation had materialised.[10] In this chapter we study the impact of multinational enterprises on the Dutch business system during the 20th century, while also taking on board the different phases of globalisation.

For a country with an open economy such as the Netherlands the study of multinational companies in relation to its national business system is particular relevant. For much of the 20th century, the Netherlands belonged to the world's top foreign direct investors.[11] In rankings the United States and the United Kingdom always came first, but in the mid-20th century, the Netherlands followed these countries closely, ahead of most other European countries, and in other periods it easily belonged in the top five in the world (see Table 7.1). In 1938, the Netherlands had about 10 per cent of all outward stock of FDI in the world. Although the Dutch share in world FDI decreased in due course by 2005, it still had 6 per cent of the world outward stock, close to the figures of the largest economies in Europe in the 2000s. However, measured as a percentage of GDP the Dutch figures were by far the highest in the world during the greater part of the 20th century.

Table 7.1 Outward stock FDI by major home countries in 1938, 1967, 1973, 1980, 1990, 2000, and 2005 in percentages of total world FDI, and FDI as percentage of GDP

	1938 % of world	% of GDP	1967 % of world	% of GDP	1973 % of world	% of GDP	1980 % of world	% of GDP	1990 % of world	% of GDP	2000 % of world	% of GDP	2005 % of world	% of GDP
United Kingdom	40		14	14.5	7.5	9.1	15	15.0	12.8	23.2	13.9	62.4	11.6	56.2
United States	28		50	7.1	48.0	7.7	40	8.1	24.0	7.5	20.3	13.5	19.2	16.4
(West) Germany	1		3	1.6	5.6	3.4	8	4.7	8.5	9.1	8.4	29.0	9.1	34.6
France	9		5	7.0	4.2	3.8	4	3.6	6.1	9.0	6.9	33.5	8.0	40.5
Netherlands	10		10	33.1	7.5	25.8	8	24.5	6.0	36.3	4.7	82.4	6.0	102.6
Belgium and Luxembourg	n.a.		n.a.	n.a.	n.a.	n.a.	1.1	4.9	2.3	19.4	2.8	72.5	3.6	103.8
Japan	n.a.		1	0.9	4.9	2.5	7	1.9	11.2	6.6	4.3	5.9	3.6	8.5
Australia	n.a.		n.a.	n.a.	n.a.	n.a.	0.4	1.5	1.7	9.8	1.3	22.0	1.5	22.5
Developed economies			97.3	4.8	97.0	5.1	96.8	6.2	91.7	9.6	86.2	22.8	86.8	27.9

Sources: G. Jones, The Evolution of International Business. An Introduction (London and New York: Routledge, 1996), 46–49; 1980 figures are based on: J. H. Dunning, Multinational Enterprises and the Global Economy (Cheltenham: Edward Elgar, 2008), 24.

DUTCH MULTINATIONALS AND THE RISE OF THE COORDINATED MARKET ECONOMY

During the period 1895–1914, business life was surprisingly international, and Dutch business made ample use of the international opportunities. The prospering colony in Asia contributed to business in general and to the international outlook of businesspeople in particular. Banks, trading companies, agricultural enterprises, and shipping companies all profited from business relations with the Dutch Indies. In this period, in 1907, Royal Dutch Shell was formed through the alliance of the Royal Dutch Petroleum Company (60 per cent) and the British 'Shell' Transport and Trading Company (40 per cent).[12] It was and remained the largest multinational headquartered in the Netherlands. Apart from the colonies, in particular the Dutch East Indies, Germany became an important host country for Dutch companies. In due time, Germany became one of Royal Dutch's key markets and evolved into a major host for the oil company's investments. The margarine manufacturers Van den Bergh and Jurgens, Unilever's forerunners, set up factories in Germany as early as the 1880s after the Bismarck administration levied a tariff on margarine.[13]

The First World War disrupted international trade and thus seriously affected the Netherlands, even though the country remained neutral throughout the war. The war had an impact on how government, business, and employees interacted with each other. For a country greatly relying on the import of raw materials and intermediate goods, this disruption needed to be addressed by a joint effort from government and business.[14] As the government had not much experience in managing the economy, it relied to a large extent on the expertise of the companies.[15] In harnessing this experience, the government encouraged businesses to work together. At the same time, multinationals suddenly found their operations situated in countries that were at war with each other. They were confronted with difficult questions of loyalty towards the home or host country. For instance, Royal Dutch Petroleum Company underlined its positioning in a neutral country, and allowed its German subsidiary to support the German war effort, while its British partner 'Shell' Transport and Trading supported the British war effort.[16] Nationality became an important issue that companies had to address seriously.

In the chaos created by the war, the government of each country wanted to look after its own citizens as well as it could, and the economy should serve the country. Multinationals were encouraged to integrate their production chain within national borders. Before the First World War, the margarine producers Van den Bergh, predecessor of Unilever, imported its raw materials via Great Britain, then produced the margarine in the Netherlands and Germany, and exported most of it again to Great Britain. Such a division of labour was no longer possible during the war. In this case, it led to local production in Britain.[17]

The war also led to closer collaboration between employers and employees and a better regulation of labour conditions. In some industries, in particular the printing industry, employers and employees experimented with collective labour agreements in combination with cartel agreements on prices and terms of delivery to organise the sector.[18] Rethinking capitalist organisation got a new sense of urgency after the Russian Revolution in 1917, which demonstrated the power of the Marxist ideology. A year later, the Dutch labour movement succeeded in getting the eight-hour working day they had campaigned for so long.[19]

The end of the war did not bring the longed-for return to normality. The continued economic chaos disqualified the 'free market' ideology and the absent government. The economy seemed to need some guidance either from businesses through agreements or from government. The state had taken on some responsibilities for social welfare, and progressive managers did the same. The electronics company Philips was among the modern companies that wanted to give social work a prominent place.[20] As chairman of the Dutch employers' organisation, Anton Philips explained that in companies in which ownership and management had become separated, managers had a greater measure of freedom to look after the interests of the workforce. After all, managers were part of the workforce. They felt no need to pursue the interests of the shareholders with the same single-mindedness as owners might have done.[21]

In the interwar years, foreign trade did not return to its prewar levels. However, foreign direct investment continued to grow, and this was also true for the Netherlands. Good financial results during and right after the war enabled the large Dutch companies to invest abroad. In addition, at the beginning of the 1920s, the strong Dutch guilder was a great advantage compared to the weak mark of the German rivals. After the mark's depreciation, the Dutch took over numerous German companies.[22] Besides, the Dutch big companies had access to cheaper capital than their local rivals via the Amsterdam and London stock exchanges and the expansion of the Dutch banking system during the 1920s.[23] German acquisitions were mostly financed through the Dutch capital market. Van den Bergh and Jurgens bought oil mills and other margarine factories, but they expanded also in other directions of the supply chain in Germany in this period.[24]

Rough estimates suggest that the Dutch share in the world's stock of foreign direct investment increased from 6 per cent in 1914 to 10 per cent in 1938. However, the majority of these investments were in the Dutch East Indies. Germany and the United States ranked second and third. In 1938, the Netherlands was the third largest direct investor in the United States, after the United Kingdom and Canada (see Table 7.1).[25] International investments took the form of greenfield investments and acquisitions, as well as cross-border mergers. Through another Anglo-Dutch merger, Unilever was formed in 1929. In the same year the artificial silk company ENKA merged with the much larger German company Glanzstoff into the Dutch holding company AKU. Thus three of the large Dutch manufacturing multinational companies had been a result of a cross-border merger. The fourth large multinational company that developed rapidly during the interwar years was the electronics firm Philips. Alongside these large multinationals a number of smaller companies set up foreign activities. Dutch companies expanded abroad because the Dutch market was too small for further expansion. In the 1930s, they frequently felt obliged to set up production abroad because of protectionist measures in foreign markets.[26]

In the 1930s, the large Dutch manufacturing multinationals had the feeling that their special interests in the increasingly protectionist international world, particularly in Germany, were not adequately understood by the government. Philips, therefore, organised a meeting between representatives of the major Dutch multinationals to discuss their issues with regard to international tariffs, fiscal rules, work permits, and licenses to establish a business. The meeting was intended to discuss how the companies could explain these issues to the government officials and enlist their help. This initiative led to establishment of an informal group in 1934 that focused on providing information to the government. During the 1930s, the Contact Committee was not very effective in their lobby towards the Dutch government.[27] This would change rapidly.

During the Second World War, the Netherlands was occupied by the Germans. The country was no longer neutral in this conflict, as it had been during the First World War, and as a consequence, communication lines within the multinationals were cut off. Dutch headquarters could no longer reach their overseas subsidiaries. Management that resided overseas could no longer contact headquarters. However, through the establishment of overseas trusts and legal provisions of the Dutch exile government in London Royal Dutch, Philips and Unilever were able to continue their activities in Allied countries, Axis, and neutral countries. The goodwill between the Dutch big multinationals, the British government, and the Dutch government in exile helped the companies to defy the challenges of the British Trading with the Enemy Act during the entire war. Philips proudly claimed in an advertisement in London in August 1940: 'A world organisation carries on!'[28] The disruption of the war meant that once again the foreign subsidiaries had to deal with the local situation as best as they could. It fostered their independence and reinforced the decentralised structures of the Dutch multinationals.[29]

Company executives from the major Dutch multinationals residing in London (mainly Shell, Unilever, and Philips) discussed the important economic and social issues that would face the Netherlands after the end the war. In fact, the meetings of these industrialists, organised by Unilever's chairman, Paul Rijkens, were partly a continuation of the prewar Contact Committee of Dutch large multinationals. They were convinced that close contacts with Great Britain and the United States would be essential for the future economic prosperity of the Netherlands. The country had focused too long on Dutch-German trade relations.[30] They were also of the opinion that securing sustainable full employment would be the key responsibility of companies after the war. The senior managers had also become convinced that in a free market economy the state had to play a crucial role in safeguarding sound economic development.[31] Managers in the Netherlands had very similar ideas about the need for a joint effort to rebuild the country after the war. During the last months of the war, the managing director of Heineken, D.U. Stikker, gathered representatives of the employees' and employers' organisations, which had been dissolved by the Germans. They worked together in the creation of a private organisation for collaboration between employers and employees. Two days after the liberation of the country, Stikker announced the establishment of the Stichting van de Arbeid (Foundation of Labour). Employers were asked to 'keep their factories open', and employees were encouraged to 'do their duty'.[32]

FOREIGN MULTINATIONALS BEFORE WORLD WAR II

The Netherlands was not only the home country of several multinationals, but it also became host to several foreign companies, from neighbouring countries like Germany, Belgium, France, and Great Britain, as well as US multinationals. For instance, Standard Oil dominated the Dutch market for kerosene in the early 20th century. Until the formation of the Dutch State Mines in 1902, the Dutch government had a rather liberal attitude towards foreign investors in coalmining—and to foreign investments in general. The private mines were for the greater part in the hands of French, Belgium, and German mining companies. Foreign companies invested in new technology and new industries, like telegraph, railways, telephone, chemicals, and oil. They were responsible for the necessary technology transfer to the Netherlands and therefore generally welcomed by the Dutch government, which only occasionally discriminated against foreign companies.[33]

German investments in the Netherlands originated in the conditions of integrated economic relations between the Netherlands and Germany since the end of the 19th century. Their geographical position, connected by the Rhine and several railways, had led them to cross-border economic cooperation. From the 1870s on, the Ruhr area developed into the most important industrial centre of Europe, while the port of Rotterdam became the most important deep sea port of Europe.[34] Around 1900, 68 per cent of Rotterdam's transit traffic was directed towards the German hinterland.[35] These extensive trade relations also led to mutual cross-border investments.

The First World War transformed the global investment patterns dramatically. After the First World War, the Netherlands would become an important safe haven for German companies. As a result of the war and the ensuing Treaty of Versailles, German companies had lost their assets in the Allied countries. Through participations in Dutch sales organisations and Dutch banks, German international business created new opportunities on the world market.[36] Many German banks found their way to this neutral country after their foreign branches in London, Brussels, Antwerp, and Paris had liquidated. In 1924, according to a high-ranking officer of the German Foreign Office, Amsterdam had become the most important financial centre for German banking.[37] In conclusion, during the 1920s, despite economic nationalism, trade and financial relations between the Netherlands and Germany increased tremendously. In general, the Germans adapted largely to the Dutch business system, as most activities were done under Dutch disguise, hidden from the Allies. The crisis at the end of the decade caused an unprecedented shock in Dutch-German economic relations; economic nationalism and Nazi autarky undermined the position of the Netherlands and its commercial activities with its hinterland, but would not end the extensive cross-border investments.

Compared to the German foreign investments, the number of American companies in the Netherlands was relatively small before 1940. The first American company that had started manufacturing operations in the Netherlands in 1896 was food manufacturer Quaker Oats. A little earlier, Singer Company, Pure Oil, Mobil Oil, and Standard Oil had set up storage facilities and sales offices in the Netherlands.[38] In the 1920s, IBM had appointed agents, and movie and radio companies Fox, MGM, and RCA had set up their sales offices. Eastman Kodak established a Dutch subsidiary in 1929, while Ford built an assembly plant in Amsterdam in the early 1930s, which was exceptionally large.

Henry Ford's foreign investment strategy was to make only greenfield investments for new assembly plants, and wherever possible, tracts of land were purchased. Ford's strategy was to maintain complete control of all foreign subsidiaries. He was, however, well aware of the lingering anti-American feeling in Europe, and he therefore decided to allow local investors to participate in subsidiaries up to less than 50 per cent. The first Board of Directors of Ford Netherlands (*NV Nederlandsche Ford Automobiel Fabriek*) thus included several important Dutch businessmen. Ford also felt that this move would make it easier to find local capital for building new factories. In 1931, Ford decided to build a completely new factory in Amsterdam. Although the municipality of Amsterdam pursued a policy of land leases, it was willing to make an exception for Ford Netherlands because of the rising unemployment in the early 1930s. Ford Netherlands acquired, almost free of charge, a large tract of land fronting water. The Amsterdam assembly plant was, like the earlier Rotterdam factory, wholly designed by Detroit engineers. Work methods and procedures were copied straight from the American factories.[39] The Ford case clearly shows that the American multinational was adapting itself to the Dutch business system, using a Dutch company name, Dutch board members, and even Dutch capital, which fitted also perfectly in the nationalist atmosphere of the interwar period. However, Ford's adaptation was only partial. Ford invested according to his own requirements and introduced American production and management methods in the Netherlands. The local government was rather flexible and prepared to meet the requirements of the foreign investor.

MULTINATIONALS AND THE COORDINATED DUTCH BUSINESS SYSTEM AFTER WORLD WAR II

In the second half of the 20th century, both inward and outward investment flows in the Netherlands increased substantially, as Figure 7.1 shows. From 1948 on, outward investment flows were nearly always higher than inward flows. Particularly striking in the FDI figures is the huge increase of both inward and outward direct investment during the 1990s, and the volatility of these figures in the 21st century.

After the Second World War, many people in the Netherlands considered a close and constructive cooperation between government, employers' organisations, and trade unions as an essential condition for economic growth and prosperity. Within the context of the coordinated market economy the entrepreneur had the duty to contribute to the overall objectives of economic policy. Economic growth and full employment were the two main objectives to which the companies certainly wished to contribute. Philips gives a good illustration of this point of view. In its 1946 articles of association, the company formulated two goals: a long-term welfare policy and the creation of as many useful jobs as possible, to serve the best interests of all those who were involved with the company.[40]

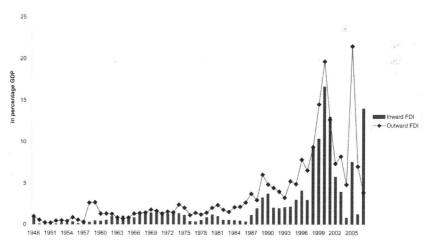

Figure 7.1 Dutch inward and outward foreign direct investment, 1948–2005

Source: Sluyterman, *Dutch enterprise,* 9; *Annual Reports De Nederlandsche Bank*, 2002–2007 (www.dnb.nl); and CBS, Statline: http://statline.cbs.nl/statweb/ (Accessed December 12, 2013).

Top management placed the interest of the employees above those of the shareholders. In their own public presentations the companies tended to underline the importance of the continuity of the company rather than making profits. Continuity had become important due to the increasing capital intensity of the production, which required large investments that only delivered income on the longer term. Moreover, continuity made it possible to build up a lasting relationship with the employees. Company leaders appreciated harmonious relationships with their employees who were informed via the work's council in which their representatives were allowed to give advice but initially didn't otherwise have much say. The employers' organisations and the trade unions worked together with the government to establish a welfare state with an extensive social security system. At the same time, companies had their own internal 'welfare policy' in the form of social funds, holiday trips, and corporate events. The package of measures often included a 'social worker'.[41] The company took care of its employees 'from cradle to grave'.

In contrast, shareholders were not considered particularly important stakeholders that deserved special attention. In 1952, the four large Dutch (or partly Dutch) multinationals asked two university professors to write a report on the importance of the company for the national economy. However, the professors did not come up with the hoped-for answer. In their report from 1953 they argued that managers had become too powerful in relation to the shareholders. Because companies were able to finance expansion from their profits, managers seldom needed to turn to the capital market. As a consequence managers paid insufficient attention to the interests of the shareholders. The four multinationals found the observations of these academics of 'little relevance' because the trade union leaders asked for more power to the workers, some political parties demanded more power for the state, but nobody was asking to give power back to the shareholders. The outcome of the report was not widely distributed.[42]

During the interwar years, Dutch multinationals had developed decentralised organisations based on national boundaries. Subsidiaries in various countries were given a great deal of local autonomy as well as a great measure of local identity. This strategy had been useful in times of protectionism in the 1930s and during the Second World War. National autonomy persisted in the 1950s and 1960s, particularly in companies such as Philips and Unilever, which produced locally for local demand.[43] The Philips concern was seen as an 'industrial democratic world federation'. The various national organisations in which the Philips subsidiaries in each country were brought together kept their considerable local autonomy, though they were also required to remain loyal to the company as a whole. Not only were products adjusted to local taste in order to satisfy local consumers, but national organisations were also embedded in the business systems of the countries in which they were working, assuming some of their characteristics. This decentralisation worked well as long as markets were fragmented, as was the case in Europe but also in Latin America, where Philips set up many factories in the 1950s. Latin America attracted considerable investment as a consequence of its import-substituting policy. Philips's factories in Australia and India too worked predominantly for local markets.[44]

To describe the organisation of Unilever, Fieldhouse also used the word 'federation'.[45] Within the Unilever concern, national organisations had a great deal of autonomy, a tendency strengthened by the Second World War.[46] This was particularly true for Unilever's operations in the United States. Despite the fact that its once flourishing businesses in the United States began to fall behind the performance of its main competitors after 1945, Unilever maintained an arm's length relationship with its US affiliates, leaving them entirely under American management. According to Geoffrey Jones, Unilever in general lagged behind the competition in the postwar years, especially in detergents. He blamed this, among other reasons, on the company's business culture that viewed making profits as only one of several considerations.[47] In 1966, Unilever introduced a system of 'product co-ordination' in Europa. However, local management kept a large measure of freedom, and that was certainly true for the United States as well as for developing countries. AKU also underlined the national identity of its foreign subsidiaries, many of which had outside shareholders in any case.[48]

Dutch multinationals were slow to explore the potential advantage of one coherent European market, perhaps because this process of integration moved forward so slowly. The reallocation of production was not a major preoccupation for most continental firms prior to 1971.[49] When in the 1970s Philips and Akzo, a merger of AKU and Koninklijke Zwanenberg Organon (KZO), tried to create a greater European integration of their production facilities, they met with fierce opposition from governments and trade unions, which wanted to the safeguard national employment.[50] Giving a fair amount of independence to the various local subsidiaries formed part of the general strategy of embedding the subsidies in their local environment. In this way the Dutch multinationals supported the national business systems, in which their subsidiaries worked.

In the late 1960s, Dutch society became critical of multinationals companies, including the Dutch companies. Multinationals were criticised for their powerful position, the damage to the environment, the exploitation of third world countries, and the shifting of employment to low-wage countries. To better inform and thus influence the public, the Dutch multinationals set up the SMO (Stichting Maatschappij en Onderneming [Foundation Society and Company]). The multinational companies had the impression that their continued contribution to economic growth and employment in the Netherlands was taken too much for granted. It was difficult to get permission for reducing the number of employees unless the company was in dire financial straits.

In 1975, when the government came with legislation that threatened their freedom of investment, the multinationals took the unusual initiative of writing an open letter to the government. They complained that the Netherlands had lost its competitive position, while its continued prosperity rested on its international trade. Wages were too high and the system of social security had become unsustainable, they argued. They asked for more market and more room for entrepreneurship. The government and the socialist labour union dismissed the letter as reactionary, but the letter could also be interpreted as a pointer to the future.[51] A few years later, when the economy slipped into recession, the government felt forced to rethink the organisation of the economy. Retired CEOs of the Dutch multinationals were invited to chair governmental committees. One of these committees studied the question of how to bring a new dynamic to the manufacturing sector, and another one offered a new design for the national health insurance in order to contain its rising costs.[52]

FOREIGN MULTINATIONALS AND THE COORDINATED DUTCH BUSINESS SYSTEM AFTER WORLD WAR II

At the beginning of the 1950s, the Dutch government had launched an industrialisation policy to transform the country into a modern industrial nation and to create employment. Part of the ambitious government programme was to attract foreign direct investments in the Netherlands.[53] Through a combination of investment subsidies, accelerated depreciation schemes, and fiscal measures, foreign investors were attracted.[54] Because the United States was one of the few countries with a capital surplus, the Dutch government focused on the attraction of US multinationals at the time. As a result, US direct investments grew rapidly during the 1960s and 1970s. The number of US affiliates quadrupled, and the value of the total investments even increased more than tenfold in that period.[55]

During the 1960s, the public image of US multinationals in Europe deteriorated. Therefore, the Council of American Chambers of Commerce (AmCham) in Europe conducted a public relations campaign.[56] The Amcham was a private interest group set up by US companies in Europe with affiliates in all major host nations of US investments. A 1967 report pointed out three main problems: the colossus concept (the fear of 'economic colonization' by the United States), the technological gap between European and American companies, and the need for adaptation of American practices to European conditions.[57] The AmCham advised its members to keep low profiles and to adapt to local conditions and national business systems.

According to the AmCham in the Netherlands, the United States had become the largest foreign investor in the Netherlands at the end of the 1960s.[58] The country provided easy access to local and world markets through the Rotterdam and Amsterdam port, and it had excellent rail and trucking infrastructures. The Dutch government continued to welcome US investments and offered special incentives to foreign companies prepared to establish production facilities in less developed areas of the country. Dutch attitudes towards open trade and free enterprise were strong and due to the widespread use of English, the language barrier was low. For US companies the Netherlands therefore remained 'the open gate to Europe'.[59]

According to the US firms, the Dutch investment climate deteriorated rapidly after the first oil crisis. The newly elected government, headed by the Social Democrats, announced new measures including an extension of worker co-determination and capital gain tax. The AmCham wrote in its annual report of 1976: 'Holland's attractiveness for US investment has considerably diminished, particularly in view of proposed legislation which would lead to loss of control and managerial freedom in business decisions'.[60] The tax plan was never realised, but workers' co-determination was extended. During the late 1970s and early 1980s, as a result of rapidly rising unemployment figures, subsequent cabinets started an economic policy, the aim of which was to stimulate investments in the Netherlands, including those of foreign companies. To that end the Ministry of Economic Affairs set up the Netherlands Foreign Investment Agency (NFIA).[61] So at the beginning of the 1980s, the Netherlands had returned to its open and welcoming policy towards foreign companies.

American multinationals did not only show their collective discontent with the direction in which the Dutch business system was moving during the 1970s, but individual companies also distanced themselves from Dutch ways of doing business. A particular interesting case in this respect is Dow Chemical Benelux, which started up its largest chemical complex in Europe in Terneuzen in 1964.[62] The location was chosen because it offered Dow an opportunity to develop an industrial complex well away from centres of population, but with good transport links to European markets. Ownership of the building lot was an absolute condition for Dow, whose wish could not be met in the Rotterdam area because of Rotterdam's long-term ground lease constructions. In addition, the Dutch regional industry policy, including subsidies, helped Dow in selecting Terneuzen as preferred location.[63]

In labour relations, Dow never liked the influence of trade unions inside its Dutch subsidiary. Tradition and atmosphere inside the American company did not match with the collective bargaining culture in the Netherlands at the time. In 1975, the whole Dow staff in Terneuzen received a bonus of 10 per cent on top of their annual wages. The trade unions disapproved of the bonus, as it was a denial of the Dutch system of Collective Labour Agreements (CAO). Among other things, Dow's bonus was meant to show Dutch trade unions that the company could pursue its own remuneration policy. Beginning in 1979, Dow did not sign a CAO anymore. Contrary to the common pattern in the Netherlands, Dow has not negotiated with trade unions on employment conditions since then.[64] Massive union campaigns could not bring alteration as 75 per cent of Dow's staff voted (under pressure) for the abolition of the CAO.[65] From 1982, Dow introduced its own remuneration system in the Netherlands, which was more performance related and incompatible with the Dutch collective bargaining culture at the time.[66] The new labour contract was called IAO (Individual Labour Agreement) and was discussed with the Works Council (OR), which had been mandated by law in the Netherlands since 1950.[67]

MULTINATIONALS IN A GLOBALISING WORLD

While the Netherlands were studying the need for change at the end of the 1970s, in other countries changes had already been implemented. This was in particularly true for the United States. In his book *Supercapitalism*, Robert Reich explains how the United States in the 1950s and 1960s experienced an unprecedented prosperity, which was widely shared. Inequality in income was reduced by progressive income taxes, good public schools, and trade unions bargaining for higher wages. Large companies considered it their duty to take into account the interests of all stakeholders, not just their shareholders, and CEOs were seen as 'corporate statesmen', who judiciously balanced private and public demands. But, according to Reich, this system came to an end somewhere in the 1970s when 'supercapitalism' was born. The result was more job insecurity, increasing inequalities of income, less regulation, and more global warming.[68] Reich argues that change in the system began with the revolution in international communications with regard to transport (containers) and the flow of information (IT). As a consequence, large national companies experienced fierce international competition, often from US companies themselves, who reduced production costs by creating global supply chains.[69]

The study of the Dutch multinationals demonstrates how the globalisation of markets impacted the organisation of these companies, which in turn changed the impact they had on the national business systems. The strategy of competing globally required stronger coordination at the level of business units rather than the traditional national organisation. For instance, Unilever, Philips, and Akzo all worked hard to get a tighter grip on their US businesses. From the mid-1970s, Unilever reasserted control over its failing US businesses. Loss-making activities were divested, and entirely new ventures, sometimes with exactly the same activity, were bought. The company no longer hesitated to send in European managers to sort out problems in the United States. At the same time, the global company obtained better access to innovation and knowledge available in the United States. In this process of restructuring, the US businesses became fully integrated in Unilever's worldwide structures. Unilever also reorganised its many fragmented production units in Europe in order to achieve a more favourable scale.[70] In 1982, Akzo acquired all the remaining shares of its US subsidiary Akzona in order to integrate its activities in the pharmaceutical and specialty chemical fields worldwide.[71] Otherwise, the company had already introduced a multidivisional structure in 1970, when AKU and

KZO merged into Akzo.[72] The majority of shares in Philips's main subsidiary in the United States, North America Philips Corporation, were still in the hands of the US Philips Trust, set up just before the Second World War to keep this part of the business out of German hands. The Trust had a large measure of independence from Philips. However, in 1987, after legal skirmishes, the Trust was ended. At the same time, Philips bought out the remaining shareholders of the North America Philips Corporation, taking full control of its US activities.[73] Ending the independent position of the US affiliates made it easier for Philips and Unilever to move from a national-based organisation to one focused on business units. For Philips this was a problem of long standing, because in the past local embeddedness had been one of its strengths. However, national variations in product specifications and marketing were no longer considered desirable in the developing global market. The same products were to be marketed worldwide and produced wherever it was most advantageous to the company. This strategy led to a major shake-up of the company in the late 1980s, when the business (product) organisations at long last triumphed over the national organisations.[74]

In the 1980s and 1990s, the relationship between managers, employees, and shareholders changed substantially. Shareholders or their representatives kept a closer watch over company performance and put greater pressure on top management. While in the 1950s and 1960s, senior managers had underlined their broader responsibilities to take care of the interests of all stakeholders, including employees, customers, shareholders, and society at large, in the 1990s, they unreservedly placed the emphasis on shareholders as the most important stakeholders.

Though managers and shareholders were obviously aware that the long-term interests of the shareholders were best served by a broader stakeholder approach, and for that reason the contrast should not be exaggerated, there was undeniably a shift in emphasis both in verbal expressions and in actions. Important in this context was the introduction of reward systems directly linked to increases in shareholders' value. The multinationals had to develop reward systems that satisfied their increasingly international top management. For instance, when Heineken engaged in a number of large international acquisitions in the early 21st century, it had to find a middle way between different national reward systems, some of which were decidedly more ambitious and generous than the Dutch system.[75]

Employees were no longer encouraged to remain their whole working life with one employer. In 1946, Philips had included the provision of employment in the Netherlands as an important company goal in its articles of association. In the 1980s, this goal was removed from the articles of association.[76] As it was no longer deemed necessary to shape lifelong relationships with employees, social programmes such as housing, medical care, and entertainment were ended or turned into a sponsorship relationship.[77] Unilever imposed higher demands on its managers, on the one hand ending managers' employment if their achievements were considered sub-standard, and on the other hand generously rewarding managers for good performances.[78] Employees were encouraged to increase their own employ-ability by following up with training and courses. Flexibility and employ-ability became keywords in human resource policy. Overall, employment numbers went down. When the trade unions in the Netherlands became concerned about the loss of employment in 1995, they demanded shorter working days. The director of human resources of AkzoNobel in the Neth-erlands argued that the problem of unemployment could only be solved by adapting the labour force, lowering labour costs, and creating broader employability and more flexibility. As a compromise both parties agreed to more flexibility by giving employees more choice in the length of their working day.[79] The changes at the company level had their impact on the collective labour agreements in the Netherlands, which became more flex-ible and more decentralised.[80]

FOREIGN MULTINATIONALS IN THE NETHERLANDS GOING GLOBAL

During the second half of the 1980s, 1990s, and 2000s, the inward and outward flows of foreign direct investment in the Netherlands skyrock-eted (see Figure 7.1). Dutch multinationals invested abroad more than ever before, but also foreign companies found their way to the Netherlands. Table 7.2 shows the growth in the stock of inward investment between 1985 and 2005.

Despite the enormous importance of US multinationals in the Dutch econ-omy, investments from the European Union became far more important.

Table 7.2 Geographic breakdown of FDI stock in the Netherlands as percentage of total FDI stock, 1985–2005

	1985	1990	1995	2000	2005
European Union (2004)	36	46	52	62	60
United States	34	25	22	22	19
Switzerland	11	9	9	5	5
Dutch Antilles and Aruba	10	10	7	3	2
Japan	3	4	3	4	2
Other countries	6	6	7	4	12
Total stock FDI in million euros	31.068	52.686	84.274	261.937	382.499

Source: www.dnb.nl De Nederlandsche Bank accessed March 23, 2009, Table 12.6s: Standen van Directe investeringen in Nederland

The average growth of European FDI amounted to 19 per cent, compared to 12 per cent growth of US investments. Key home countries were Belgium, Luxembourg, Britain, and Germany. Japan was the most important Asian investor, followed by Taiwan and South Korea.[81] The arrival of Japanese companies in the Netherlands was closely linked to the internationalisation of Japanese business, stimulated by the Japanese Ministry of Trade and Industry.[82] The Japanese entered the protected European market to serve a wealthy internal market by local factories.[83] Investments from Mid- and South America came for the greater part from the Dutch Antilles, Aruba, and other Mid-American offshore centres like Bermuda, the Cayman Islands, Panama, the Bahamas and Barbados. The countries were often used as intermediaries for investments from other western industrial nations.

From 1985 to 2005, investments came thus from all over the world, but for the greater part from the European Union and the United States. Total inward investments increased more than twelvefold in this period. Can we see an effect of this huge inflow of FDI on the Dutch business system? That is not so easy to assess because on the one hand the enormous flow of US investments might have pushed the Dutch system in a more liberal direction, while on the other the increasing flows of European investments would, in theory, have pushed the Dutch system in a more coordinated direction. This, however, is a too simple and mechanistic conclusion because other European coordinated economies were at the same time moving in a more liberal direction, and, even if multinationals came from a more coordinated environment, it does not mean automatically that they would transfer the elements of their home situation to a foreign subsidiary. What we can say, however, is that foreign multinationals in the Netherlands looked more and more to their Dutch operations from a global perspective and treated their subsidiaries as part of their global organisation structures, and relied less and less on the particular circumstance in the Netherlands.

NedCar is a good example of a company becoming increasingly dependent on global developments and international corporate structures after the direct investment of Sweden's largest car manufacturer, Volvo Car the Netherlands, since the 1970s. Initially, Volvo's investment proved not particularly successful. NedCar's factory was too small to be competitive on a car market that was severely hit by the oil crisis. As a result, at the end of the 1970s, Volvo wanted to divest its Dutch subsidiary. Thereupon, the Dutch state acquired the majority of the shares and saved the small car manufacturing plant in Born. After an enormous capital injection, Volvo's Dutch subsidiary began to develop new car models. As of 1983, for the first time since Volvo's takeover, the company became profitable.[84]

By 1990, the Dutch state—as part of its privatisation policy—wanted to sell its participation back to Volvo Car Corporation. However, after severe protests of the Dutch trade unions, another solution was found. In 1991, a joint venture was set up between Volvo Car Corporation, Mitsubishi Motors Corporation from Japan, and the Dutch state. In 1996, a completely newly equipped factory started to manufacture Volvo and Mitsubishi cars simultaneously. Three years later, the Dutch state sold its participation, as agreed before, to the Japanese and the Swedes. However, in the same year, Ford Motor Company acquired Volvo's car division in Sweden.[85] The take-over of Volvo thwarted the growth path of the joint venture because Ford's Board in Detroit decided to divest from the Netherlands.[86] In 2001, Volvo Car Corporation sold its Dutch participation to Mitsubishi. The future of NedCar became now completely dependent on the global strategies of Mitsubishi Motors Corporation in Tokyo. In 2012, Mitsubishi sold the Dutch plant to the local bus manufacturer VDL for 1 euro under the condition that the 1.500 employees would keep their jobs.[87]

Another example of the impact of global strategies is IBM, which had first established itself in the Netherlands through an agency agreement at the beginning of the 1920s.[88] From that time, the Dutch subsidiary played a major role in the development of the computing industry in Europe.[89] IBM showed a great adaptability to the Dutch environment, but simultaneously the business was managed according to IBM's international corporate strategy. Since the late 1930s, the Dutch company was embedded in IBM's strong corporate culture. IBM's human resource management in the Netherlands nonetheless matched very well with the development of Dutch postwar labour relations. Dutch management had been introduced to IBM's social policy, of which job security was a most distinguishing feature.[90]

In 1992, for the first time in its entire history, the IBM Corporation was loss making. The technological revolution had changed the relation between the customer and the company profoundly. On a corporate level a cost-reducing programme was set in, mainly through a retrenchment in staff. By 1994, IBM had to reduce 170,000 staff worldwide. The company had to give up its old policy of lifetime employment. Furthermore, the company adopted new principles, among others: 'the marketplace is the driving force behind everything we do' and 'our primary measures of success are customer satisfaction and shareholder value'.[91] Forty-five per cent of the staff in the Netherlands was made redundant. IBM's new method to inspire its workforce was from that moment on more through issuing bigger bonuses and handing out stock options, also to the lower management levels.[92]

IBM also restructured many corporate processes—including, among others, its financial systems. With supply chain management, the flow of goods and the logistics were modernised. IBM's subsidiary in the Netherlands had been made responsible for IBM's corporate distribution and became a key distribution centre for many products into Europe, the Middle East, and Africa. IBM established its international logistics centre in the Netherlands. In addition, the Dutch company acquired consultancy and software firms.

IBM Corporation moved from hardware to software and services. By 2005, IBM's major activities in the Netherlands were Logistics and R&D, and it employed around 5,200 staff, as it had done before the restructuring.[93] Until the 1990s, the Dutch company had relative autonomy; however, after the restructuring, IBM had become more and more a global company with global sourcing, in which the Dutch affiliate was just one competence centre among many others.

CONCLUSION

The internationalisation of companies does not necessarily lead to global integration. During the interwar years, the Dutch multinationals adjusted themselves to the fragmentation of markets and underpinned the process of fragmentation by their emphasis on nationally organised subsidiaries. In this way they accommodated the many differences in national business systems. Foreign multinationals in the Netherlands, which were mostly given a warm welcome, also adapted to a large extent to the Dutch business system, which became more and more coordinated at the time. After the Second World War, a process of international integration via new institutions competed with fragmentation as a result of the Cold War and the end of colonial empires. Moreover, the policies of western governments firmly focused on the national economy. Under these circumstances, the Dutch multinationals remained committed to the national organisations of their international activities, with a group of expatriates creating coherence within the enterprises on a personal basis. Some American companies in the Netherlands, however, started as early as the late 1970s to push the Dutch business system in a more liberal mode by introducing flexible remuneration systems, obviously inspired by rapid changes in their home institutions in this period. Their shareholders brought a new assertiveness to the annual shareholders' meetings.

The economic integration of Europe, the increasing pressure of financial markets, the IT revolution with its possibilities of global connections, and the accompanying globalisation all put pressure on the Dutch and foreign multinationals in the Netherlands to change their organisational structures into one global company based on business sectors. In this way, the multinationals responded to economic globalisation of the 1990s, and in turn enforced the process of global institution building. Two related changes took also place at the same time. First, the company was no longer seen as a vehicle to serve the interests of all its stakeholders, but it had to look after the shareholders' interests first and foremost. The pay of the senior management became more directly related to that goal. Second, employees were no longer seen as the most important stakeholders of the company, but as a flexible resource whose main task—with some exaggeration—consisted of adding shareholder value. These changes had their impact on the Dutch business system. The most striking change was that shareholders no longer felt responsible for employment, fair wages, or national interests. Getting the highest price on the stock market was what counted. Simultaneously, employees had to become more flexible. This conclusion is in line with the research results of McCann, Hassard, and Morris, who found that middle management of large companies experienced higher workloads and less job security in both coordinated and liberal market economies.[94]

Glenn Morgan suggests that multinationals brought more diversity in coordinated economies but not necessarily convergence between different national economies.[95] In the Dutch case, it is fair to say that there was certainly a move towards a more liberal market economy, and as such there was a convergence to other liberal market economies. However, the financial crisis of 2008 has discredited the liberal market as an ideology.

NOTES

1. Sluyterman and Wubs, 'Multinationals and the Dutch business system'.
2. Morgan, 'The multinational firm', 1.
3. Whitley, 'How and why are international firms different?'
4. Morgan, 'Globalization, multinationals and institutional diversity', 580–605.
5. Crouch, *Capitalist Diversity*, 22–24.
6. McCann, Hassard, and Morris, 'Restructuring managerial labour', 347–374.
7. Bordo, Taylor, and Williamson, *Globalization*, introduction.
8. Findlay and O'Rourke, *Power and Plenty*, 425–428.
9. Obstfeld and Taylor, *Global Capital Markets*, 23–33.
10. Findlay and O'Rourke, 'Commodity market integration', 13–64; Findlay and O'Rourke, *Power and Plenty*, 471–473, 525–526; Obstfeld and Taylor, *Global Capital Markets*, 26–42, 158–163.
11. Jones, *Multinationals and Global Capitalism*, 21–24; Sluyterman, *Dutch Enterprise*, 7–8.
12. Jonker and Van Zanden, *From Challenger*, 81–85.
13. Wilson, *History of Unilever*, 190.
14. Frey, 'Trade, ships and neutrality', 541–562.
15. Kruizinga, *Overlegeconomie in oorlogstijd*, 314–320.
16. Jonker and Van Zanden, *From Challenger*, 149–153, 198–200.
17. Sluyterman and Wubs, *Over grenzen*, 98–99.
18. Wieringa, *Ten dienste van bedrijf*, 73–76.
19. Kuijpers, 'Stille revolutie', 375–389.
20. Blanken, *Ontwikkeling tot elektrotechnisch concern*, 356–379.
21. Bruggeman and Camijn, *Ondernemers verbonden*, 105.
22. Sluyterman and Wubs, *Over grenzen*, 94; Klemann, 'Ontwikkeling door isolement', 308–309.
23. Euwe, 'Financing Germany', 219–240.
24. Wubs, *International Business*, 37–40.
25. Sluyterman and Wubs, *Over grenzen*, 93.
26. Sluyterman, *Dutch Enterprise*, 92–100.
27. Paulussen and Blanken, *Samenwerking*, 15–25.
28. London edition of *Vrij Nederland*, 3 August 1940.

29. Sluyterman and Wubs, *Over grenzen*, 131–134, 151; Wubs, *International Business*, 62–65.
30. Wubs, *International Business*, 137–141.
31. Paulussen and Blanken, *Samenwerking*, 31–38; Weenink, *Bankier van de wereld*, 193–194.
32. Bottenburg, *Aan den arbeid*, 15, 39–46.
33. Sluyterman and Wubs, *Over grenzen*, 55–70.
34. Klemann and Wubs, 'River dependence', 219–245.
35. Sluyterman and Wubs, *Over grenzen*, 57.
36. Euwe, 'It is therefore both in the German and in the Dutch interest . . .', 72–142.
37. Houwink ten Cate, '*De Mannen van de daad*', 75.
38. Stubenitsky, *American Direct Investment in the Netherlands*, 43.
39. De Goey and Wubs, 'US multinationals in the Netherlands', 149–184.
40. Blanken, *Onder Duits beheer*, 359; Blanken, *Industriële wereldfederatie*, 7–15.
41. Sluyterman, *Dutch Enterprise*, 134–138; Stoop, *Sociale fabriek*, 76–104, 141–176.
42. Paulussen and Blanken, *Samenwerking*, 51–60.
43. Sluyterman, *Dutch Enterprise*, 173–179.
44. Blanken, *Industriële wereldfederatie*, 15–19, 199–222.
45. Wilson, *Unilever 1945–1965*, 37–41; Fieldhouse, *Unilever Overseas*, 563–565.
46. Wubs, *International Business*, 179–180.
47. Jones, 'Control, performance', 435–478.
48. Dendermonde, *Nieuwe tijden, nieuwe schakels*, 167–175.
49. Franko, *European Multinationals*, 134–144.
50. Blanken, *Industriële wereldfederatie*, 259–262, 300–303; Klaverstijn, *Samentwijnen*, 93–140.
51. Sluyterman and Wubs, *Over grenzen*, 158–159.
52. Adviescommissie inzake het industriebeleid, 'Een nieuw industrieel elan'.
53. Ministry of Economic Affairs, *Fourth Memorandum on Industrialisation of the Netherlands*, April 1953, 10.
54. Stubenitsky, *American Direct Investment*, 49.
55. De Goey and Wubs, 'US multinationals in the Netherlands'.
56. Archive American Chamber of Commerce in the Netherlands (hereafter AAMCHAM), Minutes of the Council of the American Chambers of Commerce in Europe, February 7, 1964, Madrid, Spain.
57. Ibid, memorandum Jay H. Cerf, *Attitudes of American business in Europe*, Council of American Chambers of Commerce, 1967.
58. Ibid, Annual Report 1967/1968, Den Haag, 1968, 6.
59. Ibid, Annual Report 1969/1970, Den Haag, 1969; Letters to the Board, Bijeenkomst Amchams in Europe and Med, EuroMed.
60. Ibid, Annual Report 1976, Den Haag, 1977.
61. Netherlands Foreign Investment Agency, *NFIA 30 jaar op koers 1978–2008* (Den Haag: NFIA 2008), 18.
62. Barndt, *Growth Company*, 377–381; De Schipper *Achter de Dijken*.
63. Government Memoranda Concerning Industrialisation of the Netherlands 1950–1963 (Nota's inzake de industrialisatie van Nederland, 1950–1963), passim; interviews of Wubs with President of the Board Dow Benelux, Gerard van Harten, and Vice-President of the Board Dow Benelux, Ed de Graaf, 8 March 2006.
64. Pot, *Continuity and Change of Human Resource Management*, 163.
65. Interview of Wubs with Vice President of the Board Dow Benelux, Ed de Graaf, 8 March 2006.

66. De Schipper, *Achter de Dijken*, 161. In 2007 only 5.911 employees (12.7 percent) in Dow's workforce worldwide were covered by collective bargaining agreements. Dow Chemical Company, *Global Reporting Initiative Report* (2007), 77.
67. 'De ondernemingsraad bij Dow. "Een uniek concept"', *Dow Magazine*, 2009, nr. 2, 5.
68. Reich, *Supercapitalism*, 15–49.
69. Reich, *Supercapitalism*, 50–87.
70. Jones, 'Control, performance', 472–476.
71. *Annual Report Akzo*, 1982.
72. In 1994, Akzo and Nobel Industries (Sweden) merged into AkzoNobel.
73. Metze, *Kortsluiting*, 36–54.
74. *Annual Reports Philips*, 1985–1990.
75. Sluyterman and Bouwens, *Brewery, Brand, and Family*, 480–486.
76. Metze, *Kortsluiting*, 125.
77. Stoop, *Sociale fabriek*, 95–104.
78. Jones, *Renewing Unilever*, 94–102, 230–231.
79. Miltenburg and Veerman, 'Akzo Nobel', 25–38.
80. Visser, 'CAO-vernieuwing', 141–149.
81. Van Hoensel, *New Multinational Enterprises*, 97–117.
82. Nieuwkerk and Sparling, *De internationale investeringspositie*, 46.
83. Buck, 'Marktpositie en marktattractiviteit', 29.
84. Sluyterman and Wubs, *Over grenzen*, 248–254.
85. Inge Ivarsson and Claes G. Alvstam, 'Global production and trade systems', 61–82.
86. Sluyterman and Wubs, *Over grenzen*, 254.
87. See http://in.reuters.com/article/2012/07/11/us-mitsubishimotors-nedcar-vdl-idINBRE86A05W20120711 (accessed 29 November 2013).
88. Surendonk, *IBM Nederland N.V. 60 jaar*, 11.
89. Connolly, 'History of Computing in Europe', 20.
90. Olegario, 'IBM and the Two Thomas J. Watsons', 371.
91. IBM Highlights, 1990–1995, 22. http://www-03.ibm.com/ibm/history/documents/index.html (accessed 18 October 2013).
92. Garr, *IBM Redux*, 343.
93. Interview of Wubs with Appie Reuver, Former Director External Relations, IBM Nederland NV, 2 February 2006.
94. McCann, Hassard and Morris, 'Restructuring managerial labour', 347–374.
95. Morgan, 'Globalization, multinationals and institutional diversity', 580–605.

REFERENCES

Adviescommissie inzake het industriebeleid, *Een nieuw industrieel elan* (1981).
Annual Report Akzo, 1982.
Annual Reports Philips, 1985–1990.
Barndt, E.N., *Growth Company. Dow Chemical's First Century* (East Lansing: Michigan State University Press, 1997).
Blanken, Ivo J., *De ontwikkeling van de N.V. Philips' Gloeilampenfabrieken tot elektrotechnisch concern*. Geschiedenis van Philips Electronics N.V. (Leiden: Nijhoff, 1992).
Blanken, Ivo J., *Een industriële wereldfederatie*. Geschiedenis van Philips Electronics N.V. (Zaltbommel: Europese Bibliotheek, 2002).

Blanken, Ivo J., *Onder Duits beheer*. Geschiedenis van Philips Electronics N.V. (Zaltbommel: Europese Bibliotheek, 1997).

Bordo, Michael D., Alan M. Taylor, and Jeffrey G. Williamson, *Globalization in Historical Perspective* (Chicago and London: University of Chicago Press, 2003).

Bottenburg, M. van, *Aan den arbeid. In de wandelgangen van de Stichting van de Arbeid* (Amsterdam: Bert Bakker, 1995).

Bruggeman, J. and A. Camijn, *Ondernemers verbonden; 100 jaar ondernemersorganisaties in Nederland* (Wormer: Immerc, 1999).

Buck, R. 'Marktpositie en marktattractiviteit van Nederland voor buitenlandse investeerders' in: M. van Nieuwkerk and R. Buck, eds., *Nieuwe Buitenlandse Bedrijven in Nederland. Werving in het Perspectief van 1992* (Nijmegen: Buck Consultants International 1988).

Cerf, Jay H., *Attitude of American Business in Europe* (Council of American Chambers of Commerce, 1967).

Connolly, James, *History of Computing in Europe*, unpublished report (New York: IBM World Trade Corporation, 1968).

Crouch, Colin, *Capitalist Diversity and Change. Recombinant Governance and Institutional Entrepreneurs* (Oxford: Oxford University Press, 2005).

Dendermonde, M., *Nieuwe tijden, nieuwe schakels: de eerste vijftig jaren van de A.K.U.* (Arnhem 1961).

Dow Chemical Company, *Global Reporting Initiative Report* (2007).

Dow Magazine, 'De ondernemingsraad bij Dow. "Een uniek concept"', 2 (2009).

Dunning, John H., *Multinational Enterprises and the Global Economy* (Cheltenham: Edward Elgar, 2008).

Euwe, Jeroen, 'Financing Germany: Amsterdam's role as an international financial centre, 1914–1931', in: Patrice Baubeau and Anders örgen, eds., *Convergence and Divergence of National Financial Systems: Evidence from the Gold Standards, 1871–1971* (London: Pickering & Chatto: 2010) 219–240.

Euwe, Jeroen, '"It is therefore both in the German and in the Dutch interest . . ." Dutch-German Relations after the Great War. Interwoven Economies and Political Détente, 1918–1933' (PhD thesis Erasmus University Rotterdam, 2012).

Fieldhouse, D.K., *Unilever Overseas. The Anatomy of a Multinational 1895–1965* (London: Croom Helm 1978).

Findlay, Ronald and Kevin H. O'Rourke, 'Commodity market integration, 1500–2000', in: Michael D. Bordo, Alan M. Taylor, and Jeffrey G. Williamson, eds., *Globalization in Historical Perspective* (Chicago and Londen: University of Chicago Press, 2003) 13–64.

Findlay, Ronald and Kevin H. O'Rourke, *Power and Plenty. Trade, War, and the World Economy in the Second Millennium* (Princeton and Oxford: Princeton University Press, 2007).

Franko, L.G., *The European Multinationals. A Renewed Challenge to American and British Big Business* (Greenwich, CT: Greylock, 1976).

Frey, M., 'Trade, ships and the neutrality of the Netherlands in the First World War', *International History Review*, 19, 3 (1997): 541–562.

Garr, Doug, *IBM Redux: Lou Gerstner & the Business Turnaround of the Decade* (New York: Harper Collins Publishers, 1999).

Goey, Ferry de and Ben Wubs, 'US multinationals in the Netherlands in the 20th century: "The open gateway to Europe"', in: Hubert Bonin and Ferry de Goey, eds., *American Firms in Europe 1880–1980. Strategy, Identity, Perception and Performance* (Genève: DROZ, 2008) 149–184.

Hoensel, Roger van, *New Multinational Enterprises from Korea and Taiwan. Beyond Export-Led Growth* (London and New York: Routledge, 1999).

180   *Keetie Sluyterman and Ben Wubs*

Houwink ten Cate, Johannes, *'De Mannen van de daad' en Duitsland, 1919–1939. Het Hollandsche zakenleven en de vooroorlogse politiek* (Den Haag: SDU Uitgevers, 1995).
Ivarsson, Inge and Claes G. Alvstam, 'Global production and trade systems. Volvo case', in: Piet Pellenbarg and Egbert Wever, eds., *International Business Geography. Case Studies of Corporate Firms* (Abingdon and New York: Routledge, 2008) 61–82.
Jones, Geoffrey, 'Control, performance, and knowledge transfers in large multinationals: Unilever in the United States, 1945–1980', *Business History Review*, 76, Autumn (2002): 435–478.
Jones, Geoffrey, *The Evolution of International Business. An Introduction* (London and New York: Routledge, 1996).
Jones, Geoffrey, *Multinationals and Global Capitalism: From the Nineteenth to the Twenty-First Century* (Oxford: Oxford University Press, 2005).
Jones, Geoffrey, *Renewing Unilever: Transformation and Tradition* (Oxford: Oxford University Press, 2005).
Jonker, Joost and Jan Luiten van Zanden, *From Challenger to Joint Industry Leader, a History of Royal Dutch Shell, volume 1* (Oxford: Oxford University Press, 2007).
Klaverstijn, B., *Samentwijnen. Via fusie naar integratie* (Arnhem: ENKA, 1986).
Klemann, Hein A.M., 'Ontwikkeling door isolement: De Nederlandse economie 1914–1918', in: Maarten Kraaijestein and Paul Schulten, eds., *Wankel evenwicht. Neutraal Nederland en de Eerste Wereldoorlog* (Amsterdam: Uitgeverij Aspekt, 2007) 232–271.
Klemann, Hein A.M. and Ben Wubs, 'River dependence: Creating a transnational Rhine economy, 1850–2000', in: Jan-Otmar Hesse, Christian Kleinschmidt, Alfred Reckendrees, and Ray Stokes, eds., *Perspectives on European Economic and Social History* (Baden-Baden: Nomos, 2014) 219–245.
Kruizinga, Samuël, *Overlegeconomie in oorlogstijd: de Nederlandsche Overzee Trustmaatschappij en de Eerste Wereldoorlog* (Zutphen: Walburg Pers, 2012).
Kuijpers, I.M., Een stille revolutie. *De Nederlandse arbeidersbeweging en de overheid, 1914–1920* (PhD thesis. Utrecht: University Utrecht, 1996).
McCann, Leo, Hassard, John and Morris, Jonathan, 'Restructuring managerial labour in the USA, the UK and Japan: Challenging the salience of 'Varieties of Capitalism'', *British Journal of Industrial Relations*, 48, 2 (2010): 347–374.
Metze, Marcel, *Kortsluiting: hoe Philips zijn talenten verspilde* (Nijmegen: Sun, 1991).
Miltenburg, John and Anne-Claire Veerman, 'Akzo Nobel: een experiment met gevolgen', in: Marc van der Meer and Evert Smit, eds., *Innovatie of imitatie? CAO-vernieuwing op ondernemingsniveau* (Den Haag: Elsevier Bedrijfsinformatie, 2000) 25–38.
Ministry of Economic Affairs, *Fourth Memorandum on Industrialisation of the Netherlands* (The Hague: Ministry of Economic Affairs, 1953).
Morgan, Glenn, 'Globalization, multinationals and institutional diversity', *Economy and Society*, 38, 4 (2009): 580–605.
Morgan, Glenn, 'The multinational firm: Organising across institutional and national divides', in: Glenn Morgan, Peter Hull Kristensen, and Richard Whitley, eds., *The Multinational Firm: Organising across Institutional and National Divides* (Oxford: Oxford University Press, 2003).
Netherlands Foreign Investment Agency, *NFIA 30 jaar op koers 1978–2008* (Den Haag: NFIA 2008).
Nieuwkerk, M. van and R.P. Sparling, *De betalingsbalans van Nederland: methoden, begrippen en gegevens (1946–1985)*. Monetaire monografieën, nr. 7 (Deventer: Kluwer, 1987).

Nieuwkerk, M. van and R.P. Sparling, *De internationale investeringspositie van Nederland*. Monetaire monografieën, nr.4 (Deventer: Kluwer, 1985).

Nota inzake de industrialisatie van Nederland, 1950–1963 (The Hague: Staatsdrukkerij, 1949–1963).

Obstfeld, Maurice and Alan M. Taylor, *Global Capital Markets: Integration, Crisis, and Growth* (Cambridge: Cambridge University Press, 2004).

Olegario, Rowena, 'IBM and the two Thomas J. Watsons', in: Thomas K. McGraw, ed., *Creating Modern Capitalism: How Entrepreneurs, Companies, and Countries Triumphed in Three Industrial Revolutions* (Cambridge, MA: Harvard University Press, 1997), 349–395.

Paulussen, Jan and Ivo Blanken, *Samenwerking tusschen Nederlandsche industrieën met groote internationale belangen: 70 jaar contactcommissie (1934–2004)* (Zaltbommel: Uitgeverij Aprilis, 2004).

Pot, Ferry, 'Continuity and Change of Human Resource Management. A Comparative Analysis of the Impact of Global Change and Cultural Continuity of the Management of Labour Relations between the Netherlands and the United States' (PhD Dissertation, Rotterdam, Erasmus University, 1998).

Reich, Robert B., *Supercapitalism. The Transformation of Business, Democracy, and Everyday Life* (New York: Alfred A. Knopf, 2007).

Schipper, Paul de, *Achter de Dijken. Dow in Terneuzen 1962–1997* (Terneuzen, Drukkerij Van Maele, 1997).

Sluyterman, Keetie E., *Dutch Enterprise in the Twentieth Century. Business Strategies in a Small Open Economy* (London and New York: Routledge, 2005).

Sluyterman, Keetie and Bram Bouwens, *Brewery, Brand, and Family: 150 Years of Heineken* (Amsterdam: Boom, 2014).

Sluyterman, Keetie and Wubs, Ben, 'Multinationals and the Dutch business system: The cases of Royal Dutch Shell and Sara Lee', *Business History Review*, 84, Winter (2010) 799–822.

Sluyterman, Keetie and Ben Wubs, *Over grenzen: multinationals en de Nederlandse markteconomie* (Amsterdam: Boom, 2009).

Stoop, S., *De sociale fabriek. Sociale politiek bij Philips Eindhoven, Bayer Leverkusen en Hoogovens IJmuiden* (dissertatie Utrecht: Stenfert Kroese, 1992).

Stubenitsky, Frank, *American Direct Investment in the Netherlands Industry. A Survey of the Year 1966* (Rotterdam 1970; reprint London: Routledge, 2001).

Surendonk, Huub, *IBM Nederland N.V. 60 jaar* (Amsterdam: IBM, 2000).

Visser, Jelle, 'CAO-vernieuwing bezien vanuit de vakbeweging', in: Marc van der Meer and Evert Smit, eds., *Innovatie of imitatie? CAO-vernieuwing op ondernemingsniveau* (Den Haag: Elsevier Bedrijfsinformatie, 2000) 141–149.

Weenink, Wim, *Bankier van de wereld: bouwer van Europa. Johan Willem Beyen (1897–1976)* (Amsterdam: Prometheus, 2005).

Whitley, Richard, 'How and why are international firms different? The consequences of cross-border managerial coordination for firm characteristics and behaviour', in: Glenn Morgan, Peter Hull Kristensen, and Richard Whitley, eds., *The Multinational Firm: Organising across Institutional and National Divides* (Oxford: Oxford University Press, 2003) 27–68.

Wieringa, W.J., *Ten dienste van bedrijf en gemeenschap. Vijftig jaar boekdrukkersorganisatie uitgegeven door de federatie der werkgeversorganisatiën in het boekdrukkersbedrijf in het jaar 1959* (Amsterdam: Federatie der werkgeversorganisatiën in het boekdrukkersbedrijf, 1959).

Wilson, Charles, *The History of Unilever. A Study in Economic Growth and Social Change* (London: Cassel, 1954).

Wilson, Charles, *Unilever 1945–1965; Challenge & Response in the Post-War Industrial Revolution* (London: Cassell, 1968).

Wubs, Ben, *International Business and National War Interests: Unilever between Reich and Empire* (London and New York: Routledge, 2008).

Wubs, Ben, 'US multinationals in the Netherlands. Three cases: IBM, Dow Chemical, and Sara Lee', in: Hans Krabbendam, Cornelis A. van Minnen, and Gilles Scott-Smith, eds., *Four Centuries of Dutch-American Relations 1609–2009* (Amsterdam and Albany, New York: Boom and State University of New York Press, 2009) 785–796.

8 The Performance of the Dutch Business System

Jan Luiten van Zanden

INTRODUCTION

How well did the Dutch economy perform during the 20th century? And were there notable differences between phases in which the model of the liberal market economy dominated (before 1914 and after 1980) and phases in which tendencies favouring coordination prevailed (between 1945 and 1970)? In previous centuries, the Netherlands had been one of the leading economies in the world. Indeed, during the Dutch Golden Age (the 17th century), it had developed to become probably *the* most wealthy nation in the world. According to the data compiled by Maddison and co-workers, GDP per capita in the Netherlands was (expressed in 1990 US dollars) approximately $2,000–2,500, while the average for the rest of Europe was no more than half of that.[1] From approximately 1600 onwards, the Netherlands was the productivity leader in the world economy, a position it lost to Great Britain around 1800, when the Industrial Revolution was gathering momentum there. In the 19th century, the Dutch economy was much less dynamic than in previous centuries; industrialisation came much later to the Netherlands, and the lead it had over the rest of Western Europe shrank rapidly. This can also be seen as a process of convergence within Western Europe, by which the gap between the traditional frontrunners (the Netherlands and Great Britain) and the rest of the Continent diminished.

In short, in the 19th century, the Netherlands became just another 'ordinary' European nation, albeit one with a solid commercial tradition and focus, reinforced through its intensive links with its colonies, in particular the Dutch East Indies (i.e. Indonesia). It also enjoyed the benefits of a strong agricultural sector—once again an inheritance from the Golden Age—which contributed significantly to the balance of trade. Industry was closely linked to these agricultural and commercial activities, although towards the end of the 19th century, other branches of manufacturing of some significance (e.g. electronics in Eindhoven) developed.

This was the state of the Dutch economy at the dawning of the 20th century. How can the performance of the Netherlands economy be assessed? The degree of growth of income per capita is an obvious starting point;

unemployment often comes second in such evaluations. Next I will focus on the innovativeness of the Dutch business system, measured in terms of patents and expenditure on R&D. The social dimension should also be taken into account: how did inequality evolve, and what happened to the level of socio-economic conflicts such as strikes? Those are the next two issues discussed. These criteria of success and failure can be seen in a broader context in two ways: through comparison with the rest of Western Europe (i.e. those countries west of the former Iron Curtain), and by comparing the country's performance during various periods throughout the century. In the case of the latter, the question arises as to whether the period 1945 to 1980, when the Netherlands had a more coordinated market economy, sticks out from the rest.

ECONOMIC GROWTH

The most commonly used measure of economic success (and failure) is growth of GDP per head of population. Figure 8.1 presents the GDP per capita of the Netherlands and Western Europe from the turn of the 20th century to 2008.

As Figure 8.1 shows, at the beginning of the 20th century, the Netherlands was just an 'average' European nation: its income per head of population was virtually identical with that of Western Europe as a whole (the

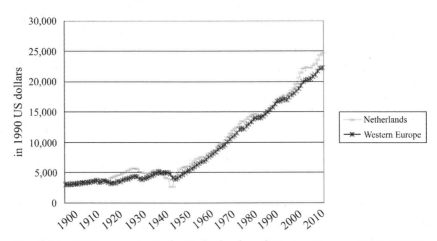

Figure 8.1 GDP per capita in the Netherlands and Western Europe, 1900–2008 (in 1990 US dollars)

Source: Maddison, *The World Economy;* the most recent summary of these results can be found in Bolt and Van Zanden, 'The first update'; see also Maddison's website: http://www. ggdc.net/maddison/Maddison.htm.

difference was less than 10 per cent), and by and large this remained so throughout the entire century—growth in GDP per capita was modest up until approximately 1940, followed by an enormous spurt in growth in the second half of the century. During the first half of the century, GDP per capita in the Netherlands increased by two-thirds, growing from $3,300 in 1900 to $5,500 in 1939 (all in 1990 US dollars); in the second half of the century, GDP per capita doubled over a period of twenty-one years ($5,500 in 1948 to more than $11,000 in 1969), only to double once again in the following thirty years (more than $22,000 in 1999), after which the economy continued to grow—in 2010 GDP per capita was around $24,000 (even despite the economic crisis of recent years).[2]

Comparison with Western Europe shows that in many respects the same trends held sway. There were, however, three periods during which the Netherlands performed better than its neighbours, the first occurring during the 1920s, when Dutch industry hurtled on, expanding at a time when many surrounding countries were facing great problems. In part, this surge in the 1920s was due to the fact that the Netherlands had remained neutral during the First World War, enabling relatively high levels of investment during those years. The country continued to profit from this in the 1920s. Although there was a financial crisis after 1920 (as in virtually all neutral countries), its effect remained limited, in part due to decisive action taken by the Dutch central bank.[3] Unfortunately the modest lead that this gave was to a large degree lost as a result of poor economic management in the 1930s. In particular, the decision to defend the gold standard to the bitter end dragged the country down.

The second period of superior performance occurred in the 1960s to 1970s. It was during these 'golden years' that, in absolute terms, income per capita grew fastest, enabling the Netherlands to perform even slightly better than the Western European average. This time, however, there was a lot of catching up to do, as the decline during the Second World War had been greater than in most neighbouring countries and recovery had begun later. Nevertheless, once underway growth in GDP per capita was very strong, continually hovering above the European growth curve. The powerful growth experienced in this period was, unfortunately, once more followed by a severe decline after 1979, dragging the Dutch curve back down to the Western European average.

Finally, once more, a positive divergence took place from 1990 onwards: in 2010, GDP per capita in the Netherlands was about 10 per cent higher than the Western European average, a positive difference that is comparable with the 1920s and the 1960s–1970s. As before, in the 1990s, there was talk of a 'Dutch miracle' and, associated with that, the Dutch 'job machine'.[4] The strong growth of the financial sector during this period was certainly of influence—although since 2008, it appears to be more of a 'liability' than an 'asset'. These favourable results were also partly due to a fairly successful reorientation focusing on the liberal market economy. However, once again the question arises: will this growth be durable, or will the positive divergence from the Western European average disappear in the financial and monetary crises in which we now find ourselves? Will history repeat itself in this respect?

A more detailed comparison with the two European countries seen as best representatives of the CME (Germany) and the LME (the United Kingdom) is possible. At the start of the century, the United Kingdom had a higher GDP per capita than the Netherlands, whereas Germany was somewhat less wealthy. This did not change fundamentally during the first half of the century, but after about 1950, we see a gradual relative decline of the United Kingdom, and an even gradual relative rise of the German economy. In the postwar period, this typical CME grows more rapidly than the United Kingdom, which, however, in this period, shares many features of the CME. The three economies more or less converge until 1970, but German relative rise continues until about 1980. Next we witness a fundamental change in the UK growth record, often associated with the Thatcher reforms;[5] clearly it profits more from the new wave of globalisation of this period. At the beginning of the 21st century, both the United Kingdom and Germany (which has by now successfully digested reunification) is doing somewhat better than the Netherlands.

How to assess this growth record? Measured in terms of GDP per capita, the level of wealth in the Netherlands in the 20th century has increased dramatically (just as in the rest of Western Europe) and is at present seven to eight times higher than at the beginning of the period. Moreover, as we shall see, up to the mid-1970s, incomes at the base of the income pyramid increased considerably more than those at the top, and the economic security of workers in the lower income brackets improved enormously.

In short, the economy has done what was expected of it, a performance in which the Dutch government has also played its role. All this is not exceptional, however. Rather, given the ideal position of the Netherlands, situated on the delta of a substantial river system, at the crossroads of large transport routes, and nestled between the economic superpowers of Great Britain and Germany, little less could be expected. The performance of, for example, the Scandinavian countries, which, despite their quite marginal geographic position, have been very successful in achieving rapid development, and that of Switzerland, which for the most part of the century has been able to generate a much higher levels of income, demand in this respect perhaps even greater admiration.

This is not to say that the Netherlands has not had to deal with some exceptional circumstances. In particular, virtually nowhere else has the population grown as rapidly as in the Netherlands. In 1900, there were approximately 5 million inhabitants in the Netherlands, amounting to 2.5 per cent of Western Europe's total population of 200 million people. In 2010, there are 16.7 million people, or 5 per cent of Western Europe's 333 million inhabitants.[6] For the purposes of comparison, while the Dutch population has more than tripled since 1900, the number of inhabitants in Belgium in the same period rose from 7 million to 'just' 10.4 million people, a 50 per cent increase. Greater levels of population growth come at the cost—at least most economists assume this is so—of 'intensive growth' because a significant part of investment capital needs to be spent on maintaining levels of capital goods per person (of course, it is much more complex than this). Nevertheless, if we look at growth in total national income, then the Netherlands makes a positive impression, since its income per capita was able to keep up with European trends.

The strong population growth was related to another notable characteristic: the—until recently—relatively low level of participation in the labour force, caused especially by the lack of participation of married women (who focused on their 'reproductive role', and thus had many children). If this factor is allowed for, then the productivity of labour in the Netherlands was by international standards very high—higher than in most of the surrounding countries, and in many cases as high as in the United States. In this respect, too, the performance of the business system during a large part of the 20th century can be classed as 'good to excellent'. This situation has changed over the past thirty years: women's participation in the labour force has increased sharply, and there has been strong growth in part-time employment, but growth in the productivity of labour has fallen behind international trends. Reference is also often made to the severe restraint on wage increases that came into effect following the Wassenaar Agreement of 1982, which improved the country's international competitiveness and created more work for its continually growing working population but weakened stimuli to innovate and increase productivity, with declining productivity of labour as a result. Obviously there was a price to pay for the strong growth of participation in the labour force, but if 'work, work, work' is the main political goal, then this is virtually unavoidable.[7]

The relative success of this policy of creating employment is clearly reflected in unemployment figures for the Netherlands (Figure 8.2).[8] These figures are not without their inconsistencies, however: before 1940, the data are only based on a limited number of European countries; and, furthermore, the definition of unemployment was not uniform across all of these countries. Nevertheless, it is clear that during the first half of the 20th century, the picture in the Netherlands was far from favourable—particularly during the 1930s, when unemployment spiked dramatically. By contrast, that picture changed radically after 1945: during the 'golden years', up until 1973, unemployment was also by international standards minimal, a situation that was to be duplicated after 1983. It was only in the period 1973–1983 that unemployment was comparable with European levels (1980 being a notable exception).

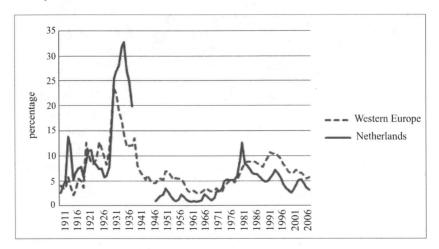

Figure 8.2   Unemployment in the Netherlands and Western Europe, 1911–2010
Source: Mitchell, International Historical Statistics: Europe; after 1993, LABORSTA Labour
Statistics Database (http://laborsta.ilo.org/).

R&D AND INVESTMENT

Growth of income and production is one criterion by which a business system
can be judged. Innovative potential is another. So how did the Netherlands
business system perform as a source of innovation throughout the 20th century? How much was invested in R&D in the Netherlands, and what fruits
did that investment bring? In fact, investment in R&D only really began to
take form during the interwar period, growing explosively after 1945 (see
Figure 8.3).[9] Around 1970, investment levelled off at approximately 2 per
cent of GDP and has since then shown a slightly declining trend. Indeed,
although around 1970 the Netherlands was still one of the largest investors
(per capita) in R&D in Europe, today its investment levels are very much
middle-of-the-road (especially the Scandinavian countries and Germany
have performed far better in this respect). The slight decline since the 1970s
is largely the responsibility of private enterprise: the contribution of private
companies to total R&D activity has declined in recent decades from more
than 60 per cent around 1970 to just below 50 per cent around 2010.

   The decline in R&D expenditure is not an isolated phenomenon, but
finds a parallel in the decline of total investment as a proportion of GDP.
The share of investment in national income in the post-World War II years
hovered consistently around 25 per cent, but from the early 1970s on, this
ebbed away to reach 20 per cent in the 1980s and 1990s, a decline that
continued into the 21st century. By 2010, a share of 15 per cent had become
more or less normal.

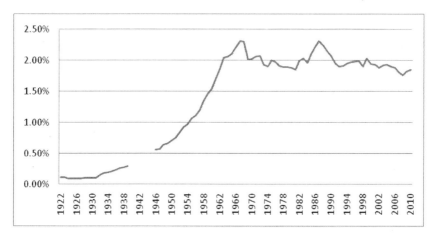

Figure 8.3   Investment in R&D in the Netherlands as a share of GDP, 1922–2010
Source: CBS, ICT, Kennis en Economie (2011); before 1992: CPB (B. Minne), Onderzoeks-memorandum, no. 116, Onderzoek, ontwikkelingen andere immateriële investeringen in Nederland.

This falling trend in investment in fixed assets and R&D since the 1970s is particularly noteworthy since the profitability of businesses has at the same time undergone strong growth, which is consistent with the shrinking share of wages in national income. It appears as if the shift from a coordinated market economy to a liberal market economy was accompanied by a declining emphasis on investment in fixed assets and R&D.

Given the complexity of the phenomenon, innovation and innovative potential is not a simple thing to measure, certainly not from an international comparative perspective, but a first impression can be gained by looking at data on applications for patents by Dutch companies (Figure 8.4).[10]

These data, compiled by researchers at the Rathenau Institute (The Hague), show a very steep increase in the number of patent applications, growing from no more than a score around 1910 (when the Netherlands once more introduced patents legislation) to nearly 10,000 applications around 2006. Between 1919 and 1940, a period during which R&D activities became professionalised, there was explosive growth (albeit starting from a very low level) in innovation. After World War II, growth in R&D took up where it left off at the outbreak of the war, culminating in a peak around 1960, only to be followed by twenty years of stagnation. A new phase of growth began in the mid-1980s and continued until around 2006. Figure 8.4 shows that Dutch patent applications have been significantly

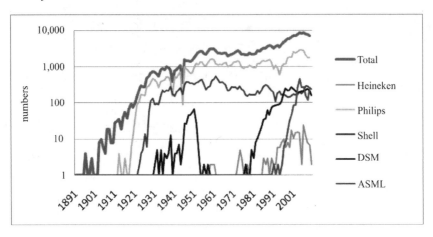

Figure 8.4   Number of patent applications worldwide by Dutch companies, 1891–2010

Source: New, yet unpublished dataset created by Edwin Horlings of Rathenau Institute who was so kind to share these data with us.

dominated by one company: Philips. Royal Dutch Shell is also a very important source of patents—contributions from other companies have been far less important.

Can conclusions be drawn about the international importance of these R&D efforts? It is possible to get an indicative answer to this question by examining the proportion of patent applications by Dutch citizens and especially Dutch companies in the United States and comparing this with the number of patents coming from comparable European countries.[11] National patent systems can sometimes be incomparable and for this reason do not give a clear impression of the innovative drive of a business system. Nevertheless, by looking solely at the output of an R&D system (e.g. that of the Netherlands) in the United States, it is possible to a modest degree to make comparisons with other European countries; moreover the physical distance from the United States is for all European countries the same.

As Figure 8.5 shows, three countries—the Netherlands, Switzerland and Sweden—grew in importance throughout the first half of the 20th century as sources of patents registered in the United States—and, assumedly, as sources of innovation. It is no accident that in these three countries large multinational enterprises are the most significant applicants for patents. In Belgium and Denmark (and Norway, which isn't shown here) businesses such as these played a less prominent role in the country's economic growth during the 20th century. Innovation in the Netherlands experienced, furthermore, vigorous development—this despite the fact that during the 19th century, it

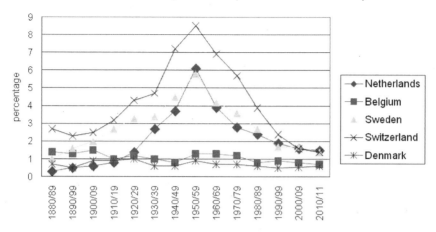

Figure 8.5 The share of five small European countries in the number of patents from abroad registered in the United States, 1880/1889–2010/2011
Source: Van Zanden, *Klein land*, 63–66.

dangled somewhere near the bottom of the list of countries ranked by R&D output. Up until 1910, then, there wasn't even a patents law—the existing law had been scrapped in 1869 as a result of liberal sentiment (see also chapter 6 in this volume). However, in the first half of the 20th century, innovative activity increased strongly, and neighbouring countries such as Belgium (that was well represented in the 19th century) were left behind.

After the 1950s, however, the relative output of the R&D systems of the Netherlands, Switzerland, and Sweden declined sharply, in part because of the rise of countries such as Japan and South Korea. In absolute terms, there was, by the way, no decline whatsoever: the number of patents awarded to Dutch applicants increased markedly from approximately 300 around 1960 to 1,743 in 2011; growth in other countries was just much stronger.[12] In relative terms, however, the decline was very pronounced, and the course this decline took in all three Western European countries was more or less identical. Around 2010, many patent applications were submitted and awarded to Dutch nationals and Dutch companies than, for example, to Belgians, but the lead has in the meantime declined steeply.[13]

The Netherlands was, therefore, in the mid-20th century, an important source of technological innovation, in particular as a result of investments in R&D by large Dutch multinationals (Shell, Philips, DSM, Akzo Nobel). In relative terms the importance of these companies has declined. This is connected to the decline in R&D investment of recent decades, just as the rising curve in the Netherlands during the period 1910–1950 was linked to the establishment of R&D labs by large enterprises. Furthermore, the rise of 'new' industrial nations in Asia has also played a role in the gradual decline that set in after 1970.

SOCIAL ASPECTS

One aspect of the business system in the Netherlands also worth considering is its capacity to resolve industrial conflict. The Netherlands has a long tradition of *polderen*—i.e. the ability through consultation and discussion to seek solutions for conflicts of interest (see also chapter 2 in this volume). The Social Economic Council is the embodiment of this tradition, although the discussion and consultation culture has deeper roots that go back to the Middle Ages.[14] Institutions such as the Social Economic Council and the Labour Foundation were established to facilitate negotiations on a national scale. The typical 'deal' was that, on the one hand, the trade unions would agree to wage restraint or accepted this if imposed by government, i.e. as was done through incomes policy after 1945. On the other hand, in exchange for this restraint, employers promised the unions more jobs, and the government contributed by expanding the system of social services—so after 1945, under Willem Drees (social democrat Prime Minister from 1948–1958), the promise of more generous social policies was delivered. For the trade unions, this also represented recognition of their role in negotiations on conditions of labour; collective work agreements were declared mandatory and became a common instrument in labour relations throughout the entire economy. Incorporation of the trade unions in this Polder Model was simultaneously an attempt to 'pacify' the workforce.

How successful were these efforts? In both the 1950s and the 1990s, the Dutch economy profited from policies of wage restraint, which made growth in employment opportunities possible (in part through improving the country's international competitive position, thus increasing exports, and by improving the profitability of businesses). But was the labour force 'pacified' by this?

Figure 8.6 shows the intensity of strikes in the Netherlands, measured in the number of strike days per 1,000 members of the working population; a value of 1,000 in the figure would indicate that the average employee has been on strike for one day. The records depicted in the figure appear to support the assertion that labour was indeed 'pacified'. During the early decades of the 20th century, workers held strikes regularly—especially around 1920, when there was a marked increase in social activism.[15] Thereafter the number and intensity of strikes decreased, until the Great Depression of the 1930s brought about a revival in activity (the following substantial peak was caused by the railway strike of 1944–1945). After 1947, however, strike intensity declined to very low levels. As Figure 8.6 shows, from the 1950s onwards, these forms of collective action occurred much less than in surrounding countries (i.e. the average of Belgium, the United Kingdom, Denmark, Sweden, and Germany, of which only the German data is at more or less the same level as the Netherlands—the rest is much higher).

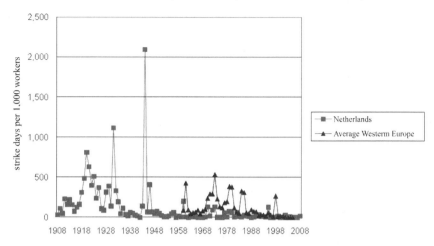

Figure 8.6   Strike frequency in the Netherlands and Western Europe, 1900–2010
Source: Sjaak van der Velden, *Stakingen;* Sjaak van der Velden et al., *Strikes.*

Even the period of social unrest that developed between the late 1960s and the early 1980s—the period that includes the two oil crises and the stagflation that followed—can hardly be found in the Netherlands data on strikes, and after, say, 1983, there have been virtually no more strikes of major proportions.

It is characteristic that in the Netherlands strikes are almost never used to achieve political goals (an important cause of strikes in, for example, southern Europe). The lesson the Dutch trade unions learned from the failed railway strike of 1903 (for that matter, a good example of a politically motivated strike) was that greater coordination of strike activity was necessary. Subsequently, first the Socialists, and then a little later the Protestant and Catholic unions, established national organisations, which, because they were able to see the big picture and could pool available resources, enabled them to play a moderating role. With the increase in national cooperation— first through the spread of CLAs, and later through the establishment of the Foundation for Labour and the Social Economic Council—came a further moderating influence from the trade union leadership. The trade union movement grew to acquire an established position in the social land- scape, with a significant decline in strike frequency as a result. Recent fig- ures for Western Europe for the period 1980–2006 assign the Netherlands fifteenth place in strike frequency, just above Luxembourg in last place and just below Germany, but far below the leaders: Greece, Spain, and Italy.[16] Conspicuously, already before the financial crisis of 2008, many politically motivated strikes occurred in these three southern European countries (with Greece lonely at the top of the list, accounting for 40 per cent of all politi- cally motivated strikes in Europe), while these rarely occur in countries such as the Netherlands and Germany. From the 1950s onwards, social stability was and still is one of the strong advantages contributing to the international competitive position of the Netherlands.[17]

Another instrument for dealing with socio-economic conflict of interest is inflation. Employers agree to wage increases—to prevent strikes—but pass these increases on in the prices for their goods and services, creating a wage-price spiral, which is actually a result of the inability of both parties to reach agreement on an acceptable distribution of income. Of course, this is not the only reason for rising prices (or price decreases)—scarcity, economic trends, and other macro-economic influences also play a role, but it is notable that the geography of inflation in Western Europe displays many similarities with the geography of strikes. Although the 20th century was subject to virtually continual inflation—accelerating during periods of war (1913–1920 and 1939–1945)—in the Netherlands it remained by international standards reasonably limited. Inflation was only less in Switzerland; it was also quite low in Germany, but only if the hyperinflation of the period 1921–1923 is excluded. Averaged over the entire century (1900–2007), inflation in the Netherlands was a bit more than 3 per cent per year, much lower than, for example, Belgium (5.6 per cent), France (8 per cent), and especially—once again—the countries of southern Europe (Italy 11 per cent, Spain 6.3 per cent and Greece 12 per cent). In recent EMU years, however, the differences have become much smaller (inflation in the Netherlands 2.2 per cent, in Greece 3.4 per cent) but still significant (only Italy's inflation was lower than that of the Netherlands).[18]

The Dutch business system has demonstrated, especially since 1945, that it possesses efficient mechanisms for resolving socio-economic conflict, resulting in greater stability in labour relations. One component of this historic 'deal' between labour and capital that developed after World War II was the creation of a system of social services meant to protect workers from loss of income as a result of, for example, sickness, unemployment, and old age. The welfare state took form slowly in the Netherlands—up until 1960, expenditure on social services was below that of neighbouring countries. But from 1960 onwards, the welfare state 'exploded' in the wake of unprecedented optimism about the future of the Dutch economy (5 per cent growth became to be considered normal and was expected to continue in the future), in part supported by the discovery of natural gas at Slochteren, in the north of the country. The welfare state that grew out of this brought about a fairly hefty redistribution of income. Inequality of income distribution and of wealth fell sharply during the period 1914–1970. In the 19th century, that inequality was quite high by international standards: the benefits of economic growth during the Golden Age were mostly bestowed upon rich traders, creating a particularly unequal distribution of income as a result.

The Gini coefficient for the Netherlands, the most common measure of inequality of income (0 indicates perfect equality; 1 indicates that one person earns all of a society's income and the others earn nothing), was between 0.55 and 0.6—comparable with countries with very high inequalities of distribution, such as South Africa or Brazil at this moment.[19] For that matter, this appears to be the normal pattern: economic growth tends to favour those with higher incomes, and to thus produce more inequality, unless all sorts of measures are taken to mitigate this development. And during the course of the 20th century, such measures were in abundance: the expansion of the welfare state, the rise of real income (in part thanks to the growing power of trade unions), and the introduction of progressive income and wealth taxes together created between 1913 and 1980 a unique combination of strong economic growth and a levelling of incomes, a phenomenon sometimes referred to as the egalitarian revolution of the 20th century. The Gini coefficient for income inequality in the Netherlands declined steadily from 0.47 in 1910, to 0.42 in 1929, to 0.36 in 1950, and 0.30 in 1980 (Table 8.1). Although levels of inequality of income distribution in the Netherlands were until 1960 on a par with those in the rest of Western Europe, after 1960, these declined to lower levels. Distribution of wealth exhibited a similar trend, with the exception of the two world wars. As a result, the Netherlands became a highly egalitarian society, comparable with the Scandinavian countries.[20] A very close link between income inequality and the variety of capitalism can, however, not be established on the basis of these data; German inequality was relatively high especially after the reunification with the east (Table 8.1), and British inequality only increased above the Dutch level after the 1970s—before 1975, its Gini coefficient was generally below that of the small European countries.

The decline in inequality of income between 1913 and 1975 occurred in large parts of the world economy, but in many cases it was followed by increases in inequality during the final decades of the 20th century, influenced by globalisation and a surge in liberal policies. The United Kingdom is a clear example: its Gini coefficient grew from 0.29 in 1970 (even a little lower than the Netherlands) to more than 0.40 in 2000; in the United States for those same years, the Gini coefficient rose from 0.36 to 0.44. Income inequality also increased dramatically in former planned economies, such as those in rapidly developing countries like China and India. The trend in Western Europe—with the exception of the United Kingdom—was much less pronounced because social legislation was reasonably resilient to the crises and pressures brought about by globalisation. The Netherlands is a good example in this respect: inequality in income distribution was minimal (the Gini coefficient rose from 0.30 in 1980 to 0.32 in 2000), and remained well below the average level of Western Europe.[21] But this situation was the result of a number of partially self-compensating trends. First, increases in real wages virtually came to a halt after 1980, so that the average worker did not experience 'ordinary' growth in welfare (while the average income per capita rose by 60 per cent). This was, however, partially compensated for by increasing employment—especially the participation of women in the

Table 8.1   Estimates of income inequality in European countries, 1910–2000 (Gini coefficients)

	Netherlands	United Kingdom	Germany	Scandinavian countries and Belgium (average)
1910	0.47	0.42	0.44	0.49
1929	0.42	0.43	0.46	0.47
1950	0.36	0.30	0.47	0.38
1960	0.45	0.29	0.39	0.40
1970	0.36	0.29	0.40	0.35
1975	0.31	0.33	0.38	0.32
1980	0.30	0.34	0.38	0.32
1985	0.29	0.35	0.37	0.29
1990	0.32	0.39	0.49	0.31
1995	0.32	0.40	0.47	0.31
2000	0.32	0.40	0.51	0.33

Source: Van Zanden et al., 'Changing shape'.

labour force (as already mentioned) increased significantly; in this way, the benefits of economic growth were felt, albeit at the price of increased work-ing hours. This picture, too, demands some subtle readjustments: part-time employment was, and still is, prevalent in the Dutch labour market; and in the Netherlands the average annual number of hours worked is the lowest in the world.

When all is said and done, the fact remains that those at the bottom of the income pyramid only profited from economic growth by being able to work more hours. Real incomes at the top of the pyramid, in contrast, underwent explosive growth thanks to the introduction of all sorts of bonuses and changing corporate culture on this issue. That development was not just confined to business either: government and semi-government sectors also experienced a strong surge in levels of executive remuneration. The rather small increase in income inequality was, moreover, accompanied by a strong increase in inequality of the distribution of wealth (although data for this item are much less comprehensive). Here, too, government policy also played a role (among other things, through the lowering of wealth and inheritance taxes), although ultimately the influence of the market dominated: share prices (in the 1960s–1980s, these were continually under pressure), grew dramatically from 1982 onwards, as did the value of real estate (including residential properties). Owners of capital profited exceptionally well, while those with only savings were barely able to keep up with inflation.

Changes in the business system brought about two opposing influences on income equality during the period of globalisation from 1980 onwards: the strong growth of participation in the labour force resulted in income growth for those at the bottom of the pyramid, while the increased focus on the liberal market model magnified inequalities with those at the top of the pyramid. Furthermore, the coordination model brought a moderate influence to bear on neo-liberal policies, thus circumventing any revolution in the rigorous style of Thatcher or Reagan. As a result, ultimately income inequality remained by international standards relatively small.

CONCLUSION

How does the performance of the Dutch business system during periods of liberal (free market) economic policy—i.e. before 1913 and after 1980—compare with those in which coordinated market policies were in force (especially between 1945 and 1980)? Comparing these periods is no easy matter. Economic growth was much stronger between 1945 and 1973 than during the periods before and after, but that was an international phenomenon that cannot be easily accredited to the Netherlands business system. Nevertheless, the simple fact that economic growth in periods of globalisation and liberal economic policies was generally slower than during periods when the coordinated market economy reigned supreme cannot escape mention.

Nevertheless, there are two aspects—unemployment and strike frequency—for which a clear connection can be observed between levels of coordination and the performance of the Dutch economy. In these matters, an unmistakable shift took place in 1945 with the introduction of a system of highly regulated and coordinated labour relations: virtually from that moment onwards, unemployment and strike frequency was consistently much lower than in other European countries (with the exception of the turbulent 1970s). Under the structures of consultation that have since become known as the Polder Model, it was possible to restrain wage claims (something that after 1945 and 1983 benefited the country's competitiveness on international markets) and reach general agreement on terms of employment and social legislation. This contributed to a substantial reduction of the inequality of income distribution and, after 1980, when the international trend was rising, stabilisation at a relatively low level (although the Netherlands was not unique in this). It was indeed no accident that the marked decline in inequality of income and wealth occurred during the period of the 'coordinated market economy'. Goals of reducing differences in wealth and increasing economic security for all were integral to the deal that was the foundation of the postwar consultation economy, a deal in which wage restraint and stable labour relations were agreed upon by the trade unions.

The coordinated economy also appears to have excelled at facilitating innovation. At the beginning of the 20th century, the R&D system in the Netherlands was underdeveloped by international standards. To some extent this situation was to repeat itself at the end of this same century: there was, and still is, too little being invested in R&D in the Netherlands. In the intervening period, however, the R&D system grew and blossomed—as shown by the registration of Dutch patents in the United States. This flourish coincided with the coordinated market economy that reigned in those years, although it also coincided with a period of expansion by large Dutch multinationals, such as Philips and Shell, which were responsible for a large proportion of the patents registered. Philips was, probably more than any other company, the embodiment of the success of the coordinated market economy in the postwar period, but it is perhaps stretching credibility to claim that the Dutch business system was entirely responsible for these successes in the realm of R&D.

NOTES

1. Maddison, *The World Economy*; the most recent summary of these results can be found in Bolt and Van Zanden, 'The first update'.
2. Ibid; these estimates can also be found on Maddison's website: http://www.ggdc.net/maddison/Maddison.htm.
3. cf. Van Zanden, *Klein Land*, 141–148.
4. Visser and Hemerijck, 'A Dutch Miracle'.
5. Crafts, 'British relative economic decline revisited'.
6. Data from Maddison, *The World Economy*.
7. For this discussion, see Visser and Hemerijck, 'A Dutch Miracle'; Kleinknecht, Naastepad, and Storm, *Het nut*.
8. Taken from Mitchell, *International Historical Statistics: Europe*; after 1993, LABORSTA Labour Statistics Database (http://laborsta.ilo.org/).
9. CBS, ICT, Kennis en Economie (2011); before 1992: CPB (B. Minne), Onderzoeksmemorandum, no. 116, Onderzoek, ontwikkelingen andere immateriële investeringen in Nederland.
10. New, yet unpublished dataset created by Edwin Horlings of Rathenau Institute who was so kind to share these data with us.
11. cf. The analysis of these data can be found in Van Zanden, *Klein land*, 63–66, as well as proof that foreign application for patents in Germany show a similar pattern.
12. Recent data on US patents from http://www.uspto.gov/web/offices/ac/ido/oeip/taf/reports.htm.
13. A recent summary on this matter can be found in Frans van der Zee et al., *De staat van Nederland*.
14. Prak and Van Zanden, *Nederland*.
15. Data from Sjaak van der Velden, *Stakingen*; Sjaak van der Velden et al., *Strikes*.
16. Kelly and Hamann, 'General Strikes'.
17. Prak and Van Zanden, *Nederland*.
18. Data on inflation in the 20th century from an inflation database published by Coos Santing at http://www.iisg.nl/hpw/data.php#world.

19. Soltow and Van Zanden, *Income and Wealth Inequality*.
20. Ibid, data from Van Zanden et.al., 'The Changing Shape'; for distribution of wealth, see Wilterdink, *Vermogensverhoudingen*.
21. All data from Van Zanden et.al., 'The changing shape'.

REFERENCES

Bolt, Jutta and Zanden, Jan Luiten van, 'The first update of the Maddison project', *Economic History Review*, 2014, forthcoming.
CBS, ICT, *Kennis en Economie* (The Hague: CBS, 2011).
CPB (B. Minne), Onderzoeksmemorandum, no. 116, Onderzoek, ontwikkelingen andere immateriële investeringen in Nederland (The Hague: CPB, 1995).
Crafts, N., 'British relative economic decline revisited: The role of competition', *Explorations in Economic History*, 49 (2012): 17–29.
Kelly, John and Kerstin Hamann, 'General Strikes in Western Europe, 1980–2008'. Paper for the European Regional Congress of the International Industrial Relations Association, Copenhagen (2010).
Kleinknecht, Alfred, Ro Naastepad, and Servaas Storm, 'Het nut van ontslagbescherming', *Socialisme en Democratie*, 69, 3 (2012), 22–30.
Maddison, Angus, *The World Economy. A Millennial Perspective* (Paris: OECD, 2006).
Mitchell, B.R., *International Historical Statistics: Europe, 1750–2005* (London: Palgrave MacMillan, 2007).
Prak, M.R. and J.L. van Zanden, *Nederland en het poldermodel* (Amsterdam: Bert Bakker, 2013).
Soltow, Lee and Jan Luiten van Zanden, *Income and Wealth Inequality in the Netherlands, 16th–20th Century* (Amsterdam: Het Spinhuis, 1998).
Velden, Sjaak van der, *Stakingen in Nederland* (Amsterdam: Stichting Beheer IISG, 2000).
Velden, Sjaak van der, Heiner Dribbusch, Dave Lyddon, and Kurt Vandaele, *Strikes around the World. Case-Studies of 15 Countries* (Amsterdam: Amsterdam U.P., 2008).
Visser, Jelle, and Anton Hemerijck, *'A Dutch Miracle': Job Growth, Welfare Reform and Corporatism in the Netherlands* (Amsterdam: Amsterdam U.P., 1997).
Wilterdink, Nico, *Vermogensverhoudingen in Nederland* (Amsterdam: De Arbeiderspers, 1984).
Zanden, J.L. van, *Een klein land in de twintigste eeuw* (Utrecht: Het Spectrum, 1997).
Zanden, J.L. van, Joerg Baten, Peter Földvari, and Bas van Leeuwen, 'The changing shape of global inequality—exploring a new dataset', *Review of Income and Wealth*, 60, 2 (2014): 279–298.
Zee, Frans van der, ed., *De staat van Nederland als innovatieland* (Amsterdam: Amsterdam U.P., 2012).

9 Dutch Changing Capitalism in International Perspective

Keetie Sluyterman

As the articles in this volume make clear, capitalism is in constant flux that can be best understood as ebb and flow.[1] Capitalism in the Netherlands showed ebb and flow in liberalism and coordination, and in the convergence and divergence with other countries. Ebb and flow were also visible in the international interconnectedness that deeply influenced the organisation of the national economies, which does not necessarily imply that globalisation created convergence between all countries.

From the preceding chapters we learned that over the course of the 20th century in the Netherlands, welfare arrangements for employees and the rest of the population first increased substantially, then became contested, and then were sobered. The intensity of collaboration between companies increased and then diminished, while government became an increasing part of that interaction and then gradually withdrew. Expenditures on innovation and the knowledge infrastructure rose and fell. The choice for entrepreneurship instead of a company career increased, fell, and increased again. In some periods, multinationals aligned their interest with the national countries in which they worked, but in others they focused on their own global strategies. Shareholders moved from important stakeholders in the company to being just one of many stakeholders—and not even the most important ones—to once again the party whose interest should be the main concern for managers.

However, some elements in the organisation of the Dutch economy remained in place. The representation of employees in the works' council continued, and the rights of the works' council remained undiminished. The power of shareholders to exert real influence over managerial decision making remained modest over the whole century. The collaboration between trade unions and organisations of employers, which had become antagonistic in the 1970s, returned in a new form with less government and tripartite negotiations and more direct agreements between unions and business. Constant remained also the willingness to reach consensus between different points of view through careful, and sometimes lengthy, negotiations. The new mix of market and coordination worked for the Netherlands in the 1990s because economic growth picked up and unemployment went down drastically.[2] But there were also critical voices arguing that the society was becoming harsher and less coherent and that income differences were on the rise.[3]

Peter Hall and David Soskice expected the liberal and coordinated market economies to be stable systems because of the institutional complementarities.[4] Though changes clearly took place over time, they did not happen entirely at random. One form of coordination—for instance, labour agreements—called forth other forms of coordination—for instance, cartel agreements. Strengthening the position of workers in work's councils at the same time weakened the position of other stakeholders—for instance, shareholders.

The changes that occurred in the Netherlands during the 20th century did not take place in isolation but happened in response to international economic and political developments that were shared by many countries. Moreover, the Dutch often looked abroad for 'best practices' and used them selectively and creatively. This concluding chapter offers some international comparisons to put the Dutch experiences in perspective. Was the evolution of Dutch capitalism in the 20th century unique, or did it form part of a general pattern? Can the comparisons tell us more about the drivers behind the changes?

This chapter will look first at the influence that the ideas and examples of two important neighbouring countries, Great Britain and Germany, exerted on the Netherlands. Furthermore, the influence of the dominant political and economic power of the 20th century, the United States, will be included in the comparison because in the Varieties of Capitalism literature the United States and Germany are seen as prototypes of respectively the coordinated and liberal market economy. In the next paragraph the experiences of four other small open European economies—those of the Nordic countries— will be examined because they are a logical choice for comparison with the Netherlands. Finally, the recent experiences of four Eastern European countries will be discussed. This comparison is interesting because these countries have recently become open economies and therefore face some of the same dilemmas as the Nordic countries and the Netherlands.

LEARNING FROM GERMANY, GREAT BRITAIN, AND THE UNITED STATES

The two neighbouring countries, Germany and Great Britain, which were both important business relations for the Netherlands, had two different forms of capitalism. In the late 19th century, Great Britain was an imperial power and an advocate of free trade. Freedom was also the keyword in labour relations. Employers had a large measure of freedom in how they treated their workers, though in the years 1830–1840, the British Parliament had posed limits on child labour and introduced some requirements regarding working conditions. In the second half of the 19th century, the industrial workers united themselves in strong unions, and the skilled workers defended their traditional abilities against attempts to rationalise the work. Employers and managers were willing to make concessions for the sake of industrial peace. Some employers, in particular those in capital-intensive industries, introduced 'welfare work' to bind the employees to the factory.[5] While Britain preached free trade, the German states, in 1871, combined in the German empire, were in favour of tariff barriers to protect their fledgling industries. Typical of the German banking system was that the banks, unlike the British banks, provided trade credit as well as long-term investment. Through their role in financing the industry, banks developed close relationships with companies strengthened by bankers holding seats on company boards. Companies had many forms of collaboration, including cartels, though the strength of cartels should not be overrated. In labour relations Germany had an unusual combination of early introduction of social security by the state and late recognition of the rights of workers to organise themselves. The social security funds were administered by employers and employees together, which created an early collaboration between both parties. Thus, around the turn of the 20th century, Germany already had many characteristics of a coordinated market economy.[6]

In its adherence to free trade the Netherlands followed the example of Britain. Both countries were colonial nations, though the Netherlands had a much smaller empire than Britain. But shipping and trading were important sources of income, and those were best served with free trade. Even during the economic depression of the 1930s, the Netherlands only reluctantly and sparingly took measures to limit imports.[7] In this respect, the Netherlands did not follow Germany, which preferred protection to build up its industry. But Dutch entrepreneurs shared with German businesspeople their interest in cartel arrangements, on the local, national, and international level.[8]

In the late 19th century, Germany set an early example in introducing state-supported social welfare measures. This example was studied in the Netherlands. The need for some kind of social arrangement was felt in society, but the way in which the risks of income loss as a result of unemployment, sickness, old age, and death, had to be countered was a matter of long debates and studies of foreign examples. Should the state arrange it all, or should those involved, the employers and employees, have the freedom to make arrangements themselves? The result of this debate was that the state passed legislation, but left employers and employees to create the necessary institutions to comply with the laws.[9] In thinking about social welfare arrangements for their workers, Dutch employers also studied British and American examples of company arrangements for security funds, model factories, and company housing. This was in particular true for the large manufacturing companies that developed in the first decades of the 20th century.[10]

Dutch businesspeople worked closely together with their international counterparts. They sent their children abroad for internships and university studies. Around the turn of the 20th century, an international business elite had grown that had contacts through friendships as well as exports, cartel arrangements, foreign direct investment, and board seats. The outbreak of the First World War suddenly forced the international business community into two hostile camps, while the Dutch tried to keep neutral and keep in touch with both camps.[11] The war disrupted the economic globalisation. Nationalism and protectionism put an end to the easy flow across borders of goods, capital, and people. The war and its aftermath caused political and economic upheaval in which some businesses thrived and many others suffered.

As a consequence of the war, governments became actively involved in the economy, and that was true for both warring and neutral countries. The Russian Revolution of 1917 and the subsequent survival of the new communist regime added to the political and social unrest in European countries. The establishment clearly could not permit ignoring the voice of labour. Although governments by and large reduced their participation after the war, they kept a more active role than before.[12] Moreover, the economic turmoil directly after the war seemed to justify more steering by governments to reduce the negative effects of competition. Rationalisation became the new keyword, which stood for both standardisation and for concentration through mergers and cartels to achieve the most rational (efficient and effective) use of the means of production. Taylorism and rationalisation more generally became an international movement. The Dutch management consultant Ernst Hijmans spoke of the organisation of producers as 'the third way' between the anarchy of capitalist competition and the bureaucracy of socialism.[13]

Comparing capitalism in the United States, Britain, Germany, and Japan, Ronald Dore, William Lazonick, and Mary O'Sullivan argued that the rise of the managerial company seemed to lead to convergence in national business systems in the 1920s. The large investment in fixed capital asked for continued production and thus stimulated the companies to forge lasting links with their employees through social arrangements and housing projects. Managers of the large US companies considered it part of their corporate social responsibility to arrange welfare work for their employees, which could include matters as pension funds, life insurance, unemployment insurance, and medical care.[14] However, in the Depression of the 1930s, the four countries moved in different directions: Germany and Japan countered the unemployment problems with authoritarian regimes, while in the United States industrial conflict intensified. The New Deal legislation in America made it possible for labour to force large companies to conclude collective labour agreements, but the large unemployment undermined the bargaining power of the workers.[15] The New Deal opened the door (slightly) to cartel agreements and set an example of government action to deal with problems of unemployment and economic stagnation that resonated in other countries.[16]

In the Netherlands, the state sanctioned and promoted collaboration between businesses and between employers and employees to help counter the problems of unemployment. During the Second World War and the German occupation of the country, the state dictated how business should be run, and set all the preconditions, though the state still needed business to do the actual running. As war progressed, problems of scarcity and the increasing violence of the occupying regime became the overriding concerns.[17]

Even more than after the First World War, the United States came out of the Second World War as the leading political and economic power. At the same time, the Soviet Union, with its totally different way of organising the economy, also seemed to be able to achieve impressive economic growth. After 1945, led by the American example and motivated by monetary incentives (Marshall Aid), Western European countries rebuilt their economies and started a process of economic European integration. The countries introduced 'mixed economies' that were basically market economies with some measure of government planning and government steering to steady the economy and secure full employment. Natural monopolies such as postal services, electricity, and railways were often in the hands of the state or provincial or municipal governments. Some industries that were considered to be vital to the economy such as coalmining and steel production were nationalised.[18]

In Britain, directly after the war, a labour government came to power that regulated business, nationalised key industries, and expanded government expenditures to keep up purchase power. Its two objectives were to maintain full employment and to provide the whole population with basic needs such as housing, health care, and education. The conservative governments of the 1950s and 1960s supported these aims.[19] Germany came out of the war as an occupied nation, which in 1949, led to the division of the country into East and West Germany. East Germany became part of the Soviet Union's sphere of influence, while West Germany became part of the Atlantic alliance. West Germany sought a middle way between capitalism and socialism with room for free enterprise and a system of social security. Labour relations were characterised by cooperation between unions and employers in reaching collective labour agreements and avoiding strikes. The 'social partnership' between labour and business also included work's councils and co-determination of employees in certain large businesses. German business remained organised in business associations, but under American pressure, cartels were curtailed and in many cases forbidden.[20]

It could be argued that the Great Depression and Second World War only temporarily halted the convergence between national economies that seemed a logical consequence of the rise of large manufacturing companies and their needs. The large manufacturing companies needed a workforce that was constantly available to keep the engines running, and that earned enough money to buy the products manufactured by those companies. They needed stable supply and demand. A stable economic development would benefit all. In this view, voiced in the 1950s study *American Business Creed*, companies had the responsibility to look after the interest of all stakeholders, including consumers, employees, stockholders, and the general public. Managers had the power to decide the future of the company, but they were supposed to use this power to balance the various interests. CEOs were seen as statesmen who looked after the general well-being, not as hirelings of the shareholders to service their interests exclusively.[21] In many respects, in these years, the United States looked more like a coordinated than a liberal market economy. Michael Hogan described the US market economy as 'an American brand of corporate neo-capitalism that went beyond the laissez-faire political economy of classical theory but stopped short of a statist syndicalism'.[22]

The Netherlands with its four large manufacturing multinationals, which also had important subsidiaries in the United States, was fully exposed to the American ideas about management and the best way of organising the economy, though that doesn't mean Dutch managers agreed with all American choices. The managers followed the logic of the large manufacturing companies and attached more importance to creating growth and employment than to increasing shareholders' value. The Netherlands followed the American lead, which in many respects fitted with the way the organisation of the economy had developed during the interwar years and in which coordination between employers and employees was central.[23]

The Netherlands was only too happy to follow US pressures for free trade. With its focus on international trade, including Asia and the Americas, the Netherlands was, however, cautious about becoming part of a European Economic Community that might lower inside tariffs but would raise outside tariffs. But as a small country that recently had lost its most important colony, Indonesia, it did not want to stay outside a European Economic Community (EEC). Once it had become a member of the EEC in 1957, it continued to promote lower tariffs. Dutch business did not follow the Americans in their antagonism against cartels. When under debate in 1957, a study group of the Social Economic Council in the Netherlands called cartels a 'traditional Dutch way of doing business'.[24] Despite American pressure to act tougher against cartels, Dutch business did not give up their cartels until the European Union explicitly forbade these arrangements, and even then some businesses continued them or were accused of having done so.[25]

The final mix between state and free enterprise differed between the Western European countries, but the international growth of the 1950s and 1960s seemed to make all the combinations equally successful. The 1960s formed the heyday of managerial capitalism.[26] The difference between the company bureaucracy of the large managerial companies and the bureaucracy of the government seemed small. In both cases good planning would make it possible to ascertain continued economic growth and welfare. The reality turned out differently.

The 1970s, with high inflation, two oil shocks, and economic recession put the national economies in Europa to the test. Exports became difficult; some manufacturing companies became uncompetitive and had to lay off their workers. As a consequence, unemployment started to rise. Stable prices and full employment had been important objectives of the mixed economy, but those objectives became difficult to realise. The system was clearly in trouble. What would be the best way out of the problems? Here countries started to diverge again. Writing in the early 1980s, the Belgian economic historian Herman van der Wee argued that the mixed economy had no answers to the risen problems. Structural measures were necessary, and he suggested three alternatives: back to the free market economy (neo-liberalism), forward to a fully centralised plan economy as some socialist parties advocated, and as third option, a move towards decentralised planning with ample room for the market and more self-management by workers as took place at that time in Yugoslavia. He thought the third alternative was the most likely to happen.[27] Events turned out differently.

Initially, countries differed in their responses to the challenges of the 1970s, with Britain and the United States reducing the role of government, while other countries, such as the Netherlands, stepped up government spending to help overcome the economic crisis. But in the course of the 1980s, the neo-liberal response from Britain and the United States began to impact the policies of many other European countries, including those of the Netherlands.

In Britain the antagonism between labour and capital, also visible in the two political parties, created a deadlock that made economic recovery hard to achieve. The power of the labour unions was broken by Margaret Thatcher, but she was able to do so only because of the dismal economic situation. Thatcher believed strongly in free market and private initiative for creating economic growth. She privatised state-owned enterprises, lowered taxes, and reduced social spending. The deregulation of the financial service sector led to a rush of foreign banks and investors to the financial centre of London.[28]

The increased international competition as consequence of the changes in the global economy after 1973 had a negative impact on employment in West Germany. The problem of structural unemployment led Chancellor Helmut Kohl in 1982 to propose similar measures as Margaret Thatcher had taken, such as less state intervention, lower wages, and more flexibility in labour relations. However, not very much really happened. Politicians were reluctant to address politically sensitive issues such as a reduction in the social safety net or vacation time. Instead, politicians put the greening of business and society high on the agenda. To make their business more competitive, industries focused on higher value-added products and flexible production methods. A new situation arose in 1990 when East Germany was successfully unified with West Germany and the difficult process of integration could start.[29] The Netherlands, thus, had again two contrasting models to choose from. But the most dominant new model came from the United States.

In the 1970s, the United States faced two major problems: rising inflation and Japanese competition in manufactured products. The inflation of the 1970s compelled pension funds to seek higher, though riskier, returns through investment in corporate equities and venture-capital funds. The consequence was that they also needed to pressure companies in reaching higher returns. Not growth or employment, but the return on investment became an important criterion to judge companies. To make sure the interests of shareholders would be foremost in the managers' minds, the managers' earnings were coupled to the shares' value. The Japanese competition stimulated a move into hardware and software for the new communication technologies.[30]

William Lazonick identified the changes in the United States as a move from the 'old-economy model' towards a 'new-economy model'. The old business model was characterised by a separation of share ownership and managerial control and top executives who saw themselves as 'organisations men', who acted in the interest of their organisation rather than just for themselves and whose careers were linked to the growth of the company. To support growth the companies paid a lot of attention to internal research and development and patenting of the results. In contrast, the 'new economy model', of the 1990s was based on a flexible organisation of labour and capital. Large parts of production were outsourced and moved abroad. Managers moved easily from one company to the next, and shareholders bought their loyalty with high bonuses linked to the price of shares. To keep share prices high, managers designed schemes to buy back shares. The new-economy model, therefore, led to less investment in new technology and less growth, while incomes became far more unequal. In this move to the new-economy model, the competition of Japanese business during the 1980s acted as a catalyst, but it was not the underlying factor. Lazonick agrees that the new model fits into Hall and Soskice's characterisation of the liberal market economy. But he doubts whether this model will be successful in creating economic growth in the long term.[31]

The government of the Netherlands initially tried to spend its way out of the crisis of the 1970s. Government involvement increased rather than diminished. Businesses received financial support to safeguard unemployment, while wages and social benefits continued to increase to compensate for inflation. The hope that the maintenance of income levels would result in more demand for the goods produced in the country was in vain. The support to ailing business did not have the expected results. Business failures and the accompanying rising unemployment led government and the organisations of employers and employees to reconsider their options in 1982. Employers and employees agreed on wage restrictions, shorter working hours, and a sobering of social arrangements to deal with the huge problem of unemployment. The new policies took shape gradually and succeeded in bringing down unemployment in the 1990s.[32] The 1990s also saw the rise of the service sector and the internationalisation of banks and insurance companies.

The success of the US economy and its IT companies in the 1990s acted as recommendations to other countries to follow the neo-liberal course. The fall of communism in Eastern Europe and the dissolving of the Soviet Union added to the feeling that capitalism as a system was superior to communism. The inefficiencies of bureaucracies were highlighted, while the efficiencies of the market were more or less taken for granted. The policies of Britain and the United States were discussed in the Netherlands, but not wholly followed. Still, elements of the neo-liberal model were introduced, as we have seen in the previous chapters. The financial sector was deregulated, and it became an industry in its own right. As happened in the United States, the Dutch pension funds started to invest in company shares to increase revenues, including shares in foreign companies. Moreover, Anglo-American asset managers were hired to manage the Dutch funds.[33] Shareowners became more vocal, and company managers began to talk about serving the interest of the shareholders first and foremost. Safeguarding employment was no longer the highest priority, but increasing profitability was. Multinationals, which were put under pressure by shareholders, at the same time became advocates of new values such as flexible labour relations and employability.

COMPARISON WITH THE FOUR NORDIC COUNTRIES

In the preceding chapters we noticed two big movements in the Netherlands: one from a basically liberal market economy to a coordinated economy in the first half of the 20th century, and from 1980s onwards, a move in the opposite direction to a more liberal economy, though to what extent the country has become a liberal market economy is still a matter of debate. As we have seen above, the Netherlands was influenced by what happened in other countries, in particular large countries such as the United States, Britain, and Germany, and by the ideas brought forward in those countries.

Are the Dutch experiences comparable to those of other small open economies? The book *Creating Nordic Capitalism* provides an excellent opportunity to put the Dutch experiences further in perspective.[34] *Creating Nordic Capitalism* compares the development of capitalism in Denmark, Norway, Sweden, and Finland from 1850 to the present. What becomes immediately clear is that those four countries experienced an ebb and flow in the way they organised their economy, similar to the Netherlands, moving from a liberal market economy in the mid-19th century to a coordinated market economy in the mid-20th century, and back (to a certain extent) to a more liberal economy after 1980.

Though the broad movement was similar, the timing differed between the four Nordic countries, and also their starting points in the 19th century differed. The economy of Denmark was characterised by agrarian cooperatives, large exports, and a German-based social security system. Martin Iversen and Steen Andersen typified Danish capitalism therefore as 'cooperative liberalism'.[35] Norway, rich in natural resources, had large imports and exports, many local initiatives, and an active role for the state. Lars Thue used the term 'democratic capitalism' to describe Norway.[36] Sweden combined international trade with a focus on the industries of the second Industrial Revolution. To characterise the Swedish model, Hans Sjögren chose the expression 'welfare capitalism'.[37] Of the four Nordic countries, Finland, a country strong on forestry and export, was in many respects an outlier, and for that reason Susanne Fellman addressed the capitalism in Finland simply as 'Finnish capitalism'.[38]

As exploiters of natural resources, the four countries benefited from the economic growth and internationalisation in the late 19th century. Economic liberalism was the dominant ideology, but governments supported economic growth by investment in infrastructure. As industrialisation took off, poverty and bad working conditions became recognised as social problems that needed to be addressed. Building up a coordinated market economy took time.

As was the case in the Netherlands, in Denmark the First World War played an important role in bringing the state, business, and employees closer together. After the war, the liberals contested the cooperation between the state and the business sector, but in practice the collaboration continued. It became even closer during the Depression of the 1930 when the state regulated imports and protected the agrarian sector. During the Second World War, the state and employers' and employees' organisations controlled the labour market and economic policy.[39]

The First World War had a huge impact on Swedish international position. After the war, industrial growth declined, capital export increased, and a process of concentration took place in the industry. Cartels were frequently used and generally accepted. In the 1930s, in order to safeguard employment, economists and politicians agreed that state intervention was necessary. They advocated a 'Swedish Way', which was synonymous with a middle way between socialism and unfettered capitalism.[40]

In the period 1890–1920, Norway saw an influx of foreign investment in mining and other natural resources, which led to a call for the national control of national resources to reap and distribute the resource rent. The establishment of large industries also created an industrial proletariat and class struggle in Norway, which in turn led to the rise of labour unions and employment organisations. During the economic crisis of the early 1920s and the early 1930s, the country struggled with class conflict, but it also saw the rise of rationalisation, coordination, and more focus on social welfare and the regulation of markets. Norway moved from a liberal to a coordinated market economy.[41]

Finland had a different trajectory from the other three Nordic countries. In the First World War, the country won its independence from Russia and subsequently experienced a civil war that created a strong antagonism between labour and business. The rift was so deep that not until the Second World War were both parties prepared to collaborate. From 1950 onwards, Finland had a very successful economic development, a state-led growth, and a highly coordinated market economy.[42]

In all four Nordic countries, during the 1950s and 1960s, economic growth and increasing social welfare went hand in hand. In particular the manufacturing industry contributed to the economic growth. In Denmark the rise of the manufacturing industry also signified more focus on the production for the home market. The welfare state expanded in the 1960s and 1970s, based on notions of solidarity and equality.[43] In Norway, the postwar appetite for socialist planning quickly diminished under international, in particular American, influence. Instead, state participation in the economy increased, and extensive coordination and cooperation between various interest groups on the national level developed. The Social Party pressed for social and national solidary. Norway succeeded in combining full employment with an extensive welfare arrangement.[44] The same was true for Sweden. A strong relationship between the financial-industrial elite and the major political parties was considered acceptable because it brought political stability, strong economic growth, extended social security, and full employment.[45] Finland entered in the 1950s the stage of state-led economic growth, and it developed into a highly coordinated market economy.[46]

The economic crisis of the 1970s, with its two oil shocks, and deep recession in the early 1980s, was in all countries a moment for reflection and debates about the role of the state, the extent of the welfare state, and the liberalisation of the capital markets. Again, timing differed. Denmark experienced a crisis in the early 1980s, Norway in the late 1980s, and Sweden and Finland in the early 1990s. Denmark stepped up government spending in the 1970s to overcome the recession but experienced an economic crisis in the early 1980s. This led to deregulation and more competition. From a strategy of exports, Danish business switched to participation in the global division of labour.[47] In Norway, state ownership was reduced and the power of unions diminished, in part because trade unionism was weak in the service industries that were the new growth sectors. Moreover, globalisation reduced the possibilities of (local) managers and employees to influence board decisions. Nonetheless, the trade unions remained a force to be reckoned with.[48]

In the 1970s, the Swedish economy performed poorly. The government gave support to ailing businesses, but that aggravated the problem of high government spending. Powerful trade unions continued to demand higher wages and better social security arrangements. In the 1980s, Sweden ended monopolies on railways, postal services, energy, media, and telecommunications, and the country seemed to have overcome the economic slump of the early 1980s. However, Sweden experienced a huge financial crisis in the early 1990s. The Swedish model came under threat because the desirability of equality became less self-evident and private firms felt less loyal to their country. They did not feel the need to sustain full employment in Sweden but moved their investments to low-wage countries if that would increase shareholder value.[49] In comparing the Dutch and Swedish institutional change, Jeroen Touwen argued that in Sweden the actors stopped following the practices described by the institutions and thus forced change, whereas in the Netherlands the institutions were reinterpreted.[50] In Finland the successful formula of the 1950s continued into the 1970s. Even in the 1980s, the economic development was more favourable than elsewhere in Europa. Still, the 1980s saw changes such as liberalisation and privatisation. In the early 1990s, Finland experienced a crisis that had external and internal causes. External was the disintegration of the Soviet Union, which had been an important market for Finland. Internal was the lack of adjustments in earlier years, which made more radical changes necessary in the 1990s. Finland also became part of the European Union in 1995, at the same time as Sweden.[51]

But by the end of the 1990s, in all four countries the international involvement had grown, the role of the government was reduced, labour unions had become less powerful, the welfare state had become less generous, and interests of shareholders received more attention. There was a clear move towards a more liberal market economy, but older notions of solidarity and social security had not entirely disappeared. The authors of *Creating Nordic Capitalism* conclude that in the 20th century, the four Nordic countries converged towards one 'Nordic model', characterised by political stability, competitive economies, and generous welfare systems. The reason that the four moved towards a similar model is—cautiously—explained by the fact that the economic interaction between the four countries greatly increased through imports and exports, mutual foreign direct investment, and cross-border mergers. Nordic institutions and joint membership of the European Union further strengthened the convergence.[52] Without arguing that globalisation will lead to one similar business system, this conclusion seems to suggest that closer economic interaction can lead to convergence in the way national economies are organised.

The comparison between the four Nordic countries and the Netherlands offers many similarities and thus greater understanding of the joined drivers of change. The starting points in the 19th century were very different for the four Nordic countries. If anything, the Netherlands resembled Sweden with its large companies of the second Industrial Revolution the most. The interwar period showed already many similarities between three of the four Nordic countries and the Netherlands, and these became more marked from the 1950s onwards. The two world wars and the Great Depression contributed each time to a greater coordination of the economy. The coordinated market economies thrived during the 1950s and 1960s, when economic growth was fuelled by expanding international trade. However, the recession of the 1970s and the globalisation of markets, including the financial markets, put the achievements of the welfare state under pressure. Preserving the welfare state seemed difficult to combine with maintaining the international competitiveness of business. The countries initially fiercely defended their welfare arrangements, but as time went by, all made adjustments. The systems became less generous with the intention of making them more robust.

In his book *Small States in World Market*, published in 1985, Peter Katzenstein explained how the small open European countries had been very good at combining international competitiveness with a high level of social security. He characterised these countries as 'democratic corporatist'. For small countries economic protectionism was no option, and therefore the countries had to choose for international openness. But to protect their citizens from the ups and downs of the international economy, the states needed to combine economic openness with 'domestic compensation', that is: generous social welfare systems. These systems were created in tripartite negotiations between the state, employers, and employees. At the same time, the countries had to react flexibly to international changes and challenges because they could not protect their economy from outside pressures, nor afford structural transformation. Katzenstein conceded that the small and flexible adjustments these countries made during the 1970s looked 'confused and disorderly', but they were in fact, he argued, a new contribution to the repertoire of modern capitalism.[53] He even recommended the approach of small European countries to his American readers: 'Democratic corporatism merits study for its response to economic change. Exposed to global markets that they cannot control, the small European states have accommodated themselves to a situation that Americans are now beginning to experience as crisis'.[54]

As we have seen above, the authors of *Nordic Capitalism* have a somewhat less positive view of the muddling through policies of the Nordic countries in the 1970s, which they consider as 'too little too late', and a missed opportunity to adjust timely to the new international competitive environment. This difference in appreciation may have to do with the fact that the countries were facing a different kind of internationalisation in the 1980s and 1990s. As Iversen and Andersen remarked about Denmark, Danish enterprises moved from exporting to truly participating in the global division of labour.[55]

Returning to his study in 2003, Katzenstein underlined that one vital part of his argument had been insufficiently understood, and that was his argument that the feeling of vulnerability of small states with regard to the international economy generated the ideology of social partnership that 'acted like a glue for the corporatist politics of the small European states'. Not only economic factors, but also sentiments such as 'vulnerability' and ideas such as 'ideology' served as explanation for the formation of specific institutions.

He argued that in the 1990s, the small European states had demonstrated the kind of flexibility, now termed 'learning capabilities', consistent with the ideas he had set out in 1985. He was optimistic that the countries in Eastern Europe would follow a similar route towards a social market economy.[56]

COMPARING RECENT DEVELOPMENTS IN EASTERN EUROPE

Inspired by the Varieties of Capitalism debate, Andreas Nölke and Arjan Vliegenthart have analysed the economies of four East-Central European countries, the Czech Republic, Hungary, Poland, and the Slovak Republic, to decide whether these countries would fit the model of the liberal or coordinated market economy. The authors concluded that the economic and political shock of the end of communism after 1989 led to the formation of a new set of institutions that is consistent with neither a liberal market economy nor with a coordinated market economy, but can best be characterised as 'dependent market economy'.[57] Why dependent? Because the economies of the Czech Republic, Hungary, Poland, and the Slovak Republic have become greatly dependent on investment decisions by multinational companies headquartered in Western Europe and the United States. These multinationals were looking for cheap but skilled labour in order to outsource the assembly of semi-standardised industrial goods. These companies have invested in new production facilities and, as a consequence, modernised the economic infrastructure. But for the four countries, the innovation came at a price: increasing dependence on the needs of these multinational companies and their decisions.

The notion of dependence is linked to the hierarchical organisation of transnational companies. In this respect, the dependent market economy has some similarities with the hierarchical market economy that Ben Ross Schneider identified for the countries in Latin America. In this model, the foreign multinational enterprises aligned their interests with the local family business groups to the detriment of the workers, who are for the most part unorganised and highly mobile. The coordination mechanism is mostly nonmarket and hierarchical.[58]

According to Nölke and Vliegenthart, the logic of transnational companies demands low labour costs, the tacit knowledge embedded in local industrial districts, and easy hiring and firing conditions. They have no need for local finance and are not interested in investing in education or vocational training because they can transfer innovation from headquarters, and they tend to lobby for government preferential treatment and advantageous investment conditions. These needs and conditions led to the business system that Nölke and Vliegenthart coined as 'dependent market economies'.[59] Because multinational companies are supposed to behave in certain predictable ways consistent with their economic logic, the model contains a set of institutional complementarities that are supposed to strengthen the model.

The model is both coherent and successful in certain sectors linked to export industries. But it does not increase the standard of living of the whole population and is also considered vulnerable because of its dependence on the decisions of multinationals from outside the country, who may decide to move to other countries with a lower cost structure. The model is based on a clear set of suppositions on how multinationals behave. This set of suppositions, however, calls for further historical research because there may well be more variety in the strategies of multinationals.[60]

While Katzenstein underlined the fact that the small European countries were able to combine international openness with national welfare systems thanks to their capacities of making flexible adjustments to changes in the international economy, Nölke and Vliegenthart are less optimistic about the Eastern European countries (not all of them small). Their economic competitive advantage is geared towards a certain type of production (assembly lines of semi-standardised products), and if the production costs might rise, multinationals could move to countries with lower (labour) costs.

One can argue that there are differences between the Eastern European countries and the Western European countries. In the first place some of the small European countries, in particular the Netherlands, Sweden, and Switzerland, had strong multinationals of their own. The top managers of the large multinationals were involved in the local economy and formed part of the local business elite that took part in the consultation and coordination process. This situation was different in Eastern Europe. But with the growth of some multinationals and in particular, with the increase of cross-border mergers and acquisitions, the business elite in Western European countries has also become more internationalised, and it is no longer self-evident that their loyalties are with the country in which the headquarters are located.

Secondly, the character of the internationalisation changed in the 1980s and 1990s. The internationalisation has become more intense. The multinational companies no longer limit themselves to establishing subsidiaries abroad as alternatives to producing export products at home or to acquire raw materials, but the whole production chain has lengthened and become more fragmented. This has created a long and complex set of dependencies that involve many different countries and even more different companies. The recent experiences of the East-Central European countries show that the way in which countries are connected to the global economy can have important implications for the way the national economy functions. This conclusion is particularly relevant for small countries with open economies like the Nordic countries and the Netherlands.

VARIETIES OF CAPITALISM AND GLOBALISATION

The Varieties of Capitalism debate started with the argument that globalisation does not necessarily mean that all countries will move towards the same organisation of their economy.[61] This overview confirms that there remain many different systems. At the same time, it is clear that many economies underwent changes in recent years and that these changes meant a move in a more liberal direction. Markets have become more important, companies seek to serve more exclusively the interest of shareholders, labour relations have become more flexible, and welfare arrangements have become less generous. Governments act less directly but are more involved indirectly in rule setting. Movement in the same direction is also stimulated by international agreements and standard setting in international organisations, such as international audit standards, that tend to be geared towards neo-liberal points of view.[62]

National economies are constantly changing and adjusting themselves. The fact that the economies all move in the same direction, though at different speeds, underlines the supposition of institutional complementarities because the liberalisation of one sphere of the economy put pressure on other spheres in the same way that in the interwar years, the coordination of the economy gradually took hold of more and more spheres of the economy. The recent experiences of four East-Central European countries seems to suggest that new coherent models can develop in a relatively short period.

It is clear that the liberalisation of markets and the subsequent increasing internationalisation have become the main drivers for change in the last decades. What still needs more understanding is how the different ways in which the national economies are connected to the international economy influence their room for manoeuver and their policy options. In particular the role of multinationals and the impact of cross-border mergers deserves more attention. While national governments compete to attract foreign companies to their countries, at the same time, multinationals compete for the best investment opportunities. It is not self-evident that in these negotiations multinationals will always have the upper hand, as is often supposed. More business history research into the precise relationship between governments and multinationals is clearly welcome. Important for identifying the impact of openness on the national economy are also the supplier relations between local and international business.

The Varieties of Capitalism literature argued that different capitalist systems could all work well in their own way. The present concern is that perhaps none of them work really well. The Asian crisis of 1997, the dot-com crisis of 2000, and the Enron scandal in 2001 that also caused the end of auditing firm Arthur Andersen, showed the instability of the global economy, yet it took the financial crisis of 2008 to start a process of rethinking the paradigm of neo-liberalism. Some of the warnings came again from the United States. Michael Sandel posed the question of whether there was anything money couldn't buy. 'Without quite realizing it, without even deciding to do so, we have drifted from having a market economy to being a market society', he argued. As a society, we have 'outsourced' our ethical choices to the market, while in the end, a society should set its own priorities through debates.[63] In his book *The Globalisation Paradox*, Dani Rodrik argues that deep globalisation, national sovereignty, and democracy are incompatible. If there is a conflict of interest between the three, then national sovereignty and democracy have to come first. Instead of embracing deep globalisation, the world should move to 'sane globalisation', that is, a situation in which the reach of global markets is limited by the scope of their (mostly national) governance. National governments should continue to be able to set their own priorities in social welfare arrangements.[64] The need as a society to take some action is also underlined by the French economist Thomas Piketty in his book *Capital in the Twenty-First Century*. His analysis of the past leads him to the conclusion that the reduction of inequality during the 20th century was an exception and that the economy, left to itself, will lead to more inequality in wealth and income. To avoid such a scenario unfolding, he advises high taxes on capital, although he is fully aware of the practical problems of such measures in a global world.[65] The popularity of these books, and in particular the amazing response to Piketty's volume, shows that the feelings of unease about the increasing globalisation, the paradigm of the free markets, and the inequality between people and countries are broadly shared in the western world. Will the financial crisis of 2008 become a new turning point in the evolution of capitalism, such as the crisis of the 1970s, in hindsight, turned out to be for the cooperative market economies? Or is the world going 'back to business' with more international mergers and acquisitions, more globalisation, and more dependence of individuals on the outcome of free markets?

NOTES

1. For the idea of ebb and flow in convergence, I am indebted to the article by Ronald Dore, William Lazonick, and Mary O'Sullivan; see Dore, Lazonick, and O'Sullivan, 'Varieties of capitalism', 103.
2. See chapters 2 through 8 in this volume; see also Sluyterman, *Dutch Enterprise* and Prak and Van Zanden, *Nederland en het poldermodel*, 211–274.
3. *In het zicht van de toekomst*, 5–7.
4. Hall and Soskice, 'Introduction', 17–21.
5. Botticelli, 'British capitalism', 51–93; Blackford, *Rise of Modern Business*, 59–79.
6. Fear, 'German capitalism', 135–182.
7. Jones, *Multinational Traders*; Sluyterman, 'Dutch multinational trading companies', 87–90.
8. Bouwens and Dankers, *Tussen concurrentie en concentratie*, 59–67.
9. Schwitters, *Risico's van de arbeid*, 246–250.
10. Nijhof and Van den Berg, *Menselijk kapitaal*, 113–133.
11. Sluyterman, *Dutch Enterprise*, 75–90.
12. Wrigley, *First World War*, 1–33.
13. Bloemen, 'Scientific management en ideologie', 291–310; Hijmans, 'Productievraagstukken', 211.

14. Mitchell, *Generous Corporation*, 10–25.
15. Dore, Lazonick, and O'Sullivan, 'Varieties of capitalism', 106–107.
16. Blackford, 'Rise of modern business', 142–144.
17. Bouwens and Dankers, *Tussen concurrentie en concentratie*, 106–120; Klemann, *Nederland 1938–1948*, 565–577.
18. Nolan, *The Transatlantic Century*, 193–201.
19. Botticelli, 'British capitalism', 85–88.
20. Fear, 'German capitalism', 172–178.
21. Jacoby, *The Embedded Corporation*, 85.
22. Hogan, *Marshall Plan*, 1–3.
23. Sluyterman, *Dutch Enterprise*, 126–129.
24. *Verslag van de werkzaamheden van de commissie Europese Economische Integratie*, 55–56.
25. Bouwens and Dankers, *Tussen concurrentie en concentratie*, 215–226.
26. Dore, Lazonick, and O'Sullivan, 'Varieties of capitalism', 109–111.
27. Van der Wee, *Gebroken welvaartscirkel*, 250–256.
28. Botticelli, 'British capitalism', 85–93.
29. Fear, 'German capitalism', 178–182.
30. Dore, Lazonick, and O'Sullivan, 'Varieties of capitalism', 111–117.
31. Lazonick, 'Innovative business models', 681–684, 691–700.
32. Prak and Van Zanden, *Nederland en het poldermodel*, 263–274; Hemerijck, Unger, and Visser, 'How small countries negotiate change', 209–230.
33. Engelen and Konings, 'Financial capitalism resurgent', 609–616.
34. Fellman et al., *Creating Nordic Capitalism*.
35. Iversen and Andersen, 'Co-operative liberalism: Denmark', 265–267.
36. Thue, 'Norway: A resource-based and democratic capitalism', 394–397.
37. Sjögren, 'Welfare capitalism', 22–24.
38. Fellman, 'Growth and investment: Finnish capitalism', 139–142.
39. Iversen and Andersen, 'Co-operative liberalism: Denmark', 283–303.
40. Sjögren, 'Welfare capitalism', 33–45.
41. Thue, 'Norway: A resource-based and democratic capitalism', 417–434.
42. Fellman, 'Growth and investment: Finnish capitalism', 154–171.
43. Iversen and Andersen, 'Co-operative liberalism: Denmark', 303–312.
44. Thue, 'Norway: A resource-based and democratic capitalism', 434–459.
45. Sjögren, 'Welfare capitalism', 43–52.
46. Fellman, 'Growth and investment: Finnish capitalism', 168–171.
47. Iversen and Andersen, 'Co-operative liberalism: Denmark', 313–323.
48. Thue, 'Norway: A resource-based and democratic capitalism', 459–481.
49. Sjögren, 'Welfare capitalism', 52–64.
50. Touwen, 'Varieties of capitalism and institutional change', 171–202.
51. Fellman, 'Growth and investment: Finnish capitalism', 188–205.
52. Fellman and Sjögren, 'Conclusion', 575–578.
53. Katzenstein, *Small States in World Markets*, 39–70, quote 58.
54. Katzenstein, *Small States in World Markets*, 38.
55. Iversen and Andersen, 'Co-operative liberalism: Denmark', 324.
56. Katzenstein, '*Small States* and small states revisited', 11, 17–21.
57. Nölke and Vliegenthart, 'Enlarging the Varieties of Capitalism', 679–697.
58. Schneider, 'Hierarchical market economies', 553–556; Miller, 'Latin American business history', 653–657.
59. Nölke and Vliegenthart, 'Enlarging the Varieties of Capitalism', 670–679.
60. Wilkins, 'Multinational enterprises and the Varieties of Capitalism', 638–645.
61. Hall and Soskice, 'Introduction', 54–60.
62. Even Switzerland, which did not participate in many of the international agreements, still felt the pressure of the norm setting encompassed in those

218   *Keetie Sluyterman*

agreements: David et al., 'Einleitung Teil 4: Die schweizerische Variante des Kapitalismus', 827–828.
63. Sandel, *What Money Can't Buy*, 3–15, quote 10.
64. Rodrik, *Globalization Paradox*, 188–206, 250.
65. Piketty, *Capital in the Twenty-First Century*, 1–16, 515–530.

REFERENCES

Blackford, M. G., *The Rise of Modern Business in Great Britain, the United States and Japan* (Chapel Hill and London: University of North Carolina Press, 1998).
Bloemen, Erik, 'Scientific management en ideologie: de internationaal management congressen 1924–1938', *Jaarboek voor de geschiedenis van bedrijf en techniek*, 3 (1986): 291–310.
Botticelli, Peter, 'British capitalism and the three industrial revolutions', in: Thomas K. McCraw, ed., *Creating Modern Capitalism* (Cambridge Mass. and London: Harvard University Press, 1997) 51–93.
Bouwens, Bram and Joost, Dankers, *Tussen concurrentie en concentratie: belangenorganisaties, kartels, fusies en overnames* (Amsterdam: Boom, 2012).
David, Thomas, Bernard Degen, and André Mach et al., 'Einleitung Teil 4: Die Schweizerische Variante des Kapitalismus', in: Patrick Halbeisen, Margrit Müller, and Béatrice Veyrassat, eds., *Wirtschaftsgeschichte der Schweiz im 20. Jahrhundert* (Basel: Schwabe Verlag, 2012) 823–829.
Dore, Ronald, Lazonick, William, and O'Sullivan, Mary, 'Varieties of capitalism in the twentieth century', *Oxford Review of Economic Policy*, 15, 4 (1999) 102–120.
Engelen, Ewald and Martijn, Konings, 'Financial capitalism resurgent: Institutionalism and the challenges of financialization', in: Glenn Morgan et al., eds., *The Oxford Handbook of Comparative Institutional Analysis* (Oxford: Oxford University Press, 2010) 601–624.
Fear, Jeffrey, 'German capitalism', in: Thomas K. McCraw, ed., *Creating Modern Capitalism* (Cambridge Mass. and London: Harvard University Press, 1997) 135–182.
Fellman, Susanna, 'Growth and investment: Finnish capitalism, 1850s–2005', in: Susanna Fellman et al., eds., *Creating Nordic Capitalism. A Business History of a Competitive Periphery* (Hampshire and New York: Palgrave Macmillan, 2008) 139–217.
Fellman, Susanna, Martin Jes Iversen, and Hans Sjögren et al., eds., *Creating Nordic Capitalism. A Business History of a Competitive Periphery* (Hampshire and New York: Palgrave Macmillan, 2008).
Fellman, Susanna and Hans Sjögren, 'Conclusion', in: Susanna Fellman et al., eds., *Creating Nordic Capitalism. A Business History of a Competitive Periphery* (Hampshire and New York: Palgrave Macmillan, 2008) 558–578.
Hall, Peter A. and David, Soskice, 'An introduction to varieties of capitalism', in: Peter A. Hall and David Soskice, eds., *Varieties of Capitalism. The institutional Foundations of Comparative Advantage* (Oxford: Oxford University Press, 2001) 1–68.
Hemerijck, Anton, Brigitte Unger, and Jelle Visser, 'How small countries negotiate change: Twenty-five years of policy adjustment in Austria, the Netherlands, and Belgium', in: Fritz W. Scharpf and Vivian A. Schmidt, eds., *Welfare and Work in the Open Economy, volume II: Diverse Responses to Common Challenges* (Oxford: Oxford University Press, 2000) 175–263.
Hijmans, Ernst, 'Productievraagstukken in verband met crisis', *Naamlooze Vennootschap*, 15, November (1922): 159–161, 186–188, 208–211.

Hogan, Michael, *The Marshall Plan: America, Britain, and the Reconstruction of Western Europe, 1947–1952* (Cambridge: Cambridge University Press, 1987).

In het zicht van de toekomst. Sociaal en Cultureel Rapport 2004 (Den Haag: Sociaal Cultureel Planbureau, 2004).

Iversen, Martin Jes and Steen Andersen, 'Co-operative liberalism: Denmark from 1857 to 2007', in: Susanna Fellman et al., eds., *Creating Nordic Capitalism. A Business History of a Competitive Periphery* (Hampshire and New York: Palgrave Macmillan, 2008) 263–334.

Jacoby, Sanford M., *The Embedded Corporation: Corporate Governance and Employment Relations in Japan and the United States* (Princeton and Oxford: Princeton University Press, 2005).

Jones, G., ed., *The Multinational Traders* (London and New York: Routledge, 1998).

Katzenstein, P., *Small States in World Markets: Industrial Policy in Europe* (Ithaca: Cornell University Press. 1985).

Katzenstein, Peter, '*Small States* and small states revisited', *New Political Economy*, 8, 1 (2003): 9–30.

Klemann, H. A. M., *Nederland 1938–1948. Economie en samenleving in jaren van oorlog en bezetting* (Amsterdam: Boom, 2002).

Lazonick, William, 'Innovative business models and Varieties of Capitalism: Financialization of the US corporation', *Business History Review*, 84, Winter (2010): 675–702.

Miller, Rory M., 'Latin American business history and Varieties of Capitalism', *Business History Review*, 84, 4 (2010): 653–657.

Mitchell, Neil J., *The Generous Corporation. A Political Analysis of Economic Power* (New Haven and London: Yale University Press, 1989).

Nijhof, Erik and Annette van den Berg, *Het menselijk kapitaal. Sociaal ondernemerschap in Nederland* (Amsterdam: Boom, 2012).

Nolan, Mary, *The Transatlantic Century: Europe and America, 1890–2010* (Cambridge: Cambridge University Press, 2012).

Nölke, Andreas and Arjan, Vliegenthart, 'Enlarging the Varieties of Capitalism: The emergence of dependent market economies in East Central Europe', *World Politics*, 61, 4 (2009): 670–702.

Piketty, Thomas, *Capital in the Twenty-First Century* (Cambridge, Mass. and London: Harvard University Press, 2014).

Prak, Maarten and Jan Luiten van Zanden, *Nederland en het poldermodel: sociaaleconomische geschiedenis van Nederland, 1000–2000* (Amsterdam: Bert Bakker, 2013).

Rodrik, Dani, *The Globalization Paradox: Democracy and the Future of the World Economy* (New York: W.W. Norton & Company, 2011).

Sandel, Michael, *What Money Can't Buy: The Moral Limits of Markets* (London, etc.: Allen Lane, 2012).

Schneider, Ben Ross, 'Hierarchical market economies and Varieties of Capitalism in Latin America', *Journal of Latin American Studies*, 41, 3 (2009): 553–575.

Schwitters, R. J. S., *De risico's van de arbeid. Het ontstaan van de Ongevallenwet van 1901 in sociologisch perspectief* (Groningen: Wolters-Noordhoff, 1991).

Sjögren, Hans, 'Welfare capitalism: The Swedish economy, 1850–2005', in: Susanna Fellman et al., eds., *Creating Nordic Capitalism. A Business History of a Competitive Periphery* (Hampshire and New York: Palgrave Macmillan, 2008) 22–74.

Sluyterman, Keetie E., *Dutch Enterprise in the Twentieth Century. Business Strategies in a Small Open Economy* (London and New York: Routledge, 2005).

Sluyterman, K. E., 'Dutch multinational trading companies in the twentieth century', in: G. Jones, ed., *The Multinational Traders* (London and New York: Routledge, 1998) 86–101.

Thue, Lars, 'Norway: A resource-based and democratic capitalism', in: Susanna Fellman et al., eds., *Creating Nordic Capitalism. A Business History of a Competitive Periphery* (Hampshire and New York: Palgrave Macmillan, 2008) 394–493.

Touwen, Jeroen, 'Varieties of capitalism and institutional change in New Zealand, Sweden and the Netherlands in the 1980s and 1990s', in: H. Egbert and C. Esser, eds., *Aspects in Varieties of Capitalism: Dynamics, Economic Crisis, New Players* (Saarbruecken: Lambert Academic Publishing, 2010) 171–202.

Verslag van de werkzaamheden van de commissie Europese Economische Integratie van de Sociaal Economische Raad (Den Haag: SER, 1957).

Wee, Herman van der, *De gebroken welvaartscirkel: de wereldeconomie, 1945–1980* (Leiden: Martinus Nijhoff, 1983).

Wilkins, Mira, 'Multinational enterprises and the Varieties of Capitalism', *Business History Review*, 84, 4 (2010): 638–645.

Wrigley, Ch, ed., *The First World War and the International Economy* (Cheltenham: Edward Elgar, 2000).

Contributors

Annette van den Berg (Utrecht University School of Economics) studied economic history, after which she wrote her dissertation about trade union membership in the Netherlands. Her current research focuses on the effects of worker participation in Europe.

Bram Bouwens is a business historian at Utrecht University. He has written or jointly authored a large number of business histories, including histories of Amsterdam Airport, the Dutch paper and board industry, the dredging company Boskalis, and the brewer Heineken. Together with Joost Dankers he published the BINT study on competition and concentration.

Joost Dankers is a historian and manager of the commissioned research group at Utrecht University and has an expertise in applying knowledge developments to our society. He has published many books and articles in the field of business history.

Mila Davids works at the sub-Department of Innovation Sciences of the Eindhoven University of Technology. Her publications focus on innovation, circulation of knowledge, and innovation networks of Dutch firms. Her current research is focusing on knowledge transfer in international perspective.

Jacques van Gerwen is research staff member for collection development at the International Institute for Social History (IISH). His main research interests are economic history (1800–2000), business history, entrepreneurial history, and biographies of entrepreneurs. He is a member of the editorial board of *The Low Countries Journal of Social and Economic History* (*Tijdschrift voor Sociale en Economische Geschiedenis*).

Ferry de Goey is an assistant professor at the Erasmus School of History, Culture, and Communication of the Erasmus University Rotterdam. He lectures on modern western history, international relations, and global history. His main research interests are entrepreneurial and business history.

Abe de Jong is a professor of corporate finance at Rotterdam School of Management, Erasmus University, and a professor of financial accounting at University of Groningen.

Harry Lintsen is a professor emeritus in the history of technology. He was initiator of a series on technology in the Netherlands in the 19th century (TIN 19) and of a series on technology in the Netherlands in the 20th century (TIN 20). Currently he is busy with the history of the knowledge infrastructure in the Netherlands and with the theme of 'sustainability in historical perspective'.

Erik Nijhof (Utrecht University, economic and social history) is an expert on Dutch social and institutional history of the 20th century. His dissertation was on the labour relations in the port of Rotterdam. His current research regards the development of the Dutch consultative economy.

Ailsa Röell is a professor of international and public affairs at Columbia University, School of International and Public Affairs.

Keetie Sluyterman is a professor of business history at the Department of History and Art History of Utrecht University, the Netherlands. She has written extensively on Dutch multinationals, including Rabobank, Hagemeyer, Royal Dutch Shell, Royal Boskalis, and Heineken. She is one of the leaders of the interuniversity research project, Dutch Business in the Twentieth Century (BINT).

Gerarda Westerhuis is a researcher at the Department of History and Art History, Utrecht University, and a lecturer at Rotterdam School of Management, Erasmus University, the Netherlands.

Ben Wubs is an associate professor at the Erasmus University in Rotterdam and is engaged in various projects related to multinationals, business systems, economic regions, and transnational fashion industry.

Jan Luiten van Zanden is a professor of global economic history at Utrecht University and an honorary professor at the universities of Groningen and Stellenbosch. His research interests include the patterns of long-term economic development and the causes of global economic inequality. His recent publications include 'What Was Life?: Global Well-Being Since 1820' (OECD 2014).

Index

Note: page numbers in *italics* indicate tables or illustrations.